Utopia without Ideology

This book explores and proposes original definitions of central terms in political sociology and social theory, including political culture, imaginary, ideology, and utopia, in a manner that renders the individual definitions consistent with one another as part of a single and general conceptual framework for understanding social action. Through a Weberian distinction between means, ends, and values, together with the thought of Alfred Schütz and phenomenological sociology more generally, it sheds light on the ways in which the book's key concepts make sense of social action, advancing the view that, rather than some promised land or aspiration, utopia is a project of broad and far-reaching collective action realized in its own enactment. As such, the book will appeal to scholars of social theory, political sociology, and political theory.

Ambrogio Santambrogio is Full Professor of Sociology in the Department of Political Science at the University of Perugia, Italy.

Routledge Studies in Social and Political Thought

This series explores core issues in political philosophy and social theory. Addressing theoretical subjects of both historical and contemporary relevance, the series has broad appeal across the social sciences. Contributions include new studies of major thinkers, key debates and critical concepts.

Connecting Practices
Large Topics in Society and Social Theory
Elizabeth Shove

Marx, Engels and the Philosophy of Science
David Bedford and Thomas Workman

Bourdieu's Philosophy and Sociology of Science
A Critical Appraisal
Kyung-Man Kim

Nation and State in Max Weber
Politics as Sociology
Jack Barbalet

The Political Durkheim
Sociology, Socialism, Legacies
Matt Dawson

Utopia without Ideology
Ambrogio Santambrogio

Social Imaginary and the Metaphysical Discourse
On the Fundamental Predicament of Contemporary Philosophy and Social Sciences
Christoforos Bouzanis

Utopia without Ideology

Ambrogio Santambrogio

Routledge
Taylor & Francis Group
LONDON AND NEW YORK

First published 2023
by Routledge
4 Park Square, Milton Park, Abingdon, Oxon OX14 4RN

and by Routledge
605 Third Avenue, New York, NY 10158

Routledge is an imprint of the Taylor & Francis Group, an informa business

British Library Cataloguing-in-Publication Data
A catalogue record for this book is available from the British Library

Library of Congress Cataloging-in-Publication Data
Names: Santambrogio, Ambrogio, 1958– author.
Title: Utopia without ideology / Ambrogio Santambrogio.
Description: Abingdon, Oxon ; New York, NY : Routledge, [2023] |
First published 2022 by Routledge. |
Includes bibliographical references and index.
Identifiers: LCCN 2022048939 (print) | LCCN 2022048940 (ebook) |
ISBN 9781032127385 (hardback) | ISBN 9781032134673 (paperback) |
ISBN 9781003229339 (ebook)
Subjects: LCSH: Social action. | Utopias. | Sociology.
Classification: LCC HN17.5 .S293 2023 (print) |
LCC HN17.5 (ebook) | DDC 361.2–dc23/eng/20221227
LC record available at https://lccn.loc.gov/2022048939
LC ebook record available at https://lccn.loc.gov/2022048940

ISBN: 978-1-032-12738-5 (hbk)
ISBN: 978-1-032-13467-3 (pbk)
ISBN: 978-1-003-22933-9 (ebk)

DOI: 10.4324/9781003229339

Typeset in Times New Roman
by Newgen Publishing UK

The disappearance of utopia brings about a static state of affairs in which man himself becomes no more than a thing.

Karl Mannheim

Perhaps the immobility of the things that surround us is forced upon them by our conviction that they are themselves, and not anything else, and by the immobility of our conceptions of them.

Marcel Proust

Contents

Introduction 1

1 A Finalistic Theory of Social Action 7
The End of Disenchantment? 7
Clarity and Consciousness 9
Coherence and Adequacy 11
Values, Ends, Means 15
Time and Meaning 21
Project of Action 24

2 Political Culture 37
Political and Civic Culture 37
Civic Culture and Quality of Democracy 41
Immanent and Non-Immanent Analysis 46
Political Theory, Political Cultures, and Political Traditions 51
Common Sense and Social Representations 54
Symbols, Values, Options 61

3 Social Imaginaries 69
Science and Common Sense 69
Bridging Ideologies 72
Integration and Solidarity 78
Modern Social Imaginaries 82
Social Imaginaries 86
Identity without Politics 92

4 Ideology 100
Ideology and Unmasking 100
End of Ideology 107
Enlightenment and Ideology 113
Theory of Ideology 118
Project of Action and the Process of Valourization 124
Politicizing Society 133

5 Utopia 148
A Brief History of Utopia 148
The End of Utopias? 153
Real Utopias 157
Everyday Utopias 161
Freely Feasible Utopias 163
The European Utopia 175

Conclusions 181

Bibliography 184
Index 193

Introduction

As far back as 1929, as he commented on what he believed to be the end of ideologies, Mannheim wrote:

> the complete elimination of reality-transcending elements from our world would lead us to a "matter-of-factness" which ultimately would mean the decay of the human will (...). The disappearance of utopia brings about a static state of affairs in which man himself becomes no more than a thing. We would be faced then with the greatest paradox imaginable, namely, that man, who as achieved the highest degree of rational mastery of existence, left without any ideals, becomes a mere creature of impulses (...) man would lose his will to shape history and therewith his ability to understand it.
>
> (Mannheim 1997a, p. 236)

Almost a century later, these words still resonate with full force. Today, more than then, we are faced with the predicament Mannheim described. Without any ability to make sense of the future, we are no longer able to understand history, not even our own individual history. We no longer know where to look; uncertainty and distrust grow. We remain captives in our accelerated daily lives whose senseless pace – driven by an increasingly dominant neo-liberalism – leaves us harried and breathless.

Our democratic systems would be in grave danger if they were not able to once again ask the crucial question on the quality of democracy: peace, poverty, education, the environment, health, equality, and rights are issues that do not admit of further delay. Above all, we need to change our relationship with time, to free ourselves from a present pressing down upon us, crushing our ability to look back or look forward. For all these reasons, the role of utopia becomes central again. This book is an attempt, at the conclusion of a theoretical journey through other concepts (political culture, social imaginary, and ideology), to present a new vision of the concept of utopia, understood as a freely feasible project. In the awareness that without any temporal structure,

DOI: 10.4324/9781003229339-1

without a sense of feeling anchored in a past and projected into a future, the present loses all capacity to make sense.

Utopia without Ideology is a work of *social theory*. Its purpose is to propose original definitions of the concepts of *political culture, imaginary, ideology,* and *utopia,* in a way that the individual definitions are consistent with each other and can be arranged within a single and general conceptual framework. These individual concepts have been dealt with within disciplines among themselves heterogeneously (political science, sociology, philosophy, anthropology); and, especially today, in international scientific debate, they are the subject of a multiplicity of interpretations which lead to an overlapping of their meaning and their use. It is not the text's purpose to put forward a review of these approaches nor to discuss them critically and favour one over the other: bibliographical references are therefore only instrumental to the arguments and do not aim to present organically and systematically single positions or entire areas of discussion.

The basic sociological approach of the work is constituted by the *finalistic theory of social action* in its Weberian formulation, starting from the relationship between *means, ends,* and *values*. This relationship brings into play the problem of that between *sense* and *time*, a question at the centre of the subsequent reflections of Schütz and, more generally, of phenomenological sociology. Particularly useful in addressing this question are the distinctions between *intentionality* and *reflexivity* and the concept of *project of action*. The sense of social action can be investigated if it is reconstructable reflexively within a project of action that comes from the past and engages the future. Just as our identity lies in this ability to project into a future of a relatively coherent system of ends that engages significant others. Without this ability, our vital living space shrinks and compresses, our view of the world becomes blurred and myopic, every problem appears to us to have no solution. Political culture, imaginary, ideology, and utopia are diverse and complementary ways to formulate this relationship between sense and time.

To sum up in essential terms, *political culture* is a specific area, concerning the political dimension, of the common sense present in a given society. And to this, we can apply the concepts developed by Schütz regarding the common sense we share within our everyday lives (opacity, irreflexivity, typification, etc.) but also those elaborated by the theory of *social representations* as developed by Moscovici and his school (anchoring, objectification, central core, etc.). The relationship between sense and time is, in this case, intentional, but not reflexive, and is based on the automaticity and predictability of the greater part of everyday human actions. A distinction must be made between *beliefs* and *intentions*: the former may be true or false; the latter, on the other hand, may be realized or not. It follows there from that while acting, using reference beliefs, one is not reflexive with respect to the beliefs, but only with respect to the intentionally intended end.

Social imaginary is, on the other hand, not so much part of common sense (as Castoriadis and, above all, Taylor imply), but rather an incoherent deposit of symbolic elements and values produced by civil society, and especially by the work of social movements. My hypothesis is that social imaginaries, thus conceived, have replaced, since the 1970s, political ideologies, be it right- or left-leaning. The end of ideologies can sociologically be read as related to a profound transformation of the structure of social stratification, essentially to the end of social classes. While political ideologies constituted a relatively coherent system of symbols, values, and practical options, produced by relatively reflexive social subjects (intellectuals, theorists, university professors, party leaders, etc.), those from the top of the political and cultural system were 'imposed' on the base; the social imaginaries are, on the contrary, a less coherent deposit of ideas and values, of disorderly production by a multiplicity of social subjects, characterized by a non-unilateral belonging to the system of social stratification (more greatly differentiated today), that propose to the political system their new visions of the world. In recent decades many movements – youth, feminist, environmentalist, pacifist, LBGT, no-global, etc. – have urged their problems onto the political agenda, transforming them from marginal to central issues. The new forms of populism and fundamentalism can also be read in this perspective.

Thus we have, on one hand, that of the civil society, *identities without politics*; and, on the other, that of the political system and the parties, *politics without identities* (in a certain sense without ideologies). The issue of the relationship between sense and time then arises dramatically, since there lacks an ability to organize, even with minimum coherency between them, values and policies, civil society and political system, subjects and government. It is no coincidence that the Habermasian model of deliberative democracy is an attempt to heal this fracture. All this jeopardizes the idea of democracy, unable today to manage politically neo-liberal economic processes that are increasingly autonomous and independent of any form of democratic control or direction.

The concept of *ideology* proposed should serve precisely to heal the fracture. Within the current contemporary debate, there are essentially two conceptions of ideology: that of distorted and false thought, to be unmasked, and a simple cognitive model on which to build social and political identities, but considered in a merely descriptive and non-evaluative manner. The first is no longer credible, since the technique of unmasking is no longer effective and can no longer be used, especially because it presupposes that it is possible to refer to a true cognitive system, non-ideological; the second makes the concept of ideology less useful: if all are, not one of them is.

My idea is that of proposing a new notion of ideology. Taking up its Enlightenment origins, I would like to return to considering it a *science of ideas*, which has two priority purposes. (1) To show that values are not fully realizable. Only ends can be achieved, ends that are somehow consistent with reference values. This is a teaching that comes from Weber's theory of action, from the ineliminable and tragic tension between the ethics of responsibility and the ethics of conviction. (2) To be a tool capable of showing the possibility of organizing values (often incoherent among themselves) into concretely pursuable ends: in sum, a technique for *translating values into ends*. It is necessary to distinguish here between democratic values transversally shared by all (tolerance, respect, fundamental rights, solidarity, etc.) and 'partisan values', through which social and political debate is structured within the common values and institutional framework. In pursuing these two ends, the importance of the figure and the role of the intellectual re-emerge, one that must also be redesigned within this new perspective. The first is a critical purpose; the second, constructive.

For example, I am in favour of equality. With the knowledge that a society of equals will never exist (and would perhaps be a true nightmare) and with the knowledge that the value of equality may conflict with other values (e.g., that of freedom), I can try to identify a system of ends that between them are relatively coherent and politically pursuable in a project of action. Conceived in this way, a theory of ideology heals the fracture between identity and politics, between society and parties, giving the latter the task of translating into a political project the values and identities present in the former. Sense and time are articulated within a project of action definable as a programme, understood as a relatively coherent system of pursuable ends (Schütz) that testify (Weber) their reference to social values and identities.

What role can be given to *utopia* in this context? My fundamental point of reference is Mannheim's sociology of knowledge, above all his demand that the end of ideologies does not mean the end of the possibility to envisage a future. So I prefer to speak of a utopia without ideology(-ies). Like ideologies, utopia shares two models in the literature of today. The first sees utopia as a model of a perfect society, characterized by total harmony. The second sees a non-place in utopia, a place we will never reach, in the knowledge that what counts is the journey and not the arrival. On one hand, there is an end without a clear path; on the other a path without an end.

There is, however, a possible third model and that is the conception of utopia as a project of collective action – in the phenomenological sense, indicated above – particularly broad and future-oriented. It can involve several generations; its general characteristics are outlined but are realized within the project itself. Utopia is a project that is realized 'in doing it', along a path that foresees continual corrections and adjustments. It is not a promised land, a place of perfection; and it is not even a non-place, a mere aspiration. The destination exists but the road we take to reach it ends up by determining it. In this way, utopia is an expression of the ability to project ourselves collectively into the future. United Europe is a possible example of a *freely feasible utopia*. Europe is the utopia for the Europeans. Another significant example is Rawl's idea of *The Law of People*. Sense and time are articulated in a process of continuous and reciprocal cross-reference within which each of the two concepts reshapes the other: within such a forward-reaching project, in fact, the demands for sense and time – and their reciprocal reshaping – are the specific object of collective action.

To sum up: (1) I hear Trump on television and my left-leaning *political culture* dictates an intentional but spontaneous reaction: I criticize him while barely listening to him. (2) I attend a Black Lives Matter demonstration and even though I do not know exactly what the objectives or the cultural role models of the movement are (are they reformist, anti-racist, feminist, revolutionary?), I do know roughly that I am in the right place, even if it is likely that I do not entirely agree with everything that the other protesters are thinking (*social imaginary*). (3) I would be happy if a left-wing democratic party, in which I recognize myself, succeeded in articulating the values that I feel meet my political culture and my social imaginary (equality, peace, democracy, rights, work, environment, etc.) in a workable programme of, among themselves, relatively coherent ends. I know that this programme will not wholly satisfy my need for these values, but I also know that believing in being able to realize them directly and fully would only re-propose tragedies that our history has already dramatically lived (*theory of ideology*). (4) I know, however, that before me, and probably before whoever comes after me, there is the further identification of broader and more general projects to realize (*utopia*), for which whatever I have approved in voting for my chosen party's program is a small, but I hope important, contribution.

What has been said up to now can lead us to think of an intrinsically descriptive model. On the contrary, I make no secret of the fact that the reflections made here have at their basis a specifically normative approach. First of all, the idea that a politics at the service of society – meaning an expression of collective decisions – must reclaim the role that was taken away from it by the market, and more generally by the neo-liberal economy. Second, the idea that such a politics must be the expression of a real democratic participation that makes possible the expression between identity (social system) and politics (political system). An important role, in this direction, is represented by models of deliberative and participatory democracy. Lastly, the experience of so-called early modernity has taught us to moderate our *hybris*: human action has ineradicable limits, the awarcness of which is a cultural, social, and political goal of extraordinary importance. This, I said, is a social theory book: my ambition and hope is that the concepts proposed here can provide a useful framework for empirical research purposes too.

The writing of this book was able to enjoy funding provided by the Department of Political Science, University of Perugia, as part of the Legality and Participation Excellence Project, 2018–2022. Thanks go to the Department Director, Prof. Giorgio Eduardo Montanari, and the project coordinator, Prof. Alessandra Pioggia. I feel deeply indebted to Lorenzo Bruni, Luigi Cimmino, Alessandro Ferrara, Andrea Millefiorini, Massimo Pendenza, and Walter Privitera who read the text or parts of it and gave me valuable advice. Marco Damiani was most useful for his general guidance and in the work of finding bibliographical sources: a heartfelt thank you to him. Julia Boone was instrumental in fine-tuning this English edition. I cannot forget Franco Crespi, teacher and friend, who has devoted much of his scholarly work to the study of the symbolic and its limits. To him a special thanks for all he has taught me.

Perugia, 21 August 2022

1 A Finalistic Theory of Social Action

The End of Disenchantment?

The following is one of Weber's most beautiful and best-known passages:

> Scientific progress is a fraction, the most important fraction, of the process of intellectualization which we have been undergoing for thousands of years (…). Let us first clarify what this intellectualist rationalization, created by science and by scientifically oriented technology, means practically. Does it mean that we, for instance (…), have a greater knowledge of the conditions of life under which we exist than has an American Indian or a Hottentot? Hardly. Unless he is a physicist, one who rides on the streetcar has no idea how the car happened to get into motion. And he does not need to know. He is satisfied that he may 'count' on the behaviour of the streetcar, and he orients his conduct according to this expectation; but he knows nothing about what it takes to produce such a car so that it can move. The savage knows incomparably more about his tools (…). The increasing intellectualization and rationalization do *not*, therefore, indicate an increased and general knowledge of the conditions under which one lives. It means something else, namely, the knowledge or belief that if one but wished one *could* learn it at any time. Hence, it means that principally there are no mysterious incalculable forces that come into play, but rather that one can, in principle, master all things by calculation. This means that the world is disenchanted.
>
> (Weber 1969b, pp. 138–139)

If we replace Weber's streetcar with the example of the computer, we make the point even clearer.

But what exactly does disenchantment mean? What are the enchantments that gradually vanish under the domination of technical means? The first to vanish is enchantment with nature. Once nature is seen through the eyes of science, it becomes a cold and mysterious universe. The lightning bolt of Zeus is no longer an expression of divine wrath, but the result of a particular combination of electrical charges. Everything becomes more incomprehensible and

DOI: 10.4324/9781003229339-2

more reassuring: the propitiatory rite is replaced by the lightning rod. A relationship of control without understanding is established. Everything loses its enchantment and appears as a combination of forces that can be reduced to relatively coherent systems of equations. Next vanishes the enchantment of the narratives with which people have given themselves varied and multiple explanations of nature and of their reciprocal relationships: tradition, fable, myth disappear into the iron cage of technical-scientific formulations. But can science really replace these narratives and thus erase the enchantment, that produced by nature and that produced by people?

The question Weber poses is not so much about the end of narratives, but rather the relationship, within processes of rationalization, between scientific and non-scientific knowledge. For Weber's American Indian or Hottentot, the technical knowledge available to their cultures is perfectly embedded in the narratives through which they interpret the world. Nor does it constitute a challenge to other types of knowledge; rather, it represents one aspect among others, within shared cultures. Technique and magic, in some ways, do not have perfectly clear boundaries, just as there are no clear boundaries between religious knowledge and technical skills. The craftsman, the peasant, the trader living within traditional cultures are not professionals in the Weberian sense: their skills are part of a common cosmos of meaning, predominantly religious. Science, on the contrary, arises in direct opposition to these other forms of knowledge, those of religion, magic, tradition. The emergence and the affirmation of scientific method would like to make available to human cultures a qualitatively different knowledge, essentially opposing the traditional forms, and potentially able in the long run to make these latter obsolete and useless. Non-scientific knowledge resists this attempt of erasure, but it is inevitably forced to confront that challenge.

The point made by Weber is that science and scientifically driven technology are not able to completely replace, as they would like to, traditional worldviews. For one simple reason. They cannot tell us how to make sense of our world. They only tell us how to intervene when we want something from the world or in the world. When we wish to visit the moon, science can tell us how to get there but can do nothing on the central question: why go to the moon? What sense does it have to go there? From this point of view, "the intellectual constructions of science constitute an unreal realm of artificial abstractions, which with their bony hands seek to grasp the blood-and-the-sap of true life without ever catching up with it" (ivi, pp. 140–141). It is here that science is 'absurd'. Citing the words of Tolstoy, used by Weber, "science is meaningless because it gives no answer to our question, the only question important for us: 'What shall we do and how shall we live?'" (ivi, p. 143). The knowledge offered by science is incapable of giving meaning to the world, also because it would subtract importance from those forms of knowledge, which for simplicity's sake may be called narratives, but the main purpose of which has always been to give a place to humans in their cosmos.

Weber's problem may be formulated more precisely: how do narratives change when they are confronted with a form of knowledge which, independent of shared cultures, aims decisively at replacing them, at erasing them? It is both misleading and wrong to answer this question if we believe that our lives can be led without our questioning its meaning and without seeking an answer, absorbed by a merely technical-rational attitude towards things and ultimately towards ourselves. But in fact, from the point of view of history, the emergence of science has not cancelled the production of narratives; quite the contrary. In the vacuum left by lost tradition and produced by secularization, paradoxically, narratives have flourished with unexpected intensity and variety. Freed from the protective umbrella of religious narratives and spurred by the development of scientific challenge, new general and specific, concrete and abstract worldviews have proliferated, suited to the few and aspiring to dominate the minds of the many. Consider, for example, the appalling totalitarian ideologies of the twentieth century.

Disenchantment, therefore, should not be viewed as opposed to a possible re-enchantment. They are not zero-sum tendencies: an increase in one does not imply a reduction in the other. Disenchantment is the cognitive attitude of science; it characterizes its absurdity, but it does not imply the inevitable cognitive monopoly of science, nor the end of narratives. Moreover, one cannot disregard the positive role played by science. For Weber too, scientific disenchantment brings with it a broader project of enlightenment of human knowledge, aimed at overcoming, or scaling back, the role played by myths, religions, and those narratives that produce, in addition to a set of enchanting narratives, blatantly false worldviews. Weber repeatedly insisted that leading one's existence on foundations of magical or religious powers prevents humankind from developing a personal or collective autonomy and freedom.

So the question arises about the form that narratives take within a world that is increasingly dominated by science and technology, to ask in which way may we continue trying to answer the fundamental questions posed by Tolstoy. Aligned with Weber, using his perspective, and after having examined the central question of understanding the meaning of social action, we will look at the relationship that exists between value rationality and instrumental rationality, therefore between narratives and technology, between enchantment and disenchantment. To address the question of meaning in more depth, in particular the relationship between meaning and time – every narrative needs time! – we will then refer to phenomenological sociology, in particular to the work of Schütz.

Clarity and Consciousness

The concept of rationality in Weber is somewhat a hazardous minefield.[1] To frame the theme correctly, a number of premises should be introduced to provide a Weberian background framework within which to elaborate the successive reflections. The premises can be summarized in five points: (1) It is impossible for humankind to live in close tune with the world. We are not granted the knowledge that reality is rational or irrational, if it contains a meaning and if this meaning is accessible to us. (2) Humankind's task therefore is to structure an own position in the cosmos – to use Scheler's beautiful expression – trying to give an own autonomous meaning to reality. (3) Weberian individualism is thus anthropological even before it is methodological. We are such insofar as we are able to make sense of what surrounds us – cognitive level – and to what we do – practical level. To make sense, namely to give a meaning, signifies the introduction in a dark and ignorant place, of a personal imprint. (4) This ability is neither simple nor obvious. It implies a challenge that each of us faces, first of all with ourselves. At stake, in fact, is our personal vision of our existence, the attempt to give it a unitary and coherent meaning. Not everyone can meet this challenge. It is much simpler to rely on the idea that there is a meaning independent of ourselves and adapt to that. Or, on the contrary, that there is no meaning at all, and adapt to that. These are both passive options that avoid any involvement of our autonomy. The élitist and pessimist Weber is quite sceptical that the broad majority of the masses are capable of meeting such a radical challenge, that they are able to do without a Grand Inquisitor or similar figure. Just as any Grand Inquisitor will always think of themself as an absolute necessity for the good of all. (5) The destiny of the West is in keeping with this tragic element of the human existential experience: modernity, as Weber reads it, constitutes the scenario in which "the ethical irrationality of the world" (Weber 1969a, p. 122) and humankind's burden of responsible action in it, while aware that we cannot completely redeem it, are displayed in their crudest light. By irrationalism, it should be understood that ends are not rationally justifiable. The destiny of humankind and the destiny of the West are intertwined in such a way that, in advanced modernity, the tragic nature of the former appears historically in its most radical and profound clarity. In this perspective, disenchantment plays a decisive role in bringing human autonomy to the forefront.

Within this context, the theme of value-rationality links to the Weberian concept of personality, to the way in which the autonomous individual is possible inside modernity. For this reason, I believe it is essential today to rediscover, along the avenue laid by Weber, a model of 'enchanted' rationality, independent of instrumental rationality, which deals with the relationship between ends and values.[2]

First of all, it must be said that human action is rarely action in the real sense. In most cases, "actual action goes on in a state of inarticulate half-consciousness or actual unconsciousness of its subjective meaning (...) governed by impulse or habit" (Weber 1978, p. 21). Consequently, "the ideal-type of meaningful action where the meaning is fully *conscious* and *explicit* is a marginal case" (Ibidem, italics mine). Although "the difficulty need not prevent the sociologist from systematizing his concepts by the classification of possible types of subjective meaning. That is, he may reason *as if* action actually proceeded on the basis of clearly self-conscious meaning" (Ibidem, italics mine). The four ideal types of acting constitute the ways in which autonomy and passivity of acting relate: the affective and the traditional are more passive and not consciously oriented according to a meaning;[3] in the two rational ideal types, on the contrary, the meaning appears more conscious and clear, that is, evident under reflection to the actor, who makes his action the expression of his conscious, and therefore rational, ability to act in the world. Rationality, for Weber, is therefore primarily *clarity* and *consciousness*. To act rationally in the world means to act in a (relatively) autonomous way, giving an action an intended meaning that is not merely mechanical, dictated by impulses or moved by habits, but that is clear and evident to the consciousness of the actor. There is not of course a sharp distinction, that between total clarity and total opacity, but a graduated scale, ranging from a maximum of the former to a maximum of the latter.

Clarity and consciousness are indispensable in the Weberian concept of rationality, but they do not complete it. They are the presupposition of a choice between alternatives, but they do not coincide with the choice. Clarity and consciousness can also inhibit or even block a choice, or simply allow more than one choice. And precisely because of this, there is not just the cognitive dimension to an action but also the concrete, practical characteristic of intervening in the world.

This practical dimension also has a rational aspect, which Weber identifies in two different ways with which a praxis may be consciously oriented towards an end: it may be goal-rational or value-rational. In its practical end-oriented dimension, an action is rational no longer only in the dimension of clarity and consciousness (a dimension that contrasts with the opacity of those behaviours that are not actions in their own right), but, within that clarity and consciousness, we can distinguish between a maximum of *coherence* and a maximum of *adequacy*, between coherence with respect to value and adequacy of the means with respect to the ends.

To sum up: action is rational if its meaning is clearly and consciously intended,[4] but it can also be diversely rational in relation to the way the actor thinks about intervening in the world, depending on whether he adopts a logic of coherence or one of adequacy. While the first level of rationality may constitute a continuum that goes from a maximum to a minimum of clarity/consciousness, the second level does not constitute a continuum but rather an alternative. Thus, it is important to reflect upon the relationship that exists between coherence and adequacy.

Coherence and Adequacy

The requisite of coherence is typical of value-rationality. It characterizes an action defined "by a conscious belief in the value for its own sake of some (…) form of behavior, independently of its prospects of success" (ivi, p. 24). Rationality coincides here with coherence with respect to an unconditional value: it "always involves 'commands' or 'demands' which, in the actor's opinion, are binding on him" (ivi, p. 25), unconditionally, one could add. To give a Weberian example:

> The central concern of the really consistent syndicalist must be to preserve in himself certain attitudes which seem to him to be absolutely valuable and sacred, as well as to induce them in others, whenever possible. The ultimate aim of his actions which are, indeed, doomed in advance to absolute failure, is to give him the subjective certainty that his attitudes are 'genuine', i.e., have the power of 'proving' themselves in action and of showing that they are not mere swagger.
>
> (Weber 1949, p. 24)

Action here is rational for two reasons: (1) because the intended meaning is clear and evident; (2) because the meaning is considered consistent with a value felt to be imperative.

The external character of value with respect to the actor – the fact that it is not rationally available to the actor – makes the rational character of coherence possible: the actor can but judge the coherence of the relationship between the actor's action and the value, but cannot judge the rationality of the value itself. Value is not derived from reason. Judging rationality is based on a relation. Of course, the judgement of rationality – since it syndicates a relation – can be placed on a continuum, ranging from a maximum to a minimum of coherence.

Let us now look at the second model of rationality, instrumental rationality, and the different continuum on which it lies. Now the actor is no longer impelled by a value to which he must conform fairly coherently: his actions, and the meaning that is more or less clearly and consciously given to them, are determined "by expectations as the behavior of objects in the environment and of other human beings; these expectations are used as 'conditions' or 'means' for the attainment of the actor's own rationally pursued and calculated ends" (Weber 1978, p. 24). The action is rational, in this second case, if external expectations are evaluated as 'conditions' or as 'means' useful to achieve a goal. The relation with the world is now sensitive to the consequences, and not dominated by pure coherence. A lie, to give an example, may be considered a useful means to an end, even if inconsistent with the unconditional value of truth.[5] What is lost in coherence is gained in adequacy; the value of success replaces the value of intention.

And so we have two models of rationality: the first can be identified with the binomial *clarity and coherence* and the second with *clarity and adequacy*. They are two extreme models, which in their purity exclude one another: I do this because I want to be consistent with what I believe, then whatever happens, happens; or, I do this because it is the most effective way to achieve an end that I have set for myself. They also differ in two other respects.

(1) Value-rationality action makes it possible to isolate every single action from the context in which it is set. Every action is an absolute of which the underlying absolute judgement can be identified. Should I ask the question – 'Are you sincere?' – the uncomplicated answer may be, in the end, just yes or no. Context and consequence do not matter, and all justification evaporates. The actor is alone before the value in which he believes: if the action is rational, that is, if its meaning is given to him clearly and consciously, he cannot hide from himself.[6] The situation is different in the case of goal-rationality action. Adequacy must be assessed upon a chain of goals that are connected to each other, and that appear to be directly influenced by action. For this very reason, Weber argues that one is rational with respect to a goal "by rational consideration of alternative means to the end, of the relations of the end to the secondary consequences, and finally of the relative importance of different possible ends" (ivi, p. 26), but he says nothing about this complex network of relationships when he talks about value-oriented rational action.

(2) While adequacy can in some way be measured, the degree of coherence can only be witnessed. The meaning of a rationally instrumental action lies in its ability to be useful in accomplishing an end, whereas a value-oriented action is not concerned with whether or not something has been accomplished, but only with the fit between the meaning and a value external to it. Both forms of rationality can be maximized, though in different ways: one, on the ability of the criteria adopted to achieve the end; the other, on the extent of the compromises which it has been possible to avoid.[7]

From what has been said so far, the two models of rationality seem mutually incompatible. They have a few things in common: their rational nature lies in the attitude of the subject, and not in reality itself; meaning must be clearly and consciously intended. For the rest, they follow different logics: the first is attentive to coherence, indifferent to consequences, absolute; the second is attentive to adequacy, not indifferent to consequences, and relative to the context. In a certain sense, they are also antithetical: greater attention to coherence implies less attention to adequacy, and vice versa. But their connection cannot be avoided. Does it make sense to tell the truth if I later find out that it is of no purpose, simply for the sake of saving one's soul? And, conversely, what is the point of achieving a purpose if I am then indifferent to it? In Weber's words, from the point of view of goal-rationality,

> value-rationality is always irrational. *Indeed, the more the value to which action is oriented is elevated to the status of an absolute value, the more 'irrational' in this sense the corresponding action is* (...). The orientation of action wholly to the rational achievement of ends without relation to fundamental values is, to be sure, essentially only a limiting case.
>
> (Ibidem, italics mine)

Therefore, they are mutually not rational: from the point of view of coherence, it is irrational to act effectively; from the point of view of effectiveness, it is irrational to act coherently with respect to a value. It must be stressed that coherence with respect to a value appears all the more irrational the more absolute that value is: an absolute value requires absolute coherence, it becomes even more irrationally demanding. We can think of the countless examples of martyrs of the faith: the total disregard of the consequences, for oneself and for others, causes a short circuit of coherence.

I think that Weber wants to suggest a reflection of this kind: the problem of coherence – and therefore of value-rationality – appears only when there is a discrepancy between action and value. Rationality is exercised over this discrepancy, and it always involves a judgement of a relation. If this discrepancy is removed and only a value appears, then the value reveals its specific nature, which in itself is neither rational nor irrational and which, to human eyes, vanishes in the absoluteness of its inexpressibility. Managing the discrepancy, that is, witnessing value with action, means being aware – tragically aware, one might say – of the finite and contingent character of human action. A value cannot be realized, or completely achieved. A value is never directly the goal of action, otherwise, any goal would be a value. Thus, our action is value-rational if (1) the meaning is clearly and consciously intended; (2) it carries with it a judgement of coherency with respect to the value and, therefore, presumes that it cannot fully realize it.

On the other hand, an action that is completely effective, but incapable of questioning the meaning of what it is going to accomplish, would be absurd and similarly irrational. It completely severs the relationship with value, that is, with the irrationality of the world. While for value-oriented action the problem is not to presume to be able to realize value within history, to redeem the irrationality of the world, in this case the problem is total indifference to value, which entails the risk of mere adaptation. It is that irrationality whereby what is a means becomes an end, and the ethical choice vanishes. And this is precisely the world of complete rationalization, of total disenchantment, within which the horizon of the ends is defined by the technical-scientific possibilities available. The latest ultra-technological mobile phone does not respond to any need but to something that is made possible – and desirable – by its very existence.[8] Of course, these are extreme cases, which serve to clarify the extremes within which the rational dimension of human action is placed: on the one hand, a world dominated by absolute value; on the other, a world without heart, dominated by technology. Two different extreme worlds, equally inhuman.

To summarize briefly: human rationality is a flicker of light in the dark senselessness of the world. Our actions, mostly dominated by irrational forces that we do not know how to manage and of which we are mostly unaware, rarely take advantage of this flicker. When they do, they have the arduous task of dealing with these forces, without falling into subjugation, and without presuming their erasure. The task, both difficult and sublime, that Weber entrusts to reason is to attempt the impossible and not to believe naively in its realization. Therefore, and as a consequence, our rational judgement is exercised in two ways: find means adequate to an end and evaluate the coherence of ends with respect to a value. These are two independent logics that can, however, meet each other, in a way that is also rational. They cannot be separated: absolute coherence would be inhuman and ultimately irrational; absolute efficacy would also be inhuman and irrational. Too much coherence and too much efficacy erase the space that makes rational judgement possible. Consequently, it is important to reflect on the way in which the two logics – within an increasingly rationalized society – can reasonably accommodate each other.

Values, Ends, Means

Let us hold firmly to the idea that there is no rational theory of value in Weber. To return to the example of the syndicalist, "whether one should or should not be a syndicalist can never be proved without reference to very definite metaphysical premises which are never demonstrable by science" (Weber 1949, pp. 24–25). The two forms of rationality are based on the idea that a judgement that ponders a relation with the greatest possible clarity is rational: what is the relation between the means I use and the end I want to achieve, and between the latter and the value I want to bear witness to? If, in the first case, the relation is one of adequacy, then my action is rational (I use means that are more or less adequate); if, in the second case, there is coherence and not too many compromises, then here too my action is rational (I have identified ends that are coherent with the value).

Furthermore, let us at the same time hold firm to the idea that there is a methodological level, through which the two forms of rational action are analysed as ideal types and a historical level, which consists in seeing, from time to time, how the ideal typical forms concretely relate to each other in a given epoch. According to Weber, total rationalization and total enchantment are the two different, but closely related, realizations of the two abstract ideal types. These realizations – like the ideal types of reference – are also historically impossible because they are abstract extremes of a continuum upon which we find the concrete historical forms: a totally rationalized world would be one in which value-rationality disappears completely; a totally enchanted – enchanting? – world would be one in which there is no space for instrumental rationality. In practice, and historically, their relationship – the relationship between the two forms of rationality and the relationship between rationalization and enchantment – constitutes a tension present throughout the history of the West,[9] a tension that reaches a zenith in modernity. It is therefore important to clarify carefully the methodological nature of this relationship, in its most abstract and ideal typical form.

The fundamental point of Weber's analysis of the rationality of human action can correctly be made if we distinguish three dimensions: *values*, *ends*, and *means*. Since there are three elements, there will be two main relationships: that between means and ends, and that between ends and values.

As we shall see better later, value is concretely determined in ends. This determination in alternative ends, however, implies a not total coincidence between values and ends. The relationship between means and values is thus mediated by the sphere of ends. Goal-rationality expresses a judgement on the relationship between means and ends; value-rationality on the relationship between ends and values, on the way in which these are actualized into ends.

The two levels of rationality cannot be reduced to one, especially not to instrumental rationality. According to Parsons,

> Action is rational in so far as it pursues ends possible within the conditions of the situation and by the means which, among those available to the actor, are intrinsically best adapted to the end for reasons understandable and verifiable by positive empirical science (...). Since science is the rational achievement par excellence, the mode of approach here outlined is in terms of the analogy between the scientific investigator and the actor in ordinary practical activities (...). *Apart from questions relating to the choice of ends* and from those relating to 'effort' (...) there is, where the standard is applicable at all, little difficulty in conceiving the actor as thus analogous to the scientist.
>
> (Parsons 1968, p. 58, italics mine)

On the contrary, I believe a dual notion of rationality must be maintained precisely because one cannot leave aside 'questions relating to the choice of ends'. Moreover, for this very reason, the action of social actors does not coincide with that of the scientist, and science for Weber is value-free (see also Schütz 1964, pp. 64–88).

Let us pause on the relationship between ends and values. Value cannot be exhausted by praxis, since it does not coincide with the end that praxis can actually give itself. An action can, using appropriate means, achieve an end but never achieve a value that may be coherent with other later ends. *A fortiori*, a means can be adequate only in an instrumental sense to achieve an end, but never – and only indirectly – to achieve a value. To use Schütz's language, an end can be anticipated as the motive for achieving which action is enacted, but a value cannot be anticipated in the same way (Schütz 1972, pp. 15 ff.). Moreover, an end can be considered a sub-project of a larger project of action, which involves further ends, themselves sub-projects of even larger projects of action, and so on. In contrast, a value cannot be a sub-project of anything. There are no isolated ends, but there are potentially isolated values.

A value – and, even more so, a set of values – is not realized in the same way as an end, that is, by finding adequate means. It can be said that a value is never realized directly, in and of itself, but only through the realization of ends consistent with it. But even the realization of the latter is always and only an approximation to the value, which can never be wholly appropriate. It is possible to identify and realize a multiplicity of ends, even potentially incompatible with each other, that are consistent with the reference value without, however, ever realizing the value itself. Rationality with respect to value expresses the value of dignity of the end with respect to value: I can find ends that are more worthy of being pursued than others, to which I give a greater priority because they are more capable of bearing witness to the reference to value. Therefore, this is a model of rationality that does not discriminate against the means, but rather against the way in which a value is pursued.

Let us take the value of equality as a tangible example. Equality as such will never be the end of an action. In essence, there will fortunately never be a world of perfectly equal people. Realizing the value of equality means identifying ends worthy of pursuit in the light of that value. Is providing parking lots for disabled users an end that is consistent with the value of equality? Is it consistent with that value? If the answer is yes, then the most appropriate means of achieving that specific end can be found. Once the parking lots are provided, I will not have achieved equality since it can be pursued by identifying other, and perhaps more worthy, ends. For example, was it not better to provide public buses with easy access? Can both ends, buses and new parking lots, be achieved?

The distinction between the two moments may now be clear. The means/ends relationship is a question of the feasibility, of the adequacy of the means in relation to the end within a variety of available means. The ends/values relationship involves a judgement of coherency, testimony, and dignity within a variety of available ends. The concept of end is the moment when the two different forms of rationality meet and avoids their abstract and unrealistic opposition. If one chooses ends to be achieved, one must take responsibility for them and be convinced of them. Let's think about indifference to the consequences characteristic – in its ideal typical conception – of value-rationality. When an action implies a choice between ends that are equally worthy of being achieved because they are all consistent with the value, an important role in the choice can, and must, be played by attention to foreseeable consequences. If the construction of parking spaces reserved for disabled users creates unsustainable aspects for the community (excessively high costs, environmental problems, technical difficulties, etc.), responsibility would require that their implementation be combined with, or replaced by, other projects. Similarly, having the means to effectively achieve ends does not exhaust the problem of action. What is also needed is not just an instrumental evaluation of the appropriateness of pursuing these goals but a deferral to the values that choices bring into play. For example, in the city where I live a light rail was built essentially because of the opportunity to enjoy European funding, overshadowing other evaluations that later turned out to be decisive, including the environmental impact, but also the actual public utility of the infrastructure. Or, on a broader scale, the mere possibility of eugenic techniques cannot exhaust the rational discussion of issues that require in-depth reflection on the relationship between technically feasible goals and the values at stake.

Three problematic dimensions can be identified, which may come to imply conflicts: (1) a conflict between values, which are not necessarily reconcilable with each other, indeed they almost never are; (2) a conflict between alternative ends: once the value has been chosen, which end is more worthy of being pursued must be decided; (3) a conflict over the most appropriate means to achieve the chosen end: here too, technical/scientific rationality rarely outlines a framework without alternatives. These three dimensions are closely interconnected: even the priority given to one of them – as in the example of the light rail built in my city – hardly erases the issues connected to the other two. Since operationally the end is what can actually be pursued, the position that the dimension of the ends assumes among the means and values makes it the pivot around which the question of the rationality of action revolves.

Onto the concept of the end is transferred, therefore, the double tension that comes, on the one hand, from the conviction in the pursuit of a value and, on the other, from the responsibility for the foreseeable consequences. Acting in a purely strategic way is just as irrational as acting in a purely value-oriented way. Rationalization in itself is just as irrational as the absolutization of values.[10] What we desire must meet what is feasible, and vice versa. For Weber, acting rationally implies an intervention in the world that is both convinced and responsible. It is necessary to be responsibly convinced. This means not being so convinced that we become blind, that we believe we can carry out an intervention in the world that fully realizes a system of values; but being sufficiently convinced not to be dominated by the logic of simple adequacy, of simple adaptation. Only in this way can human action, even within a sphere of limited possibilities, find space for the impossible.

We thus return to the questions of philosophical anthropology from which we started. It is possible to reconstruct a certain coherence in Weber between what is methodological, historical-political, and anthropological, all of which find a place in his conception of human action. For Weber, action is a matter of doing so and not otherwise, not because 'I have to' – the value I believe in imposes it on me; nor because 'I can' – the technical possibilities allow me to do so; but because 'I want to', namely I choose to do so starting from a clear and conscious weighing of the 'I have to' and the 'I can' within which I find myself acting: with a balance between my convictions and my sense of responsibility. The context within which the choice is placed is defined – methodologically – by the possibility of rationally articulating the two ideal types of rational action, of mediating between the two logics that constitute them. The sphere of rationality is thus connected with that of freedom, understood as the expression of subjective autonomy. Interpreting Weber, Löwith writes:

> Rationality thus coincides with the freedom to act since it is, insofar as it is '*teleological*' *rationality*, the freedom to pursue an end indicated by ultimate values and by meanings of life with a free and attentive examination of the means adequate to it. In such goal-rational action,

> 'personality' takes concrete form in the constant relationship of man with his ultimate values.
>
> (Löwith 2016, p. 33, italics mine)

Teleological rationality, which is linked to a finalistic theory of action, involves a necessary and complex weighing of the two rationalities and the two ethics.[11]

At least three consequences can be drawn from this way of reading the Weberian concept of rational action. (1) It implies a rational and radical critique of any praxis that intends to implement a radical transformation. The distinction between ends and values identifies the limits within which our ability to act in the world operates. Even ends cannot be unlimited: they bring with them the idea of feasibility, the only approach that allows the assumption of responsibility and a reasoned relationship between means and ends. (2) Since a single value may be compatible with a multiplicity of different ends, this opens up the prospect of a public dialogue which, starting from common values, enables a dialectic between different ends. For example, one can share the idea of equality and then diverge over the ways to achieve it. (3) A distinction may be introduced between *value-charism* and *goal-charism*. The first requires unconditional faith and believes in the possibility of directly realizing the values of reference through practice. The second requires only a responsible faith so that politics can be seen as the process of first selecting and then pursuing ends consistent with common values and, as such, removed from decision-making. These are aspects that will be visited in the following chapters.

Of course, as discussed above, the two ideal typical models of rational action refer back to the two ideal types of ethical behaviour. Ethics of responsibility evaluates action from what it produces in the world; ethics of intention is a goal-free ethics that acts in the world but is not of the world and evaluates action only based on its meaning. An action moved primarily by the ethics of responsibility is always included in a project of action (I use here the Schützian concept); it has an uncertain outcome (from good may come evil, and vice versa); it is indifferent to ultimate positions; it is supported by a cost/benefit logic; it is attentive to the possible and identifies its ends on a logic oriented by the value of success: in short, it aspires to adequacy. An action moved primarily by the ethics of intention can be isolated from context; it has an outcome removed from discussion (good always produces good); it is indifferent to consequences; it is guided by a logic of testimony; it is aimed at the impossible; it identifies ends based on the value of intention: in short, it aspires to coherence. In their purely ideal typical form, these models are contraposed.[12]

The methodological contrast paradoxically serves to show their inevitable complementary relationship at the socio-historical level, especially if one has to analyse the modern world. As mentioned above, it is a matter of understanding how this complementarity becomes real. Where technology becomes so invasive and where there is consequently a real danger of the return of particularly dangerous forms of irrationality, the only way of giving a responsibly autonomous meaning to one's own experience lies in the ability to make the two forms of rationality and the two forms of ethical behaviour complement one another in an increasingly reflexive way. Each historical epoch connotes with its own specific modality the potential for an encounter between the two ethics, subjecting the tension that opposes them to a specific and historically determined constellation of forces. Puritan ascetic individualism, the ethics of revolutionary syndicalism as well as Bismarckian realism – just to mention some Weberian examples – are different ways of how this meeting can take place, now leaning to one side, now to the other. Complementarity certainly does not mean having to opt for one or the other ethics in absolute terms. Rather, it is a matter of considering, first, what are the objective conditions within which the problem of the relation between the two ethics arises and, second, of assessing what is the actual response, specific and particular in its uniqueness, that each person subjectively gives to the question. In between, between the objective conditions and the subjective decision, lies the unfathomable. At the same time, in the middle lies the impossibility that the question can be dissolved once and for all or that it is, on the contrary, always starting from scratch.

In the modern world, in the era of rampant rationalization, the experience of the radical ethical irrationality of the world becomes radically, and perhaps collectively evident – due to the process of disenchantment. It thus becomes even more apparent how the actor's choice is in a sense without a parachute, since the actor cannot count on and refer to an external objective meaning coming definitively and completely from a religion or scientific knowledge. Every choice becomes respectable in itself, at least as an expression of an autonomous capacity to act. A choice is such – this is what Weber seems to want to suggest – if the intention does not evade the assessment of consequences, but responsibly assumes them. Worthy of note, therefore, is that choice – typical of a subject capable of establishing their own personality – which is able to address two simple questions: is a non-blind steadfastness possible and, vice versa, is a responsibility that does not annihilate possible?

As Goldman writes,

> Weber here lays out a Kantian version of the personality in which it is opposed to, or rather lifted above, nature and merely natural determinations. It *translates* higher values into rational action; yet it is constrained by factors in the social world dictating the limits and possibilities of such action. Unlike Kant, however, from whom the dictates of pure practical reason determine the self as personality, Weber states that the 'innermost elements' of personality – 'the highest and ultimate value judgements, which determine our action and give to our life meaning and significance' – determine the self.
>
> (Goldman 1988, pp. 142–143)

Therefore, "ultimate values, an 'inner' relation to these values, constant will, and rational action are thus the hallmarks of personality" (ivi, p. 142).

Modernity brings with it a very particular challenge in mediating the two models of action and ethical behaviour. A challenge that oscillates between Scylla and Charybdis: between the impossibility of total deference to the purity of an intention or, on the contrary, submission to the rampant instrumental effectiveness of a technique without end and without an end. In his analysis of modernity, Weber fears that the possibility of an autonomous inner life may be at risk.

But the unimaginable may happen:

> It is immensely moving when a *mature* man – no matter whether old or young in years – is aware of a responsibility for the consequences of his conduct and really feels such responsibility with heart and soul. He then acts by following an ethic of responsibility and somewhere he reaches the point where he says: 'Here I stand; I can do no other'. That is something genuinely human and moving. And every one of us who is not spiritually dead must realize the possibility of finding himself at some time in that position. In so far as this is true, an ethic of ultimate ends and an ethic of responsibility are not absolute contrasts but rather supplements, which only in unison constitute a genuine man.
>
> (Weber 1969a, p. 127)

Here Weber has in mind not so much, or not only, the ideal type of the professional politician, or scientist. He envisages the theme of the autonomous inner life of each of us. And of our ability to take it on thoughtfully. Even Weber's pessimism, despite flailing inside the iron cage, with the breath of inner life persistently stirring, cannot help but melt away.

Time and Meaning

The theme of intended meaning as a central element of human action, within a finalistic theory of action, is taken up by Schütz. He recognizes that

> never before had the project of reducing the 'world of objective mind' to the behavior of the individual been so radically carried out as it was in Weber's initial statement of the goal of the interpretative sociology. This science is to study social behavior by interpreting its subjective meaning as found in the intentions of individuals.

Certainly,

> the action of the individual and its intended meaning alone are subject to interpretative understanding. Further, it is only by such understanding of individual action that social science can gain access to the meaning of

> each social relationship and structure, constituted as these are, in the last analysis, by the action of the individual in the social world.
>
> (Schütz 1972, p. 6)

This said, however, Weber "naīvely took for granted the meaningful phenomena of the social world as a matter of *intersubjective agreement*" (ivi, p. 9), which did not depend at all on the various points of view, those of ego, and those of alter, those of whoever is different from ourselves, those of whoever came before us and whoever will come after. Intersubjective agreement is only an initial approximation. It is based on a naturalistic worldview, at the centre of which meaning is identically reproduced between subjects and different groups, and from one generation to the other. It applies to a social world experienced as natural, completely regulated for example by tradition. But it is also the way in which everyday actions are lived, within an everyday life that itself appears natural. All of us live our world without detaching ourselves from it; we think that others do the same; we are convinced then that the various understandings, our own and those of others, substantially match. In other words, we live in a 'natural' world, which we take for granted.

The 'natural' social world is the world of the anonymous and obvious. It is the world of everyday life, of our everyday lives. It functions not because there is within it a functionally based attunement, an order based on means-ends efficiency.[13] It 'works' because it is that common background inside which, through

> acts of establishing or interpreting meanings there is built up for us in varying degrees of anonymity, in greater or lesser intimacy of experience, in manifold intersecting perspectives, the structural meaning of the social world, which is as much our world (strictly speaking, my world) as the world of the others.
>
> (ivi, p 15)

The intersubjective social world is therefore a world of common-sense thinking, which can become the object of interpretation. It should be underlined that, from the beginning, our world

> is from the outset an *intersubjective world of culture*. It is intersubjective because we live in it as men among other men, bound to them through common influence (…), understanding others and being understood by them. It is a world of culture because, from the outset, the world of everyday life is a universe of significance to us.
>
> (Schütz 1962, p. 10, italics mine)

For Schütz, intersubjectivity is

> *the fundamental ontological category of human existence* in the world and therefore of all philosophical anthropology. As long as man is born of

> woman, intersubjectivity and the we-relationship will be the foundation for all other categories of human existence.
>
> (Schütz 1966, p. 82, italics mine)

The constitution of meaning is an intentional operation of consciousness, an operation that cannot be separated from the question of time. Intentionality is the original element of the life of consciousness, of conscious being, as it is connected "to my awareness of the actual ongoing or passage of my life, to my duration; in Bergson's words, to my *durée*, or, in Husserl terminology, to my internal time-consciousness" (Schütz 1972, p. 36). The fact is that "in everyday life, occupying as I do the position of *natural attitude* (or *standpoint*), I live within the meaning-endowing acts themselves and am aware only of the objectivity constituted in them, i.e., objective meaning" (Ibidem). Only when "by a painful effort" I detach myself from the objectivity of external things and turn directly to myself, to the intentional flow of my consciousness, can I notice the intentional processes that characterize it. Thus emerges something that before was only experienced intentionally, but not grasped reflexively.

Within the continuous unfolding of duration, I do not notice the passing of time and meanings: I live within them, in an "irreversible unidirectional" flow. In the end, I "find myself aged": I have lived "simply the duration along its path", without noticing the flow. Something remained hidden. Therefore,

> the very awareness of the stream of duration presupposes a turning-back against the stream, a special kind of attitude toward that stream, a *reflection* as we shall call it. For only the fact that an earlier phase preceded this now-and-thus makes the Now to be Thus, and that earlier phase which constitutes the Now is given to me in this Now in the mode of remembrance (*Erinnerung*). The *awareness of the experience* in the pure stream of duration is changed in every moment in *remembered* having-just-been-thus.
>
> (ivi, p. 47)

Reflection enables 'the awareness of experience': the intended meaning within the stream of duration of consciousness thus emerges reflexively.

A different attitude towards time is what distinguishes *intentionality* and *reflexivity*. Within everyday life, in my natural world, actions take place in a continuous flow without the need to ask what their meaning is. The baker, seeing me early morning, does not ask me why I have come into his bakery. Our actions are intentional,[14] meaning it is not a matter of instinctive gestures: the fact is that we take for granted the meaning of our actions that does not come reflexively to us.

So, for Schütz, meaning is a reflexive excursion from temporal continuity: to grasp meaning, it is necessary to halt – metaphorically – the duration, the flow of time and life. The subject stops and reflects: Why am I here? What is the meaning of my action? In this way, one loses the flow in its unity, in its uninterrupted flow, because one separates the now from the before and reconnects the nature of the now to that of the before. The before is caught in the now as a past, appearing to me as a memory. To become aware reflexively, to interrupt the intentional flow of time and consciousness, is to break the unity of time and its flow: reflecting is always remembering. From the intentional but unreflexive flow of consciousness, through reflection, I separate units of time endowed with meaning in the form of memory. This morning I am here at the bakery because I remember that I am out of bread. Intended meaning, for Schütz, "is merely an operation of intentionality, which, however, only becomes visible to the reflexive glance" (ivi, p. 52). There is no opposition between intentionality and reflexivity: reflexivity is the way in which the intended meaning appears to me, the way in which I become conscious of it.[15]

Adopting the reflexive perspective, the intentionality present in the unreflexive experience emerges. Intention can be opaque, unreflexive, part of the taken for granted; or it can appear to me reflexively, emerging from opacity. In the first case, I do not ask myself the problem of the meaning of my action, *I act without thinking*; in the second case, it is as if I stop acting, as does the flow of my daily life, to reflect: in a certain sense, *I think without acting*. Through reflexivity, what appeared obvious is interpreted: "meaning is a certain way of directing one's gaze at an item of one's own experience. This item is thus 'selected out' and rendered discrete by a reflexive Act. Meaning indicates, therefore, a peculiar attitude on the part of the Ego toward the flow of its own duration" (ivi, p. 42). This is a process by which the subject, by turning his attention to his past experience, construes it, and no longer just lives it, as endowed with meaning. The gap between the intentionality of living in the duration and the reflexive gaze means that only the past experience has an objective meaning and not the present experience. Moreover, through the reflexive gaze on the self, the subject truly emerges. With reflection,

> my Self, which has been hidden as yet by the objects of my acts and thoughts [and emotions, we should add], emerges (...). Consequently, all my performed acts, thoughts, feelings reveal themselves as originating in *my* previous acting, *my* thinking, *my* feeling.
>
> (Schütz 1962, p. 169)

To sum up, through the reflexive gaze the subject constitutes himself because he constitutes his world, made of thoughts, emotions, and actions.

Project of Action

The close relationship between meaning and time can also be grasped from another perspective. For Schütz, "*the meaning of any action is its corresponding projected act* (...). An action (...) is oriented toward its corresponding projected act" (Schütz 1972, p. 61). Buying bread from the baker is part of a project of action that aims at an end, from which the actions useful to pursue it acquire meaning. Action is *meaningful because it is planned*.[16] The meaning does not emerge immediately through the information that is presented objectively to the observer, but it always requires a reflexive interpretation of the unreflexive intentionality: whoever observed me at this moment would only see someone writing words – or rather, just, letters! – one after the other. The meaning lies in the project that this writing aims at.[17]

The structure of human action, taking up Weber, is finalistic. The meaning of an action, in its processuality, lies in the sense of the end to which it is directed. According to Schütz, there are intermediate ends and final ends. But the distinction is merely operational and discretionary: it depends on the intervention of the reflexive gaze on the intentional flow of duration. It is an inevitably arbitrary intervention. It depends on our way of making meaning of what we do, separating within our everyday life – along its uninterrupted flow – segments endowed with meaning: "if one is in earnest about seeking the subjective meaning of an action, one will find it in that which is the action's own principle of unit. The latter is always determined subjectively and only subjectively" (ivi, p. 216). The chain of ends can be broken in such a way that, through the identification of a project of action, final ends emerge, each of which, however, is always included in broader projects of action. The true final end is our own life, and better that it should not coincide with a single end.[18]

The relationship between intermediate and final ends can shed light on the nature of the concept of value, as it is applied by Weber himself. It seems to me to be completely improper – especially in a Weberian perspective – to think of a value as an autonomous entity, endowed with its own specific, I would say almost metaphysical, nature. So in what sense can we talk about values? In what sense do they constitute a pole within that problematic dialectic between means, ends, and values described above? The only reasonable answer can be to think of values as final ends, in Schütz's sense. A value, if understood as a final end – as such, unattainable – allows us to activate the mechanism of evaluation of intermediate ends, which are in effect evaluated on the basis of the value they assume pursuant to the final end. Value is not an entity, but rather the result of an activity that consists in evaluating, that is, in placing a value on intermediate ends. Weber identifies this activity in a value of testimony and coherence: the end of the action has value – and the actor gives value to it – inasmuch as it bears witness to an ultimate end beyond praxis. In light of the ultimate goal, the intermediate goal can therefore take on more or less 'value'.

The question of disenchantment is grafted onto this matter. In a natural world, that of common sense or that of traditional societies, the common goal is essentially opaque, because it is shared, and removed from reflexivity. Every intermediate goal is then seen as a means to the final shared goal. Think of the Christian-Catholic doctrine of good deeds: adequacy and coherence, success and testimony coincide. A good deed is objectively an instrument of salvation. When St. Martin divides his cloak and gives half of it to the poor man, his action is instrumentally effective both to protect the poor man from the cold and pursuant to the saint's redemption. The instrumental content and the value content of the action are both objectively assessable. Disenchantment and rationalization have to do not so much with the end of values, with the disappearance of the process of evaluating the ends and the actions that aim to achieve them, but with the definitive breakdown of this unity, of the possibility of an objective evaluation. The modern world is that world which experiences the end of the unity of the world. In Scaff's words, "the disenchantment thesis holds that modernity represents a loss of the sacred meaning of the wholeness and reconciliation between self and world provided by myth, magic, tradition, religion, or immanent nature" (Scaff 2000, p. 125).

Also in the modern world, however, subjective intentionality continues to refer to a shared repository of sense. Intended meaning is a product of the individual in a very distinctive way. The subject rarely *produces* meaning: mostly, they *reproduce* common sense, adapting it to their own projects of action. Today, at the bakery, I bought more bread than usual because I have friends over for dinner tonight. I used common-sense thinking for a project of action of mine, which fits into the flow of my life. Having mentioned a dinner party, the following quote from Schütz falls into place. For him, the common sense is 'cook-book knowledge'. In fact,

> The cook-book has recipes, lists of ingredients, formulae for mixing them, and directions for finishing off (…). Most of our daily activities from rising to going to bed are of this kind. They are performed by following recipes reduced to automatic habits or unquestioned platitudes.
>
> (Schütz 1964, pp. 73, 74)

There are of course recipes that we know well, others less well, and still others that we do not know at all.

Common sense is recipe knowledge that is taken for granted. Its salient feature is that it is shared, that it constitutes a community. At the level of the solitary Ego, as Schütz calls it, the reflexive gaze captures past individual experiences. In the same way, if the we-relationship becomes the object of reflection, I observe past collective experiences: common sense always involves an already constituted We. And just as the subjective meaning does not coincide with the lived experiences of my natural experiences, in the same way the shared meaning is not the natural We. The same duplicity that characterizes the I emerges: I can *live the We* in the shared living intentionality; I can *think the We* if my reflexive gaze rests on past experiences of the unreflexive We. The decisive aspect is that, within the world environment of everyday life, the I and the You are both present in the now-and-thus, that is, they live within the same real world of the We. This is an environment that belongs to no one: it is the *common world*, which is added to *my world* and *your world*. The reciprocal orientation takes place in the specific form of living together, within a world made up of meaning, or rather that is meaning: an unreflexive meaning, in pure common living intentionality. It is an understatement to say that the common world is meaningful: there is no such thing as a meaningless relationship.

The tension between intentionality and reflexivity, in practice between living and thinking, opens up the question of change. It is a way of conceiving change: in the everyday flow of common sense there is normality and repetition. But we need to look better inside common sense, in light of that tension, so as to avoid the radical alternation between stability and change. Change can be rapid or very slow, superficial or profound, shared or opposed. However, it is always a process, sometimes visible, sometimes hidden, depending on the role played by intentionality and reflexivity. *Intentional change* assumes the form of the continuous and invisible change of a river bed: the flow of unreflected duration, like the flow of the current, produces change in a mostly unreflected, opaque, invisible, slow way. Superficial changes, over time, can become profound: I may one day notice that the river bend is no longer the same. Instead, the reflexive highlighting of common sense can trigger change more consciously, quickly, and transparently, turning it into an object of conflict. Hence, we can talk of *reflexive change*.

It may be helpful to reason upon the internal structure of common sense. Typically, common sense is seen as something homogeneous, unstratified internally, characterized by opacity and impersonality. On the contrary, it can be seen as a universe within which lies a range of differentiation, that is, characterized by elements of greater resistance and opacity and others of greater volatility and transparency. On these latter, a greater degree of subjective discretion is exercised but with regard to the former, the processes of change are more radical and profound, requiring the activation of a considerable and articulated collective reflexivity across a lengthy span of time.

The dialectic between stability and change meets that between opacity and transparency: the reflexive emergence of meaning is the essential, though not sufficient, condition for the transformation of the universes of common sense. As we have seen, reflection, on the one hand, is always exercised on specific and delimited contents of meaning; on the other hand, so as to operate it also needs to lean on, to leverage and refer to, common sense: something must remain obscure in any case. A completely transparent world would no longer be a social world.[19]

One can then think of a connection, within common sense, between contents that are more sedimented, more insensitive to reflexivity, and others that are more exposed to it, that are less profound. I have used a geological metaphor, which envisages layers that are more resistant and others that are more exposed to change: in short, there is always something less visible, less at the disposal of the autonomy of subjective reflexive consciousness, and something that is more so. One can therefore distinguish, within common sense, between *deep common sense* and *ripples of meaning*. These are two extremes that identify a continuum, ranging from a maximum of resistance to reflexivity to a maximum of meaning available to the subject's reflexive consciousness.[20]

In this way we obtain an enriched interpretation of everyday life and common sense: they are not only routines and predictability but also places of the unexpected, of contradictions, of fractures, all realities that exist against a background that remains stable in substance. Everyday ordinariness is a varied and complex expression of normality and extraordinariness, of predictability and unpredictability: it is a rich and ineludible dialectic that concerns both the subjective sphere and the relation between the subject and the subject's world,[21] involving both the autonomy of subjective consciousness, the internal relationship between intentionality and reflexivity, and the autonomous interactions between universes of meaning that have become autonomous, that of ego and that of alter. Always, of course, beginning with a taken for granted, which constitutes the pre-reflexive basis of reflection, what I propose to call deep common sense.

Common sense is internally structured along another path too. When I send out a package, I expect different parties (clerks, mailmen, etc.) to behave in a way that is consistent with my plan of action. In these cases, my specific relationship with my mailman friend, or the relationship between ego and alter, should not matter: the important thing is that all the subjects involved direct their actions (with all, and in spite of all, possible ripples of meaning) in a typical way, which concerns not only mine but all other possible parcels. It is a matter of activating anonymous and typical forms of meaning synthesis: "in communication or in social intercourse each appresentational[22] reference, if socially approved, constitutes merely the kernel around which fringes [subjective meaning] are attached". But "all this already presupposes an existing typification of social relations" (Schütz 1962, p. 350).

Common sense presupposes within itself some typical universes of meaning – which concern the various social spheres – available to subjects, independently of the real relationship in its particularity. From the actual social world, from the interaction between ego and alter, we thus move on to the social world in general, anonymous and diffuse: it is a set of typifications that are actualized in real experience, moving from their merely typical form to their specific manifestations. This is why the process of meaning production, in the form of pre-reflexive intentionality, appears mostly as mere replication. Typifications are a stock of knowledge that "has its particular history. It has been constituted in and by previous experiencing activities of our consciousness, the outcome of which has now become our habitual possession. Husserl (…) speaks graphically of the 'sedimentation' of meaning" (Schütz 1964, p. 283). In the anonymous relationship, the I/you relation remains the original source of meaning. We are thus faced with a kind of *circle of representation*.[23] On the one hand, meaning is always subjective meaning, linked to the reflexive capacity of consciousness to break the unreflexive flow of duration; on the other hand, since intersubjectivity has a foundation independent of ego, then the latter is also always constituted by alter and, within the constitutive intersubjective relation, is always already social. The reflexive act of consciousness is always embedded in an intersubjective intentionality from which it cannot free itself and of which it cannot do without.[24]

Finally, one last important aspect must be stressed. The typical living experiences that make up common sense have the implicit task of maintaining a certain amount of coherence, so that everyday life, even with all its contingencies, can take the form of relative stability and predictability. This is a fundamental problem: a 'rational' social order and therefore comprehensible – to subjects and sociologists – must contain a minimum dose of coherence. In short, this is another way, in addition to the relationship between transparency and opacity, of looking at the problem of change: a disjointed and incoherent common sense will in fact be more prone to processes of transformation that grow ever deeper the greater the incoherence.

At the cognitive level, we thus have three dimensions that allow us to articulate an understanding of the mode of production and preservation of intended meaning: cognitive intentionality, common sense, typifications. Together with the concepts of reflexivity and project of action, they compose a theoretical framework capable of providing a theory of society based on an understanding of the intended meaning within a finalistic theory of social action.

The relationship between time and meaning can be seen in a final perspective, by pondering the fate of Tiresias. Tiresias has seen Athena naked, so the gods punish him by taking away his sight and, as a form of compensation, they give him the ability to predict the future. From then on, Tiresias lives in the future. He lacks the typical connection between past, present, and future that characterizes the structure of time for each of us, of everyday life. Unable to live his existence as an expression of projects of action, Tiresias can witness something that will happen, but he can no longer influence the future he foresees. He becomes an inactive observer of the ineluctable. He does not act, and cannot act, because he is unable to build connections of meaning from an end. He lacks the dimension of the original intersubjectivity, made up of social actors placed in time. In a way, Tiresias is alone. The future he can foresee is real, sooner or later it will come true, but it is disconnected not only from his personal individual motivations but also from the flux of that everyday life endowed with meaning that should lead to the future, to *a* future. His prediction appears meaningless, inexplicable and, therefore, out of human reach: it is *the* future that depends on the gods. And that, consequently, cannot be understood. It is incomprehensible because it is not the result of action.

Schütz uses Tiresias to show, on the contrary, how different is the experience of the common individual living everyday life: the latter acts because he or she does not know the future, because he or she cannot foresee it with the eyes of the seer. The individual can construct it because he or she does not know it. Tiresias has a knowledge that disarms, that takes away the meaning of action. Certainty is not the modality of our daily life, which is instead the home of doubt, of possibility, of unpredictability and, therefore, of meaningful action. Divine compensation is not properly a gift. It underlines and reinforces the nature of the chastisement: it foresees only those who do not see! The total emotional indifference that the seer feels in communicating his verdict is an expression not so much of awareness, of a resigned and fatalistic view of things, but also of his inability to feel the future: not being able to act, he is at the same time condemned to the impossibility of feeling emotion in response to the things that will happen. They are there before him, inescapable and final, in a vision that blocks the mind and heart. Tiresias is a typical example of the 'solitary Ego'. His prescience is a gift that excludes him from the common world.

For the common individual of our times, forced to predict without the gift of foresight, within a strongly rationalized world, where science is not able to replace the prophet or the oracle, the need for a reflexive effort appears more and more evident, capable of managing the tension between the two Weberian forms of rational action and the Schützian relationship between intentionality and reflexivity, in far-reaching projects of action.

Notes

1 It is also one of the central, unifying themes in all of Weber's work. According to Brubaker, "the idea of rationality is a great unifying theme in Weber's sociology. Weber's seemingly disparate empirical studies converge on one underlying aim: to characterize and to explain the development of the 'specific and peculiar rationalism' that distinguishes modern Western civilization from every other" (Brubaker 2006, p. 1).

2 My proposal sets itself within the framework of the Weberian re-readings initiated above all by the texts of Schluchter (1985; 1989; 1996). As Ferrara writes, while "keystones of the traditional image (…) were the neo-Kantianism of the methodological writings, the supposed centrality of the influence of Rickert, the analytical propensity of large sections of *Economy and Society*, the absence of a unifying theme for the entirety of Weber's work, the anti-evolutionist polemic, and finally, the strongly realist accentuation, almost to the point of a quasi-elitism, of his political sociology (…), the shift in perception concerns a vast range of aspects. The analytical-conceptual and methodological aspects have become less important, interest in the influence of Rickert has given way to interest in the influence of Nieztsche, there is an emerging interest in comparison with Simmel, but first and foremost, center stage has been occupied by the theme of the *rationalization of cultures and social action* as a *letimotif* in the story of humanity" (Ferrara 1995, pp. 7–8, translation mine).

3 As Weber writes, "strictly traditional behavior, like the reactive type of imitation (…), lies very close to the borderline of what can justifiably be called meaningfully oriented action, and indeed often on the other side. For it is very often a matter of almost automatic reaction to habitual *stimuli* (…). Purely affectual behavior also stands on the borderline of what can be considered 'meaningfully' oriented, and often it, too, goes over the line" (Weber 1978, p. 25). Two brief observations here. In order for an action to be recognized as traditional, a reflexive gaze outside the tradition is needed. This gaze can be that of the social scientist, but also that of a

society that has become more reflexive overall. Inside tradition there is no tradition. With regard to affective action, the contemporary sociology of emotions has made it clear that emotions contain a significant cognitive dimension, which distinguishes them from mere sensations (Hochschild 1983; Nussbaum 2001). This does not mean that this cognitive component is rational in the Weberian sense.

4 The scientist is a subject who acts predominantly at the cognitive level. For this very reason, his task is cognitive clarity, at a level impossible to achieve when the action of the everyday person constitutes a complex union between cognitive and practical dimensions. While in the classical world knowledge always has practical ends, tied to the identification of the right choice, of the right action, in its modern conception science presupposes the idea of objective knowledge because it is ethically neutral: the scientist produces 'mere knowledge', of which the requirements of scientific nature are independent of its possible practical outcomes. In this sense, science is absurd: insofar as it is predisposed not to deal directly with practical issues, in search of a level of value-free objectivity independent of ethics. At most, it can shed light on the conditions within which an ethical, practical choice is made, so as to make it as conscious as possible, but always with an awareness that is different from that of the scientist. This latter can "force the individual – or at least help him – *to give himself an account of the ultimate meaning of his own conduct*" (Weber 1969b, p. 152). Resorting to science thus remains a discretionary option: human action, and consequently political action as well, does not have an end in itself, unlike science. In this direction, science, from objective knowledge *super partes*, can become a tool to wield in the clash between the two sides: in a world dominated by scientific logic, it is increasingly imperative to give an equally scientific justification to all new standpoints. The use that politics has made of science during the recent pandemic is a good example. It is also appropriate to offer two important clarifications. The first is that Elster makes it clear that the distinction between value rationality and instrumental rationality does not match the distinction between formal and substantive rationality. This is because "formal rationality is essentially a procedural concept (…). Formal rationality is not a consciously chosen means to anyone's end, nor is it itself a form of means-ends efficiency (…). Economic, legal and bureaucratic systems are substantively rational when they aim at creating a specific distribution of goods, income or life-changes, or aim at bringing about some other substantive end (…). The substantive rationality of legal and bureaucratic institutions is a form of instrumental adaptation" (Elster 2000, pp. 22 23). For example, "one might say about the Protestant sects what Weber says about the animists: their behavior was rational, but only within their framework of magical thinking" (ivi, p. 38). That is, there can be no instrumentally rational action avulsed from the non-instrumentally rational context in which it is embedded. The second is that we must also distinguish between subjective and objective rationality: "subjective rationality depends on the clarity and self-consciousness of the actor's inner orientation; objective rationality on the extent on which action measures up to an objective standard (…). Judgments of objective rationality, Weber argues, are possible only from a purely technical point of view – only when the problem is to determine the most rational means to a precisely specified end" (Brubaker 2006, p. 5). But if so, it follows that "the most pressing problems of social life (…) cannot be solved in a objectively rational manner" (Ibidem). Both distinctions presented – that between formal and substantive rationality, as well as that between subjective and objective rationality – emphasize the inevitable intertwining of instrumental and value rationality.

5 Of course, speaking the truth can also be a means to an end: I can tell the truth to make a good impression on someone I care about. What matters is not the thing itself, but the nature of the subjective choice, an expression of the way we position ourselves towards the world. The world, as we have seen above, is neither rational nor irrational, neither right nor wrong. Right and wrong, as well as rational or irrational, are qualities that our actions take on through the choices we make. This is also true for value: rational is never the value itself, but only the attitude with which I am disposed to act with regard to it.

6 The dialogue between Jesus and the Grand Inquisitor or rather, more precisely, the latter's monolog is an excellent example of this absolute confrontation with the absolute, in search of a justification for one's actions. In Weber's words "the proponent of an ethic of absolute ends cannot stand up under the ethical irrationality of the world. He is a cosmic-ethical 'rationalist'. Those of you who know Dostoyevski will remember the scene of the Grand Inquisitor, where the problem poignantly unfolds. If one makes any concessions at all to the principle that the end justifies the means, it is not possible to bring an ethic of ultimate ends and an ethic of responsibility under one roof or to decree ethically which end should justify which means" (Weber 1969a, p. 122). Later, in the chapter on ideology, the question of bad faith will be discussed.

7 With thanks to Alessandro Ferrara for this observation.

8 According to Habermas, "[Weber's] hierarchy of concepts of action is designed with an eye to the type of purposive-rational action, so that all other action can be classified as specific deviations from this type. Weber also analyze the method of *Sinnverstehen* in such a way that complex cases can be related to the limit case of understanding purposive-rational action (…). Finally, the connection of these conceptual and methodological decisions with Weber's central theoretical question – how Occidental rationalism can be explained – is evident. This connection could, of course, be contingent; it could indicate merely that Weber was personally preoccupied with these problems and that this – from a theoretical point of view – contingent interest affected his theory construction down to its foundations. One has only to detach modernization processes from the concept of rationalization and to view them in *other* perspectives, in order to free the foundations of action theory from connotations of the rationality of action and to free the methodology of interpretative understanding from a problematic intertwining of questions of meaning with questions of validity" (Habermas 1984, v. I, p. 6). For Habermas, in Weber there is an ineliminable link between the methodological predominance of goal rationality and the analysis of Western rationalism, with the concept, that is, of rationalization. Moreover, Habermas seems to read Weber through the eyes of Horkheimer and Adorno, even if he then develops a completely separate path. And it is a reading to its own use and consumption. On the contrary – given that for Weber there is no rationality inside history, and rationalization cannot be confused with the idea of the presence of an inevitable historical progress – I think that in Weber there is no hierarchy among the concepts of action, that he has a rather complex and articulated theory of rational action and that, consequently, his reading of modern rationalism, and of the fate of the West, cannot be identified completely with the concept of rationalization. In short, there is life outside the iron cage, and the iron cage does not coincide with the world, not even the modern world. Western rationalism will never be completely disenchanted: this seems to me the crux of the argument.

9 Even magic, to give an example, syndicates the relationship between means and ends, with a clarity, and therefore with an adequacy, inferior to that which science can bring into play. This latter is increasingly heading in a direction that makes possible the transformation of the world. This is the historical process which, through rationalization, produces disenchantment. First, religion must historically emancipate itself from magic. This is already a first form of rationalization, which produces disenchantment: "religion must, so far as possible, have given up the purely magical or sacramental character of the *means* of grace. For these means always devalue action in this world as, at best, merely relative in their religious significance, and they link the decision about salvation to the success of processes which are *not* of a rational everyday nature. When religious virtuosos have combined into an active asceticist sect, two aims are completely attained: the disenchantment of the world and the blockage of the path to salvation by a flight from the world. The path to salvation is turned away from a contemplative 'flight from the world' and towards an active ascetic 'work in the world'. If one disregards the small rationalist sects, such as are found all over the world, this has been attained only in the great church and sect organizations of Occidental and asceticist Protestantism" (Weber 1969c, p. 290). The process of disenchantment can thus be seen as an increase in effectiveness in view of the transformation of the world.

10 On this point, I find extremely significant Mannheim's analysis of totalitarianism. Taking up Weberian theory of action, he shows how the two forms of irrationality can even coexist, giving shape to the totalitarian nightmare. The regimes of the fascist type, but also Soviet communism, efficiently combine the maximum of instrumental rationality – if we think of the use made by media to indoctrinate the masses, or to the use of completely centralized and rationalized forms of economic planning and of power – with the absolutization of values, which take the form of new irrational mythologies, as are the myth of race or of the working class. For Mannheim, totalitarianism is a tragic mixture of instrumental rationality and substantive irrationality (Mannheim 1997b). This seems to me the best terrible example of how the Weberian question of disenchantment does not simply mean the end of narratives, but rather the need, in a world dominated by technique, to rethink the relationship between technique and narratives.

11 It is possible to apply the reconstructive logic used here for the two ideal typical models of rational acting also to the two ideal typical models of non-rational acting. In fact, in the latter, values are either linked to tradition and therefore appear as merely given, not the object of possible reflection; or they are part of the cognitive content present in every affective action (on this important point I refer especially to Nussbaum 2001). In both cases, the relationship between the three dimensions – of means, ends, and values – continues to be present, even if not so clearly and consciously.

12 Their irreconcilability as ideal types is well emphasized by Schluchter: "it is (...) evident that in Weber's formulation there is no complementarity between an ethics of responsibility and an ethics of intention (...) in the end he used these two concepts to characterize two diametrically opposed political ethics, and in evaluating them he took into account their 'actuality'" (Schluchter 1985, p. 39).

13 This is the perspective embraced by Parsons, a perspective that, in the end, betrays the authentic Weberian inspiration, which I find instead preserved in the phenomenological approach.

14 On the concept of intentionality, see Searle (1983). For Searle, intentionality "is that property of many mental states and events by which they are directed at or about or of objects and states of affairs in the world" (ivi, p. 1). It is "a ground floor property of the mind" (ivi, p 26) and is concerned with a dimension of directionality relative to something. Very similarly to Schütz, "intentionality is not the same as consciousness. Many conscious states are not Intentional, e.g., a sudden sense of elation, and many Intentional states are not conscious, e.g., I have many beliefs that I am not thinking about at present and I may never have thought of" (ivi, p. 2). In Schütz's vocabulary, this distinction means that I can act intentionally without reflecting on my intentionality, that is, without reflexivity. The distinction between intentionality and reflexivity does not identify two different ways of being of consciousness, but only a different direction of gaze towards the flow of consciousness. Reflexivity is also intentionality: in the language of Searle, it is an intention directed towards itself. And it is always, to keep with Searle, an action, not a belief. Belief and intention, according to Searle, have to do with two different directions of adaptation between mind and world. A belief "is a propositional content in a certain psychological mode, its mode determines a mind-to-world direction of fit, and its propositional content determines a set of conditions of satisfaction" (ivi, p. 15). An intentional action "is simply the conditions of satisfaction of an intention"; thus, "there are no actions without intentions" (ivi, pp. 80, 82). The intentional action, in its finalistic structure, "has the world-to-mind direction of fit" (ivi, p. 88). For example, 'I believe it's raining outside' is a belief that can be verified by opening the window (a condition of satisfaction): my mind 'adapts' to the reality of the world (mode or direction of adaptation). 'I'll go get a coffee' is instead an action because it requires the activation of all those conditions that make it possible for me to have a coffee (conditions of satisfaction): the world adapts to the mind (mode or direction of adaptation). I find that Searle's approach is in line with Weber's finalistic theory of action and, in particular, with Schütz's development of it. One last remark. Intentions need justifications and therefore rely on beliefs. From the first-person perspective of the agent subject, it is therefore meaningless to argue, as Weber does, that the world is meaningless. What then is the point of view from which Weber speaks of the groundlessness of values, and therefore of intentions? The point of view cannot be the first-person point of view. Weber, during his life, took a position, always and very decisively. Only two alternatives are given. Either it is the third-person point of view of the scholar, who recognizes that in the modern world the conditions – be they metaphysical or religious – for a foundation of values are no longer given. Or it coincides with a view that is also metaphysical, close perhaps to that of Nietzsche. I believe that Weber always maintains an ambiguous attitude between these two alternatives, the methodological and the ontological.

15 I become aware of it, altering my normal – 'natural' – relationship with time: this is one of Schütz's great contributions to a general theory of action and understanding, a contribution that develops Weber's notion of intended meaning using the philosophy of Husserl and Bergson.

16 "What distinguishes action from behavior is that *action is the execution of a projected act*" (Schütz 1972, p. 61): action, as it unfolds, is oriented in the direction of planned action, and it is precisely the project of action, which gives the orientation of action, that makes it possible to speak of action in the proper sense and not mere behaviour.

17 This is an assumption with considerable methodological implications for the ways, and conditions, through which it is possible to understand action and intended meaning, both by alters and by the particular alter that is the social scientist.

18 An example: My students take my classes (intermediate end) to pass the exam (final end). However, passing the exam is for them an intermediate end of a larger project, namely to graduate. Graduating, for forward-looking students, can be part of an even larger project, such as becoming a sociology professor at a university. Devoting one's entire life to sociology, making it the broader culminating end of all, may, and through no fault of sociology, eventually prove frustrating. In this articulation of progressively greater ends, which are assumed to be relatively coherent, the scope is given to replace the unit of unreflexive system of the flow of experience (living without thinking) with a unit of reflexive system, operated by the subject who thus gives meaning to his actions. Therefore, Schütz can argue that "*rational action can therefore be defined as an action with known intermediate goals*" (ivi, p. 61). My far-sighted student behaves rationally if he constructs a project of action, whose goal is to become a professor of sociology, within which the intermediate goals are consciously organized and managed. Rationality, again unlike Parsons, lies not only in the objective and instrumental adequacy of means to ends, but in the reflexive capacity to give coherence to a system of ends, a capacity that is not objectively measurable, but only subjectively identifiable. An intermediate end is a means with respect to the final end in a sense other than a merely technical instrumental one. In fact, completed action is very often different from planned action. Our projects of action, and the meaning contained in them, only partly come to fruition as we intended. This fact is, on the one hand, the result of the complex intertwining of subjective cognitive, practical and emotional dimensions; on the other, the result of the unpredictable relationship with the world. Rationality, for Schütz, has to do not with the objective realization of the ends pursued through technically adequate means, that is, it is not instrumental but is rather linked to subjective reflexivity, to the ability to give our actions a relatively coherent and conscious meaning, even independently of the final ends achieved.

19 This aspect is well-evidenced by Habermas: "communicative actors are always moving *within* the horizon of their life-world; they cannot step outside of it". Hence, "only the context directly spoken to on a given occasion can fall into the whirl of the problematization associated with communicative action; by contrast, *the lifeworld always remains in the background*" (Habermas 1984, v. II, pp. 126, 131).

20 Still in the words of Habermas, "a *situation* is a segment of *lifeworld context of relevance* that is thrown into relief by themes and articulated through goals and plans of action; these contexts of relevance are concentrically ordered and become increasingly anonymous and diffused as the spatial-temporal and social distance grows" (ivi, pp. 122–123).

21 To cite Schütz, "using the terms *in their strictest meaning* we may therefore say paradoxically that in the common-sense thinking of everyday life whatever occurs could not have been expected precisely as it occurs, and that whatever has been expected to occur will never occur as it has been expected" (Schütz 1964, p. 287).

22 I would point out that Schütz takes the concept of appresentation from Husserl. To appresent something means to grasp it even if it is not directly manifest. For example, if I see a tree, I also appresent what it looks like from behind, namely what I do not see.

23 On the notion of the circle of representation, see Santambrogio (2006).

24 Also on this point there is an interesting affinity between Schütz and Searle. For Searle, "no set of 'I Consciousness', even supplemented with beliefs, add up to a 'We Consciousness'. The crucial element of collective intentionality is a sense of doing (wanting, believing, etc.) something together, and the individual intentionality that each person has is derived *from* the collective intentionality that they share (...). Why are so many philosophers convinced that collective intentionality must be reducible to individual intentionality? Why are they unwilling to recognize collective intentionality as a primitive phenomenon? (...). The requirements of methodological individualism seems to force us to reduce collective intentionality to individual intentionality. It has seemed, in short, that we have to choose between reductionism, on the one hand, or a super mind floating over individual minds, on the other. I want to claim, on the contrary, that the argument contains a fallacy and that the dilemma is a false one. It is indeed the case that all my mental life is inside my brain, and all your mental life is inside your brain, and so on for everybody else. But it does not follow from that that all my mental life must be expressed in the form of a singular noun phrase referring to me. The form that my collective intentionality can take is simply 'we intend', 'we are doing so-and-so', and the like (...). The intentionality that exists in each individual head has the form 'we intend'" (Searle 1995, pp. 24–26).

2 Political Culture

Political and Civic Culture

The study of political culture has long been associated with the topic of democracy. This connection is at the heart of the first major study in political culture, that of Almond and Verba on civic culture (Almond, Verba 1963). The purpose of their research is to discover the nature of political culture that can maintain and support a democratic regime. A more general purpose is to highlight, in an international situation marked by the Cold War, those settings in which such political culture thrives, so that these settings – not surprisingly, USA and UK – may serve as a model for countries under fragile democracy.

Despite its ideological bias, the research still provides an excellent starting point for the study of political culture, if only because it defines the object and raises a series of related issues. The fundamental topic of the research takes up the Weberian question from which we started: what relationship is given, within the processes of rationalization, between structure and culture, and between technical-scientific development and cultural development? According to Almond and Verba,

> while the movement toward technology and rationality of organization appears with great uniformity throughout the world, the direction of political change is less clear. But one aspect of this new world political culture is discernable: it will be a political culture of participation.

It remains to be understood what form the demand for participation takes: "the emerging nations are presented with two different models of the modern participatory state, the democratic and the totalitarian" (ivi, p. 4).

Since the processes of rationalization and technical-economic development seem to be similar in all countries, the cultural variable becomes central. It may be that it has a decisive importance in understanding what direction that demand takes, whether towards democracy or totalitarianism. The growing demand for participation implies a model of democracy more exacting than the mere presence of classical democratic institutions, such as free elections, parties, and elected parliaments, all of which can be present even in regimes

DOI: 10.4324/9781003229339-3

that are not properly democratic. Hence the focus on political culture, rather than on other structural elements, whether economic or political. And, again, the focus on subjective attitudes rather than the logic of rational choice. These are two crucial theoretical and methodological innovations: "what must be learned about democracy is a matter of attitude and feeling, and this is harder to learn" (ivi, p. 5).

By political culture, Almond and Verba mean

> The specifically political orientations-attitudes toward the political system and its various parts, and attitudes toward the role of the self in the system. We speak of a political culture just as we can speak of an economic culture or a religious culture. It is a set of orientations toward a special set of social objects and processes.
>
> (ivi, p. 13)

The political culture of a nation is instead a composite set of subjective attitudes towards politics, characterized by specific and variously articulated connotations. For Almond and Verba, it has three dimensions: *cognitive*, which includes knowledge and beliefs about politics; *affective*, which includes feelings and emotions towards political leaders and political structures; and *evaluative*, which includes the set of judgements and opinions towards political phenomena and facts. Starting from these dimensions, the authors define three types of attitude: *parochial*, characterized by no or low knowledge of the political system; *subject*, characteristic of subjects who, despite having some basic knowledge of the political system, do not actively participate in political life; and *participant*, typical of an attitude that participates in political life on the basis of good knowledge. Depending on the varying presence within a given society of these three types, three different political cultures are obtained: *parochial*, typical of non-western countries, especially in Africa; *subject*, typical of non-western countries, especially in Latin America and pre-modern Europe, to include examples from the past; and *participant*, present in Europe, especially in the UK, and the USA. The three political cultures correspond to three different political-institutional structures. In this way, we have a traditional and local political structure, an authoritarian and centralized one, and a democratic and representative one.

Within this theoretical scenario, civic culture is characterized by a balanced mix of diverse and contrasting attitudes, including participatory spirit and apathy, but also deference and respect for institutions and trust in authorities.[1] The USA and UK have stable democracies partly because, as the data collected in the research shows, they are characterized by the presence of civic culture. Germany, Italy, and Mexico (the other three countries surveyed) are characterized by unstable democracies because they have political cultures that express little trust and attachment to democratic institutions. The demand for participation across the world finds, on one hand, balanced cultural foundations capable of sustaining democracy, and on the other, there are generalized attitudes of distrust and distance from the political system that do not guarantee stability. In the decisive challenge between democracy and totalitarianism – the two global responses to a new need for participation and social protagonism, associated with the processes of economic development traversing the world after the end of the war – the presence and further development of civic culture can be a useful weapon in the hands of democracy and a decisive factor for its stability. This last question hovers over the book, because the memory of the collapse of democratic regimes in Italy and Germany before the war is still strong.

Net of the accusation of ideology, the book has received countless criticisms, rarely constructive ones. The concept of political culture has been seen as confusing and full of ambiguity (Kim 1964); insufficient to explain the stability of democracy, because it is the latter that produces civic culture, and not vice versa (Barry 1970); as an empty category, capable of explaining anything that cannot be explained through other clearer and more precise factors (Pye 1972);[2] unable to explain change and supportive of the status quo (Pateman 1971; Dittmer 1977); insensitive to class and power differences in society (Levine 1974); incapable of being an explanatory variable, because it requires explanation itself (Tucker 1973); and finally one of the most "popular and seductive", but also "controversial and confused" concept, to be used, if at all, "in conjunction with other variables (…). Instead of asking whether institutions cause culture or culture causes institutions, we should look for their joint effects" (Elkins, Simeon 1979, pp. 127, 139).

An important text by Inglehart, in which the author claims the revival and usefulness of the concept, dwells especially on this last question:

> I argue that different societies are characterized to very different degrees by a specific syndrome of political cultural attitudes; that these cultural differences are relatively enduring, but not immutable; and that they have major political consequences, being closely linked to the viability of democratic institutions.
>
> (Inglehart 1988, p. 1203)

In his text, Inglehart argues that the approach related to political culture is an excellent alternative to rational choice theory (based on economic variables), to explain the stability of democratic systems, and political systems in general. He points to the most significant attitudes through which to measure the level of democraticity of a political culture: intersubjective trust: attachment/confidence towards democratic institutions, and the degree of individual satisfaction with the way things are going in one's life.

The importance of mutual trust had already been highlighted by research on southern Italy conducted by Banfield (1970). In his research, it is shown how a low level of mutual trust encloses the subjects within narrow social circles, of a familial type. Narrow circles prevent them from broadening their individual vision and their sense of involvement and active participation towards broader, general, and collective interests involving the entire community. This is an attitude that slows down, or even prevents, the development of a participatory and democratic conception of public institutions, an attitude that Banfield called, with a label that has become famous, *amoral familism*. It is an attitude of total attention to one's own limited life-world – to use a phenomenological term – incapable of producing public morality or of supporting democratic participation. The inhabitants of Montegrano – the fictitious name of the town where the survey is carried out – act on two general rules: "maximize the material, short-run advantage of the nuclear family; assume that all others will do likewise" (ivi, p. 85).[3]

Further characteristics are revealed in this general attitude, so as to constitute a real political culture. For example, it is the weaker subjects who demand a system in which order is maintained by force; there is no connection between abstract political principles and real behaviour; benefits for the community are appreciated only if they also involve individual advantage. This system thus tends to create social resentment rather than mutual trust. Electoral behaviour is based on personal benefits already received or expected. This familist ethos is considered one of the fundamental obstacles – along with other factors, of course, such as poverty, marginality, and cultural backwardness – not only to democratic participation but also to economic development.

Inglehart takes up the theme, asking the following question:

> Does southern Europe have low levels of trust because it has not yet developed modern organizational structures? Or (in a variation on Weber's protestant ethic thesis) did southern Europe industrialize and develop modern organizational structures later than northern Europe because its traditional culture was relatively low on interpersonal trust?
>
> (Inglehart 1988, p. 1204)

Of course, the conclusion he reaches is that there is a mutual causal link between the two dimensions. But this conclusion is possible only after having demonstrated that the cultural dimension exists, can be evidenced, and has its own independent influence with respect to the economic-structural dimension. The latter, in short, does not explain everything.

Collected data show that this can be empirically demonstrated for all three of the variables examined: trust, attachment to institutions, and the degree of individual satisfaction. For example, the degree of satisfaction remains stable, despite the economic crises, in all the European countries examined between 1973 and 1987, so that democratic stability seems to be the element that most influences it. Inglehart can then write that "my conclusion is very simple, but very important: there is a durable cultural component underlying these responses" (ivi, p. 1207). Alongside the economic-structural explanations, there are equally significant cultural explanations:

> The results indicate that economic development per se does not necessarily lead to democracy. Only in so far as it brings appropriate changes in social structure and political culture does it enhance the viability of democratic institutions (...). The result suggest that political culture is a crucial link between economic development and democracy.
>
> (ivi, p. 1219)

These themes are taken up and further explored in a subsequent text edited by Almond and Verba (1980) but do not add important new elements to the debate. An important critical element is underlined by Pateman: the participation that Almond and Verba have in mind, and which seems to constitute the key element of a democratic political culture, is electoral participation (Pateman 1980). But this, while essential, is too little. The model of democracy in question is the classical liberal one, insufficient to grasp the powerful emergence of civil society, as expressed, for example, in the season of social movements. Moreover, Pateman shows how abstention from voting has become a widespread phenomenon, and precisely a feature of those stable democracies that were the pride of Almond and Verba. Among other things, electoral abstention in the USA concerns mainly African Americans, women and the unemployed, and, more generally, people on the margins of the system. All this shows how the American model of democracy fails to actively involve a sizeable chunk of the population, especially the weaker classes. Marxist critics, on the other hand, insist that the concept of political culture presupposes a homogeneity that in fact does not exist, since it is necessary instead to consider the differences in class and power, which greatly influence the political culture of different and heterogeneous subjects. The social structure, with its stratification, has repercussions on the cultural dimension, and to ignore this leads to scientific oversimplification and ideological distortion (Wiatr 1980). The aspect of this critique that does appear significant is the insistence on the relationship between collective subjects, with their specificities, and the production of political culture.[4]

Civic Culture and Quality of Democracy

A decisive contribution to the debate comes a few years later with the work of Putnam. Times have changed and the Cold War is over. At stake is no longer the stability of democracy, but its quality. The question of participation becomes truly central, in all its expressions, and no longer only those around the electoral hour. As Putnam writes in the *Preface* to the Italian edition of his book, "some supposed remedies, such as economic progress or the reform of public institutions, however necessary and desirable in themselves, are not sufficient to ensure the health of Italian democracy. Two critical elements, which are required by the therapy, are at the center of the plot I have found myself weaving: the first is the *decentralization of power*, and the second is the *awakening of civic commitment*" (Putnam 1997, p. VIII, translation mine), elements that are interconnected.

The research examines the performance of democracy, through the performance of democratic institutions, and uses as an empirical sample, the recently, formally established Italian administrative regions. The hypothesis is that a connection lies between this performance – therefore the quality of democracy – and the degree of civicness present in the citizens, understood as a macro variable and not individual:

> even an individual who is endowed with a great deal of civicness (highly civic), if he is placed in a society lacking in civicness (uncivic), is destined to behave in a non-cooperative manner, to violate the highway code, to act with selfishness and distrust and so on
>
> (Ibidem, p. X, translation mine)

Thus, civicness is considered a collective and social variable, and not a summation of individual attitudes. The main theoretical reference is Tocqueville, according to whom, as Putnam writes, "the civic community is marked by an active, public-spirited citizenry, by egalitarian political relations, by a social fabric of trust and cooperation" (Putnam 1993, p. 15).

Putnam is aware of the multiplicity of factors that can affect the performance of institutions, and the multiplicity of theoretical approaches that emphasize the importance of those factors. He highlights three main theoretical approaches: *institutional*, which emphasizes the importance of elements of institutional engineering; *socio-economic*, which focuses on social development and economic well-being; and *socio-cultural*, which draws on research on civic culture. In his book, he highlights important aspects of change that are directly influenced by institutional factors. For example, he points out how "the regional government has transformed élite political culture. The most striking metamorphosis in regional politics (...) is a remarkable ideological depolarization, coupled with a strong trend toward a more pragmatic approach to public affairs" and, consequently, "as ideological distances narrowed, tolerance across party lines blossomed". Institutional reform had "nurtured a new way of doing politics" (ivi, pp. 28, 29, 38).

The heart of the book, however, lies in assessing the influence on the performance of institutions of the other two variables: socio-economic modernity and civic community. The conclusion Putnam reaches through his empirical research is that the performance gap between the various regions, especially between Northern and Southern Italy, is "wholly inexplicable in terms of economic development", so that "wealth and economic development cannot be the whole story" (ivi, p. 86).[5] The question, both theoretical and empirical, is very similar to the one addressed by Inglehart. It concerns the characteristics of a democratic civic culture which not only guarantees stability but also contributes to the development of the democratic quality of the system. As the civic culture develops, so the quality of democracy increases. We reach a point where stability is taken for granted and focus turns to the best ways to improve democratic performance. Although it was central to Almond and Verba's research, the question of participation as possibly leading to a democratic or totalitarian outcome is no longer raised. Rather, it is now a matter of understanding, within a democratic system considered stable, how to improve its quality by acting on the civic variable. Democracy is not something always equal to itself, indistinct: it can be better or worse. Its properties do not coincide only with those typical of the classical liberal conception. Once these properties take root, *making democracy work* becomes the next step to make the democratic principle fruitful.

The Italian example is very significant. It is no coincidence that Almond and Verba place Italian democracy among those that are unstable and fragile. After the end of the war, a fundamental aim of the men and the women – and of the political cultures – who wrote the Constitution was precisely that of preparing mechanisms, including institutional ones, that would protect Italian democracy. Concerns about the nation's democratic hold after fascism and the war were entirely justified. The Regions envisaged by the constitutional dictate were activated only in 1970, when the fear that decentralization could jeopardize the stability of the system had almost completely passed. Putnam is quick to recognize the issue: the establishment of the Regions is related to the development of the need for participation. Their institutional performance, even beyond economic progress is nourished above all by the ability to tap into these new needs that run through the Italian social fabric and to enhance them, within a democratic system now considered relatively stable. Without this further step forward, democracy would probably have been at greater risk.[6]

The fundamental issue is well exposed by Putnam: "Is there any connection between the 'civic-ness' of a community and the quality of its governance?" (ivi, p. 91). A question that could be formulated in this other way: can democracy only survive in an immobile stability, or does it also need to grow democratically? If there is a link between socio-economic modernization and the need for social protagonism, the answer is obvious. We are at the heart of a central question: modernity, whatever is meant by that, implies modernization, i.e., technological and economic growth, but also development, meaning an idea of a better society, which cannot coincide with modernization alone. Rationalization, Weber would say, is always accompanied by new narratives.

Returning to Putnam, based on four indicators of civicness (vigour of associative life, number of newspaper readers, turn out in referendums, percentage of preferential votes), he reaches the conclusion that in Italy there is

> A remarkable concordance between the performance of a regional government and the degree to which social and political life (…) approximates the ideal of a civic community (…). The predictive power of the civic

> community is greater than the power of economic development (...). The more civic a region, the more effective its government.
>
> (ivi, p. 98)

A few aspects should be underlined. The vitality of associationism is a qualitative dimension, not just a quantitative one. It is not enough to hold an association membership card. Association should produce vivacity: that internal participation in the associations is active and gratifying; that it stimulates interpersonal trust; that it is significantly active towards the outside world; that it pursues goals that are collectively recognizable and meritorious; that it produces interpersonal gratification and social ties based on reciprocal recognition; that it promotes equality among citizens; that it develops a sense of belonging and respect for the rules. In short, associations must be democratic, and not the Ku Klux Klan. Quality and quantity must be interconnected. Moreover, associations need not be purely political in nature and purpose but can take on many forms: sports, neighbourhood, defence of the weak, management of free time. Even "taking part in a choral society or a bird-watching club teaches self-discipline and an appreciation for the joys of successful collaboration" (ivi, p. 90). Finally, after empirically showing the inversely proportional relationship between religiosity and civic spirit, Putnam emphasizes that fundamentally "the civic community is a secular community" (ivi, p. 109).

One last important thought on the concept of civic community: In what sense is a civic democracy a community? If we stick to the idea that the *community* – characterized by small size, personal relationships, a strong sense of mutual solidarity, strong link with tradition – is gradually being replaced by *society* – characterized by large size, impersonal relationships, low level of solidarity, high level of rationalization – by the processes of modernization, the idea of civic community would seem destined to disappear. The very concept of community seems inappropriate to describe modern democracies. Putnam opposes this logic, since "modernization need not signal the demise of the civic community" (ivi, p. 115).

Putnam approaches the subject through analysis of the so-called *social capital*, exploring it in greater depth in his second text, devoted to civic culture in the United States (Putnam 2000). The basic hypothesis is that social capital facilitates cooperation and mutual trust, even in rather large contexts, based on the mechanism of generalized reciprocity. The latter is a form of bonding that does not necessarily require the exchange of equivalent values. It implies a structured and permanent relationship, not on interchange, and characterized by horizontal and non-hierarchical interactions. As such, it is opposed to the logic of rational choice. One of the clearest and most striking examples is friendship. Friendship relationships are resources that are not consumed, but, on the contrary, "depleted if *not* used" (Putnam 1993, p. 169).

Let us briefly take a closer look at this topic. First, Putnam distinguishes between physical capital (referring to physical objects), human capital (the characteristics of individuals), and social capital. The latter,

> Refers to connections among individuals, social networks and the norms of reciprocity and trustworthiness that arise from them (...) 'social capital' calls attention to the fact that civic virtue is most powerful when embedded in a dense network of reciprocal social relations. A society of many virtuous but isolated individuals is not necessarily rich in social capital.
>
> (Putnam 2000, p. 16)

Of course, social capital is a means, and like all means it can be used for noble and social purposes, but also for malevolent and antisocial purposes. We can then hypothesize different forms of social capital, including two of the most significant: *bridging* (or inclusive) social capital and *bonding* (or exclusive) social capital. The latter constitutes "a kind of sociological superglue, whereas bridging social capital provides a sociological WD-40"[7] (ivi, p. 21). All of Putnam's second research is aimed at demonstrating how in the United States the level of communitarianism – that is, the varied interweaving of social capital which opens and closes, two dimensions which are not incompatible with each other – has been changing over time, following a path which is by no means linear, but fluctuant. The fundamental idea is that American modernization is not incompatible with the endurance of a certain level of community belonging, but rather of observing its morphosis over time and what forms it takes. The concern is that – after a period, the 1950s and 1960s, characterized by strong civic engagement and a high level of associationism – Americans seem to have stopped even bowling together.

What is of interest here, from a theoretical point of view, is that modernization does not erase community. Rather, it transforms it in a new direction. The ties between people and the way of building relationships of mutual trust change, taking shape within a complex dialectic between openness and closure: "Many groups simultaneously bond along some social dimensions and bridge across others" (Ibidem).[8] This is a decisive fact, to which we will return later. The point is to contemplate the possibility of a community that is not communitarian, within which elements of openness, bridging social capital, are not excluded. Putnam seems to find comforting empirical support in the possibility of reconciling community and freedom:

> Individuals who are more engaged with their communities are generally *more* tolerant than their stay-at-home neighbors, not less. Many studies have found that the correlation between social participation and tolerance is, if anything, positive, not negative (...). Social joiners and civic activists are as a rule *more* tolerant of dissent and unconventional behavior than social isolates are.
>
> (ivi, p. 387)

In conclusion, Putnam's two studies, the Italian case and the American case, reach the same conclusion: "the health of our public institutions depends, at least in part, on widespread participation in private voluntary groups – those networks of civic engagement that embody social capital" (ivi, p. 365). The theme of civic culture is enriched by a type of participation other than merely electoral participation, capable of developing mutual trust, social cooperation, and civic consciousness. In conclusion, "civic norms and networks are not simply froth on the waves of economic progress" (Putnam 1993, p. 162).

Immanent and Non-Immanent Analysis

Of course, the concepts of political culture and civic culture continue to be as problematic as any other topic within the social sciences. Decades of study and research, briefly summarized, however, demonstrate that continuing to work on these issues is not time wasted. In summary, the problems raised within this complex debate can be listed as follows: (1) what is the relationship between cultural and structural dimensions; (2) what is the relationship between individual and collective dimensions; (3) how to explain the relationship between stability and change, in connection with the diversity of social subjects that produce political culture; and (4) what is the internal composition of political culture.

I will focus on the first point, analysing it from a sociology of knowledge approach, with reference to Mannheim's work. The topic at the heart of the sociology of knowledge is the relationship between culture and structure, between both all forms of culture, and all types of structure. This approach differs from that of Marx. According to Marx, there is a fundamental structure that determines all other 'structures' – which, for Marx, are not properly so – and all cultures. The set of relations of production, that is, the material structure of society, constitutes the real basis on which the juridical and political superstructure, with its determined and specific forms of social consciousness, arises. But, like all other cultures, economic culture depends on the material structure. It is no coincidence that Weber's research on Protestant ethics aims to highlight the autonomous role of a specific economic culture, and a specific work ethic, with respect to the material structure of the relations of production. In essence, for Marx, the productive structure determines the entire class structure of society, in its structural and cultural aspects: the windmill produces feudalism and its specific class structure; the steam-mill, the society of industrial capitalists.[9]

Mannheim changes the perspective, also with respect to Weber. It is a matter of studying the nexus that binds structures and cultures. In this way, a considerable step forward is taken, away from Marx and the Marxist tradition. The first impulse of a Marxist thinker when faced with a reflection on cultural phenomena – of whatever type – is to trace them back to economic structure. We have seen that Marxist-inspired criticisms of research on political culture emphasize the underestimation that such research makes of the relationship between political culture and social stratification. In doing so, however, they forget, for example, the relationship between political culture and political structure, quite naturally because it is taken for granted that the latter also depends on class relations, that is, on the development of the forces of production. The same thing could apply to a possible study of religious culture: the Marxist would lead these cultural forms back to the class structure of society, underestimating the relationship they maintain with the institutional structure of religions. Simplifying, perhaps excessively but I think correctly, it can be said that Marxism identifies a structure on which everything else depends, both other structures and all cultures, including economic culture.

The sociology of knowledge appositely frames the matter: it is to study the relationship between being and thought, in all their forms, within a given society. The first fundamental idea is that it is only in modern society that culture emerges as an autonomous element, differentiating itself from the medieval hierarchical structure dominated by religion, thus becoming the object of thought. This is that great historical process characterized by "a struggle of the cultural spheres for autonomy. Once each sphere (as, for example, art, science, as well as economic, political, and even purely sensual life) had got out of the systematic attachment in which it gained its whole sanction and specific meaning from a central life-value", namely religion, "a new element has asserted itself: the cultural process itself, in its characteristic liveliness, so plainly apparent, in contrast to the medieval state of things" (Mannheim 1997e, pp. 39–40). It is a process "whereby culture was itself, so to speak, discovered", so that

> *culture becomes a value where it has ceased to exist as being* (...). Only where the cultural, the meaningful no longer lies in the sphere of being has it become a value. Then it can be called into question and tested for its worth. Dependent on our will, our suppositions, it can be comprehended as movable, calling for reform (...). The designation of culture as non-nature became genuinely and internally consistent only because being and meaning, actuality and value were experienced as having departed from one another.
>
> (ivi, p. 45, italics mine)

Weberian echoes reverberate. The differentiated modern world imposes a choice, since there is no longer any participation in a 'natural' cultural sphere which, insofar as it is totally shared and opaque, lies in the sphere of being and does not appear as something to be valued. Now, "communal, collective experience arises only where and when different individuals execute within themselves an identical pattern of experience" (ivi, p. 71). This is a new situation, where "the certainties to be discovered are those demonstrable to anyone and not those evidential only for a believing community" (ivi, p. 155). Only as a consequence of this process does the whole social movement, structural and cultural, become the object of reflection. Only in this context can the sociology of knowledge arise as a study of the relationship between being and thought, where the two dimensions are mutually autonomous and mutually related.

Given these assumptions, Mannheim leads the question in three directions. First, in modern society, being increasingly becomes *social being*, as the centrality of social relations progressively emerges as the constitutive element of human bonds. In the past, first the religious sphere and then the political sphere constituted the general dimension within which human being and thought were contained. The centrality of the social dimension is a specific element of the modern era, characterizing it in its essence.

Second, those between being and thought are *nexus of mutual causation*, in all their forms. The idea is that there are nexus of various kinds between cultures and structures, and these nexus can be empirically investigated.[10] What characterizes a given society is the specificity that these nexus assume. By influencing each other, with a relevance that varies from situation to situation, structural and cultural elements end up creating a typical nexus, which constitutes something original with respect to the individual elements considered per se. To speak of the nexus of reciprocal causation means to rule out that the link existing between being and thought flows in one direction of conditioning, or even of the result. To resume Marx, it means that if there is the steam-mill, easily – but not necessarily – there is also the industrial capitalist, and vice versa. What is important to highlight, from the point of view of scientific analysis, is the link, more or less strong, between different realities, a link that can be reconstructed as an empirical regularity, in order to highlight the specific forms that, connecting variously with each other, the various cultural and social factors help to constitute.

Mannheimian *relationalism* can be read in this way. The normative question of whether a certain thought is correct or not is transformed into an epistemological question. In Marx, bourgeois consciousness is false because it tends to conceal its social determination. The technique of unmasking coincides "with the existential corroding of a theoretical proposition" (Mannheim 1997c, p. 141). On the contrary, if all thought is related to social structure, highlighting this relationship no longer involves any unmasking or even any relativization, but rather the highlighting of connections useful for understanding the nature of a given society. As Mannheim writes,

> A modern theory of knowledge which takes account of the relational as distinct from the merely relative character of all historical knowledge must start with the assumption that there are spheres of thought in which it is impossible to conceive of absolute truth existing independently of the values and position of the subject and unrelated to the social context. Even a god could not formulate a proposition on historical subject like 2 + 2 = 4.
>
> (Mannheim 1997a, pp. 70–71)

This brings us to the last question. For Mannheim, "the principal thesis of the sociology of knowledge is that there are modes of thought which cannot be adequately understood as long as their social origins are obscured" (ivi, p. 4). This means, however, that there are also aspects of thinking that can be interpreted independently of their social origins. Let's look at an example taken from Mannheim himself. The validity of the Pythagorean theorem is not an object of sociological study, because it does not depend on its social origins. The fact that the theorem was formulated in the context of the Greek culture of the sixth century BC has little to do with its validity. It pertains to mathematics and is an issue addressed within cultures that are different from each other.[11] However, the sociology of knowledge can study the nexus that exists between this specific element and the social, cultural, and structural context within which it was produced, between the mathematical theorem and the world in which Pythagoras lived. The highlighting of these nexus is useful to understand a specific social form.

Mannheim distinguishes between *immanent* and *non-immanent* study of a given cultural element. The former concerns its intrinsic characteristic and is the task of different disciplines. To take another example, the fact that Rembrandt's *Night Watch* is a work of art is not certified by sociology, nor by mathematics. The specific task of sociology is the study of the non-immanent aspects of culture, those aspects that concern the connections between culture and structure. We have a final, particularly significant example, concerning the concept of style. 'Style' is both an aesthetic and sociological category. This is because "in a purely immanent approach to the works of the Gothic period we can grasp the Gothic principles of composition and describe their development" (Mannheim 1997e, p. 86), recognizing, within this aesthetic form, the various individual contributions. Each work, as a product, always contains something different from the style to which it is attributed: this something extra is attributed to the creative individual. But behind the work of individuals lies "the common basis which is only made possible by the common experiencing of certain domains within a given age" (ivi, p. 88). The immanent attitude should therefore be replaced by the socio-genetic one, not immanent: "it no longer designates the work itself but only so much of it as is the result of the communal experiential contexture stored up in it" (ivi, p. 89).[12]

In short, while the immanent analysis of a cultural product is objective, the non-immanent one is functional: in the first case, it is a matter of assessing the validity of the object studied, while in the second, what links it to the general context in which it was produced and which it contributes to forming. In a static society, "men are attuned to the immanent qualities of the contents of meaning" (ivi, p. 49). In modern society, the *existential connection* of thought appears:

> a *general concept* is potentially valid for everyone, even if in actuality only one person thinks it; a *community-wide, conjunctive (historical) concept*

> counts only for those who participate in an experiential space, even if in actuality everyone participates on it.
>
> (ivi, p. 203, emphasis mine)

The existential connection of thought is an expression of the split between community and consciousness that characterizes modernity. Only now does the double nature of culture fully appear: the content of objective meaning and the functionality deposited within it.[13]

Once individual causal links have been highlighted, because of empirically detectable regularities, according to Mannheim it is possible to take a final step forward: to construct, nexus by nexus, the totality to which they belong and contribute to creating. If where x exists, one can reasonably expect the presence of y, and the simultaneous presence of x and y is reasonably related to the presence of z, within mutual influences, one can think that the set of the three elements constitutes a specific *social constellation*. Of course, the three elements may come into connection with other factors in different contexts: the point is that their specific connections may constitute a recognizable and characteristic totality. This is a process of *dynamic synthesis*: it tends to reconstruct a puzzle that is never definitively finished, because the search can bring to light ever-new and previously unknown connections. These totalities – depending on the number and weightiness of the connections involved – can be circumscribed and restricted, or broader and more general. Where Mannheim speaks of modernity, characterized by the emergence of the social dimension as a key feature, he means a constellation of forces and elements that is very broad and diverse, but still recognizable.

I would like to return briefly to Putnam. In his latest book, he reconstructs American history by showing, based on empirical data, that since the 1960s there has been a gradual shift from a we-based society to an I-based one (Putnam 2020). He writes that

> Between the mid-1960s and today – by scores of hard measures along multiple dimensions – we have been experiencing declining economic equality, the deterioration of compromise in the public square, a fraying social fabric, and a descent into cultural narcissism (…). In that same period we replaced cooperation with political polarization. We allowed our community and family ties to unravel to a marked extent. And our culture became far more focused on individualism and less interested in the common good. Since the 1950s we have made important progress in expanding individual rights (often building on progress made in the preceding decades), but we have sharply regressed in terms of shared prosperity and community values.
>
> (ivi, p. 17)

It thus appears that

> The story of the American experiment in the twentieth century is one of a long upswing toward increasing solidarity, followed by a steep downturn into increasing individualism. From 'I' to 'we', and back again to 'I' (...), our hope is that by presenting a new, evidence-based story spanning the past 125 years of our nation's history we might begin to bridge the 'Ok Boomer' generational divide – and the many other lines of fracture facing our nation – in order to construct a shared vision for the future that we can all work toward together.
>
> (ivi, pp. 24, 23)

As can be seen, the themes are the same as those present in his previous works, now set in a far-reaching, historical-sociological scenario.[14] It may be useful to stress a point highlighted by Putnam, which is surprisingly linked to reflections in the sociology of knowledge. He writes that

> Finally, this book is not primarily about causal analysis. It is about *narratives*. Narratives, as we use the term, are not merely entertaining tales, but events linked together in trends inter-braided by reciprocal causality. The strands of a narrative are inextricable, but still interpretable, and therefore instructive as we look to the future (...) for the arc we describe is not an arc of historical inevitability, but an arc constructed by human agency.
>
> (ivi, pp. 24, 25, italics mine)[15]

In conclusion, granted the importance of cultural factors, and granted a relationship of reciprocal influence between the various elements that make up a given socio-historical form, it is a matter of reconstructing causal links based on empirical regularities, of interpreting threads woven into a narrative.[16] In the next paragraphs, we will try to address the other issues raised above, within an original proposal for reading the concept of political culture.

Political Theory, Political Cultures, and Political Traditions

First, I propose to distinguish between *political culture* and *political theory*. Consider the proposition, "Marxism has influenced Italian political culture much more than American political culture". While Marxism can also be understood, within this proposition, as a political culture – as such autonomous from other political cultures/theories such as liberalism, communitarianism, conservatism, romanticism, etc. – it is so in a different way to which we speak of the political culture of Italians, or Americans. The political culture of the Italian working class, to give another example, was influenced by both Marxist and Catholic political culture. As much research points out, it was more heavily influenced by these two different political cultures than any liberal one. How then does the political culture of social subjects – such as Italians, workers, the middle classes, young people, etc. but also of historical periods – such as the 1960s, or 1970s, etc. – differ from the political cultures/ theories that influenced them?

Let us look first at the characteristics of political theories. They constitute theoretical constructions that contain an inevitable need for internal theoretical integrity. They aspire to internal argumentative coherence, and non-contradiction. The subjects that formulate these political cultures produce political theory within relatively autonomous *traditions of thought.*[17] These traditions are recognizable because they start from identifiable assumptions, developing them into argumentative structures aimed at resolving issues of internal integrity. Thought follows thought, immanently. The social subjects that produce theory are a restricted élite of intellectuals, bestowed with a completely specific and characteristic education. Greek philosopher-legislators, medieval monks, Enlightenment intellectuals, and even today's university professors, however different they may be, are always and in any case the incumbents of working with thought that differentiates them from the rest of citizenry. Their being different collective subjects has deeply influenced their theoretical production, if we consider the latter in a non-immanent perspective. It is not possible here to make a historical reconstruction of the various models of intellectuality that have succeeded one another over time. What is important to emphasize is that working with thought has produced, certainly in the most recent eras, different and alternative theoretical paradigms. These paradigms differ from each other not only because they too can be traced back to the social dynamics in which they were produced, but because they bring with them problems of internal coherence, starting from some basic assumptions, to which generations of thinkers have dedicated themselves.

Is Locke a bourgeois thinker? Partly yes, partly no. Let us briefly analyse, for example, his theory of private property.[18] On the one hand, yes, because the question is imposed by the times, by the need for the new rising class to be able to rely on a solid argumentative basis to justify the legitimacy of property against limits and conditions set by the previous forms of medieval and canonic law. On the other hand, no, because the argument aims to be as coherent as possible, and this coherence is totally immanent, that is, independent of the link that the author may have with a specific social subject, and with the interests of the latter. His theory can be contested, based on arguments, by a bourgeois thinker as well as by a Marxist one. Again, is Locke a typically English thinker? Again, the reasoning is the same: he may be, but his justification of private property can be challenged by an Englishman as well as by any non-Englishman. All this does not mean that Locke cannot be 'bourgeois' or 'English'. It means that, alongside these analyses of his thought, it is also possible to show the structural weaknesses of his theoretical position, if there are any. We can think of the debates that have arisen around the so-called Lockian clause, which would like to introduce limits to the private appropriation of common goods. One could collect an entire library of works around the issue, which still today has not been laid to rest.

Of course, Locke's is just one example. The same argument applies to all political cultures/theories.

There is functionality in all the examples we have given, in the sense that they are socio-genetically connected to a specific context of experience. But as far as their core element is concerned, they are meanings that can be grasped independently of the social context and can be subjected to immanent analysis. Political cultures – as expressions of political theories – are organized into fairly coherent and fairly recognizable traditions based on certain basic assumptions, which the authors make their own. These cultural traditions can also be studied in an immanent way, i.e., by analysing them from the point of view of their coherence and internal consequences, and in a socio-genetic way, and by showing their link with a specific socio-historical evolution within which they embed.

A classic example of this study is Mannheim's research on conservative thought (Mannheim 1997f). Firstly, Mannheim outlines the characteristic intellectual content of conservatism, identifying four aspects: a critique of the naturalistic-bourgeois concept of freedom, a critique of the bourgeois concept of property, an appreciation of concrete existence in its immediacy, and an understanding of the world and reality that looks backward to the past. These are elements that characterize counter-revolutionary conservatism, ensuing as a reaction to the French Revolution and its liberal and bourgeois ideas.[19] Secondly, Mannheim reconstructs the nexus between this tradition and the social context from which it issues. In the first lines of the text, he writes that "the aim of the investigations (…) is to show, in a limited section of the historical domain, that thinking is bound to existence. We shall not be talking about thinking in general, but about determinate thinking and knowing within a determinate life space" (ivi, p. 31), in order to show "that even those works which originate in the scholar's closet, seemingly totally remote from the arenas of life (…), are themselves part of a more comprehensive contexture of experience which reaches beyond them" (ivi, p. 189). The two dimensions are intertwined, and the study of culture benefits from both approaches. Thought is separable from its psychological (the creative subject) and sociological (society) origins while it is always reconnectable to the context, individual and collective, from which it arose.[20]

To summarize: political cultures/theories are the result of a 'desk' creation, while political culture is instead closely connected to everyday life, and is the result of a widespread, anonymous process. The fundamental characteristics of political cultures/theories can be summarized as follows: (1) they have a high degree of reflexivity; (2) individual creativity plays a fundamental role within them; (3) they contain a need for logical coherence and non-contradiction; (4) they are potentially transmissible to all communities, since they are partially independent even from the one that produced them; (5) they can constitute traditions (paradigms) based on typical fundamental assumptions; (6) they are characterized by the transparency of their contents, which become accessible, as objective cultural products, to processes of interpretation; (7) the collective subjects that produced them are identifiable; and (8) the change to which they are subjected is reflexive.

In the next section, to strike a contrast, the concept of political culture will be discussed, which will have opposite characteristics to those now presented.

Common Sense and Social Representations

I propose that we view political culture as that section of shared common sense that pertains to the political sphere. It is, to use Mannheim's concepts, connective, communal-historical thinking, not general, context-independent thinking. And it is typical sense, to use Schütz's phenomenology. The objectivity of connective knowledge is quite different from that of theoretical-scientific knowledge. The Pythagorean theorem, in its mathematical objectivity, tends to be always understood in the same way, while the objectivity of common-sense thinking depends on the community of experience in which it is shared and on the currents that flow through that community. It is an experience that is lived each time in its typicality, which implies both a degree of standardization and a personalization traceable to the very moment of experience, with its specificities.[21] This approach allows us to address the second and third of the problems within the literature on political culture: how do we move from the individual to the social dimension? How do we explain, at the same time, stability, and change, starting from the heterogeneity of social subjects?

The approach I propose links the phenomenological theory of common-sense thinking to that of social representations, in the direction that this theory has enjoyed under Moscovici. As is well known, the concept of social representation was introduced by Durkheim, for whom the essential object of sociology is to seek how collective representations are formed and how they combine. However, this very object is ultimately ignored by Durkheim, who could not address it without a theory of formation of meaning. Instead, we find this theory at the heart of Schütz's work, the task of which is to show how we move from subjectively intended meaning to common sense. By combining this approach with Moscovici's work, it is possible to develop a theory of social representations that explains their dual nature as *product* and *process*.

Moscovici speaks of *social representations* instead of collective representations – the Durkheimian term – precisely to highlight their dynamic and plastic character. He believes it is a question of studying representations as a bridge between the individual and society, under the view that social life is always in fieri. It is possible to summarize this terminological change in three points. First, social representations are not objects that are discovered, but *processes in action*. A social representation is a formation of meaning always undergoing a process of transformation because it is always and only actualized by an individual who lives it in their own experience. It does not exist outside this actualization. Any empirical analysis that wants to highlight a representation is akin to selecting a movie still: it is an element detached from the stream of consciousness to which it belongs. Second, a representation is a *shared social belief*. Reference must always be made to the social group that supports that belief. It is not unfounded to argue that a social group exists because it has its own set of social representations, which constitute its world of seeing itself and the world. Finally, social representations are experienced mostly unconsciously, intentionally, and not reflexively, as Schütz would say: we see ourselves and the world using our representations without reserve. In this sense, our world is social, even if we do not always know it.[22] Summing up the three points, Moscovici, with a beautiful expression echoing Schütz, argues that social representations are a thought that becomes the environment, the familiar environment within which we live.

Let us now see how such an environment is produced. This question is left unanswered by the literature on political culture. For Almond and Verba, for example, it is a matter of bringing out something that exists, without asking how it was produced. For Moscovici, a social representation is produced through two processes: *anchoring* and *objectification*. First, nothing is created out of nothing: a representation arises from a pre-existing meaning, usually extraneous.[23] This meaning may come from different social representations, characteristic of other social groups. But significantly, Moscovici highlights the role that science also plays in changing representations, especially in the modern world. It is mainly scientific and technical changes that impose changes on our shared universes of meaning. In line with the proposed reading of Weber, rationalization does not just produce disenchantment but contributes to the formation and transformation of our representations of the world. In the past, common sense was sheltered from scientific achievements: science was a world for the few, and ordinary people could continue to live in their own unknowing 'ignorance'. In modernity, however, science invades the everyday.

Moscovici's first major research studies the impact psychoanalysis has on common-sense thinking (Moscovici 1961). Psychoanalysis is a scientific invention, the knowledge of experts. What happens when it invades the knowledge of non-experts, when ordinary people must form an idea of what it is, without having to study Freud's incomprehensible books? The first function of social representations appears here: to make the unfamiliar familiar, anchoring the unfamiliar to the familiar. In doing so, psychoanalysis is transformed into something else, raising the question of the adequacy of that transformation. But a representation is not more or less adequate. Adequacy is not its problem. The central concern is to cope with the unknown, to understand it by anchoring it. According to Moscovici, "in social thinking, the conclusion has priority over the premise and in social relations (…) the verdict has priority over trial. Before seeing and hearing a person we have already judged him; classified him and created an image of him" (Moscovici 1984, p. 27).[24] An anchoring works if the element to which it anchors is credible and is endowed with symbolic resources adequate for the effort. These resources must be accessible to the extraneous element capable of producing plausible knowledge. Moreover, specific social subjects must take charge, to a degree, consciously, of this process. To return to psychoanalysis, Moscovici discovers in his research that the French, little by little, anchors psychoanalysis to the Catholic sacrament of confession. The Christian tradition, and the common sense it has produced, makes available to the French a rich and elastic symbolic heritage, historically capable of absorbing a great number of novelties.

Anchoring is only a starting point. It is a temporary solution. If psychoanalysis has a certain success, on the scientific level and on that of its diffusion, it will need to provide itself with its own autonomous representation. Now it is the moment for the process of objectification, which must construct a set of recognizable contents of meaning that can be traced back to psychoanalysis, in part even independently of the meaning given by specialists. The representation becomes 'object', beginning a life of its own. Moscovici shows that, in the course of this evolution, young French secularized citizens will come to see in religious confession a kind of psychoanalysis, thus superseding the initial anchoring. The conclusion reached by Moscovici is that

> Durkheim – true to the Aristotelian and Kantian tradition – has a rather static conception of these representations – somewhat akin to that of the Stoics. As a consequence, representations, in his theory, are like a thickening of the fog (…) like layers of stagnant air in a society's atmosphere, of which it is said that one could cut them with a knife. Whilst this is not entirely false, what is most striking to the contemporary observer is their mobile and circulating character; in short, their plasticity.
>
> (ivi, p. 18)

The two joint processes – anchoring and objectification – must ensure stability and plasticity of representations. The new representation must be in tune with the set of common sense to which it accedes. Anchoring guarantees a minimum of coherence, but it is then necessary to see whether subsequent objectifications guarantee the initial coherence. This is not, of course, the logical coherence of abstract thought – and political theories – but rather an existential coherence, internal to the logic of what is familiar. Similarly, the change triggered by anchoring and objectification is not a reflexive change and is easier to grasp when it is accomplished rather than in its making. There is no conscious subjectivity driving the process. If society 'thinks', it does so in an unreflexive way, guided by a finalism that is not grasped as such. A "thinking society", according to Moscovici (ivi, p. 14), is the expression of the continuous and daily operationalization of social representations. It is a deafening background noise that no one hears because hearing it would mean turning it off.

However, we must also see within each social representation. It must maintain a balance between the objectivations that compose it. Here again, we are faced with a long and complex process of continuous readjustment, on which it is worth dwelling. An important result, through his empirical research, has been achieved by Abric:

> The elements comprising a representation are inter-dependent and arranged in a certain hierarchical order. In our own work we have tried to analyze the nature of this organization and our results have allowed us to formulate a general hypothesis which we can express as follows: *All representations are organized around a nucleus*. This nucleus is the fundamental element in the representation as it determines both the meaning and the structure of the representation.
>
> (Abric 1984, p. 213)

The *central nucleus*, also a set of objectifications, has a double function: qualitative, because it gives form to the representation, so that if the nucleus changes, the whole representation changes; quantitative, because it orders the nature of the links between the various objectifications, establishing a criterion of greater or lesser importance. Abric calls the former creative function, the latter organizational. The objectifications included in the nucleus must have both qualitative and quantitative centrality. We can therefore imagine that the process of construction of a new representation finds a first completion with the definition of the nucleus. In the example of psychoanalysis, at first the central nucleus is built around the Catholic contents related to the sacrament of confession and then develops, becoming increasingly autonomous, around the notions of complex and repression. In a sense, the consistent presence of anchoring elements from the outside denotes a representation that is still under construction. These are elements that can then remain in the form of a cultural deposit, a kind of symbolic memory that testifies to the interests, emotions, and volitions that set in motion the process of constructing the representation.

According to Moscovici,

> when studying a representation, we should always try to discover the unfamiliar feature which motivated it and which it has absorbed. But it is particularly important that the development of such a feature be observed from the very moment it emerges in the social sphere.
>
> (Moscovici 1984, p. 28)

It is one thing to study the representation at the moment it is formed; it is quite another to reconstruct the sedimentation of meaning that has been deposited over time. Finally, the nucleus is generally the most stable element, around which the other objectifications are organized, down to the most peripheral, less stable, and less significant ones. The function of the latter is very important. They act, so to speak, as a buffer between internal coherence and the complexity of the external world, so as to absorb, and manage, the discordances that may arise between representation and reality. They protect the central nucleus, blurring and attenuating the impact of the outside, even at the expense of pure coherence. The relationship between the central nucleus and the periphery tends to establish a certain degree of internal elasticity in the representation, which can consequently appear both rigid and flexible.

The internal dialectic between the objectifications of a representation can explain the relationship between stability and change. An ideal situation which guarantees stability and coherence is difficult to achieve: every representation contains tensions and inconsistencies that make it susceptible to change. Naturally, it is the peripheral aspects that will change most rapidly, through adjustment processes that can also affect the daily dimension of the individual and his or her actual experience. Thus, the same issue that is addressed from the phenomenological point of view appears: common sense is both rigid and flexible, standardized, and unpredictable. Typifications, like social representations, are both a product and a process. Meaningfully experiencing the social world involves opacity and transparency, intentionality and reflexivity, stability and change. This is because just as the individual is a social product, at the same time society is a product of subjective reflexivity. This is a process in which *reproduction* is always accompanied by a certain degree of *production*, if only because of that minimum level of individual adaptation with which each person interprets, living in his or her daily life, the deposit of typical elements that society makes available. We could say common sense is never changed in its entirety: we never go from one common sense to another. Changes always occur within the stream of consciousness, although, of course, it is impossible for the scholar to find the first subject that anchored psychoanalysis to confession.[25]

I emphasize the point: representation is always internal to the intended meaning of an acting subject. It is always in place; it is not something that can be detached as an object independent of the context of its enactment. For the acting subject, knowledge of the normative order is the normative order. As we have seen above, while acting one is not reflexive about beliefs. For this reason, when the scholar wants to capture social representation, they can only ever do so through the analysis of subjectively intended meaning, which can be done in many ways, through questioning, interaction, interpretive observation, survey, and so forth. It is a matter of drawing out what the members of a given social group generally know. But social representations are not internalized norms that automatically dictate behaviour. They are the unintentional result of an intentionality that has become reflexive. Central to achieving this result is the role of repetition, which underlies the *cognitive success* of a representation. As Moscovici writes, a representation is affirmed when, as happened for psychoanalysis,

> Its figurative paradigm was detached from its original milieu by *continuous use* and acquired a sort of independence, just as a well-worn saying is gradually detached from the person who first said it and becomes an unmediated fact. Thus, when the image linked to a word or idea becomes

> detached and is let loose in a society it is accepted as a reality, a conventional one, of course, but nonetheless a reality.
>
> (ivi, p. 39, italics mine)

There is a circular relationship between continuous use and cognitive success. Repetition is at first the basis of cognitive success; then the opposite happens, and diffusion justifies repetition, so that the representation becomes independent of the subjects who produced it. In this way, it becomes a reality, progressively detaching itself from the reflexivity of the subjects, individual and collective, who triggered the process. These are steps that always require 'mind-bearers', as Weber calls them. The fact that a process initiated by an anchoring takes one direction rather than another depends always and only on the infinite number of actions enacted by subjects, individual and collective; on the direction these actions take; and on the perspective they make their own. It is a process that, according to Weber, leads from "subjectively intended meaning" to "socially transmitted sense connections"; and, to use Schütz's language, from the ego/alter relationship to shared common sense, so that "the cultural pattern provides by its recipes typical solutions for typical problems available for typical actors" (Schütz 1964, pp. 101–102). A reality becomes what we think it is.

The process we have briefly described varies from context to context. There are societies within which stability prevails; and societies where adaptation and change seem to dominate. In general, modern society – as opposed to pre-modern society – is of the second type. The described dynamic can also apply to more circumscribed and delimited contexts: within our society today, we can find exemplary contexts of experience that are more stable and others that are more dynamic. We may say that this heterogeneity – the presence of a complex mixture of stability and change – is typical of societies like ours, within which processes of transformation are easier to see, while the stability which underpins change remains hidden. However, we cannot forget that every change rests on something that remains stable, which provides the necessary anchorage.

In this regard, a final argument must be introduced. Within a common universe of experience, it is not necessarily the case that all representations are universally shared. According to Schütz, "all experience (*Erfahrung*) of contemporaries (…) is formed by means of interpretive judgments involving all my knowledge of the social world, although with *varying degrees of explicitness*" (Schütz 1972, p. 183, italics mine). Generalization, sharing, and determinacy are interrelated: the more a representation is universally spread, the more it can be expected to be known. But it may be that not all have the same degree of generalization. Different, specific contexts could have representations not known to all; just as representations known to all might be not universally shared. In summary: everything that is shared is also known, but not vice versa. I therefore propose to identify three different levels of generalization of representations: *individual opinion*, *group attitude*, and *social stereotype*.[26]

Individual opinion lies on the level at which the shared sense passes through the filter of subjectivity and is reactivated as a subjectively intended meaning. It is a question of evaluating, at this first level, the degree of conformism present. If we are faced with a simple reproduction, the individual opinion will only reproduce the social stereotype. But this is never entirely the case: the individual always adds his own, albeit small, 'fringe of meaning', to use Schütz's term. The individualization processes typical of modernity tend to progressively expand this individual contribution. Today, individual identity is not necessarily a mere reproduction of group membership, because the individual tends to develop his or her own autonomy. Moreover, each of us belongs to a wide and heterogeneous multiplicity of social groups. As a result, individual *identity* and *belonging* do not coincide and the former is increasingly the reflexive product of multiple belongings. This is an important aspect, which reconfigures the relationship, to remain with our theme, between political culture and social subjects. We can say that the less individual opinion is conformist, namely it is characterized as mere reproduction, the less it will be generalized and shared.

The second level of generalization is group attitude. It expresses the culture shared by a specific group within the more general common 'we'. As Schütz says, "every social group, be it ever so small (...), has its own private code" (Schütz 1964, p. 101). This private code has something in common with the 'we' and something that distinguishes it. How can that dialectic between intentionality and reflexivity that we have seen at the subjective level be interpreted at the group level? First, identifying an intermediate level of generalization of representations between the individual and society can better clarify the relationship between stability and change in a complex and diversified society,[27] raising the question of social pluralism. Second, we can say that a particular social group exists insofar as it has its own specific representations of reality. For example, in what sense does the working class exist? Is it a concept used by the social scientist; is it a representation constructed by other social subjects; or, is it a subject capable of self-representation? I believe that only in the latter case are we in front of a reflexive collective subject, capable of developing its own representations, consequently able to act as an autonomous subject, which recognizes itself in its own non-hetero-constructed identity.[28] It is thus possible to distinguish between *self-representations* and *hetero-representations*, the former characterized by greater 'social' reflexivity: a subject exists as an autonomous social protagonist when he is, first of all, capable of constructing his own autonomous self-image.[29]

The level of social stereotype corresponds with true common sense, with the highest level of generalization and dissemination of a symbolic content. The cognitive success achieved makes this sense content universally available. Of course, it is easier to see the common sense of others: stereotypes are always those of others. Very astutely, Schütz observes that "in common-sense thinking only the other fellow has prejudices" (ivi, p. 271). Stereotype, however, is only a descriptive term here: it is typical of my own and others' common sense, even though it is easier to be reflexive about others. Making the stereotype reflexive means laying the groundwork for not sharing it: the individual who is capable not only of living it but also of thinking about it is one step away from criticizing it.[30] In a sense, we can distinguish between *knowledge* and *sharing*; everyone can know everyone's stereotypes, but one does not necessarily share them. Knowledge and sharing can separate especially at this level of generalization. Knowing that others think a certain way, as is known to all, does not mean sharing their way of thinking.

The articulation between different levels of generalization (opinion, attitude, stereotype) represents a sort of index of anonymity. The more typical an experience is, the more anonymous it is and the less original and unique it is. There is a range from subjective meanings, the least anonymous, since the subject can never be considered a mere passive container; to intersubjective meanings, represented by attitudes and stereotypes, where the latter represent the highest level of anonymity. In other words, we move from individual opinions to a shared culture. In addition, the three levels allow the identification of more stable social representations – very stereotyped, in which opinion is mainly reproduction – than other more dynamic ones. One can formulate the hypothesis that the central nucleus is made up of stereotypes; that it can provide, more than other symbolic elements, the function of anchoring; that it tends to coincide with deep common sense. In general, we obtain an interpretative scheme capable of interpreting very different social realities, characterized by different levels of stability and change. For example, it becomes plausible to think that two different groups can also have the same representation of the same reality (with a common central nucleus) and different peripheral contents. And it is also possible to come across a very unstable representation because it is characterized by several alternative central nuclei.[31]

To summarize: change can be the product of the reflexive becoming of an intentional content, fostered by the cognitive dissonances present within the taken for granted. It can be more or less profound, depending on whether it affects the central nucleus or the more peripheral objectifications. In general, it can be said that existential coherence is a requirement that common sense ascribes to reality, and not reality to common sense. Therefore, an articulated and differentiated common sense offers individuals who reactivate it many more opportunities for reflexivity than one that is more standardized and stereotyped. One final issue remains open, the fourth, which will be addressed in the next section.

Symbols, Values, Options

Considering political culture as part of shared common-sense thinking and as a set of social representations allows us to address most of the issues raised in the literature. And to provide a usable theoretical framework for empirical research. The proposed approach can apply to political as well as religious, legal, artistic, etc. culture. It proposes a theoretical framework and a methodological perspective but does not define the object. In what is political culture characterized as *political*? How to identify the object, distinguishing it from others? The question also involves political theories. Liberalism is a political tradition, but not only. The same thing can be said of other political theories, since they all refer variously to religious, philosophical, anthropological, aesthetic, etc. presuppositions. It is a matter – for political culture, as well as for political theories – of identifying the nature of the political, as distinct from other dimensions.

The question, with reference to political culture, has been notably taken up by Pekonen (1989). He starts from Weber's idea that

> 'Culture' is a finite segment of the meaningless infinity of the world process, a segment on which *human beings* confer meaning and significance (…). The transcendental presupposition of every *cultural science* lies (…) in the fact that we are cultural beings endowed with the capacity and the will to take a deliberate attitude towards the world and to lend it *significance*.
>
> (Weber 1949, p. 81)

What, then, is the 'attitude towards the world' that produces political culture? If it all depends on subjective positions, one can range from the radical feminist, for whom even the private sphere is political, to the opposite extreme of the political bureaucrat, for whom politics is only administrative management. Pekonen, on the one hand, coherently writes that, for this very reason, "we cannot in advance decide the boundaries of political culture" (Pekonen 1989, p. 129), since basically every aspect of life in common can be politicized; on the other hand, he concludes that "of course, every meaning is not political culture. Only those meaning-givings which are reflected in the political arena, in the arena of political forces and power relationships, may be understood as political culture" (Ibidem). While the first proposition concedes too much, the latter may be too narrow. What exactly is the political arena? Do social forces, e.g., collective movements, have political relevance? The question addressed above returns: does participation in the political arena coincide with electoral participation, or do other forms of participation take on political and, potentially, democratic significance? The conclusion Pekonen reaches is that what is politically relevant depends on each specific historical contingency.

I will expand on this issue in the following chapters. It may be appropriate, however, to introduce a final classification concerning the different nature that the contents of a political culture can assume. I propose to distinguish between *symbols*, *values*, and *options*, with an immediate example. Let us take the political culture of a left-leaning Italian citizen: we will find reference symbols – the colour red, not black; fundamental values – equality, rather than market freedom; basic options – a statist rather than privatist attitude.

Contents that express the most symbolic dimension of politics are, for example, slogans, flags, myths, colours, songs, brands, etc. This component is presumably the least reflexive: the strength of symbols lies in constituting binding memberships, which do not require argumentation and are available to a very large number of subjects. Flags, songs, and symbols can move the feelings and belonging of entire peoples and generations.[32] Values, on the other hand, express a more reflexive dimension than symbols. Just think, to give some examples, of the contrast between communitarian and individualist values; between equality and freedom; between war and peace; etc. On these issues, widespread political culture produces arguments and stances that are translated into topics, into shared reflexivity. Finally, the dimension of options includes the set of cultural models that are more directly operational, closer to concrete political practice. These are guiding ideas for definite political praxis. A political culture with a strong component of options is decidedly in contrast with one of great symbolic values: unlike the latter, it can have at its disposal cultural models capable of dealing with real and thorny issues.

In simplicity, it can be said that symbols express the most visceral dimension of politics; values constitute the reasons of the heart; options are those of the head. It is difficult to find the options in the central nucleus of a representation: it is much easier to find a varied mixture of symbols and values. As we saw in the first chapter, values are not something autonomous from ends, but the result of a process of valourization with respect to alternative ends, the values being general affirmations determined in ends. Similarly, I start from the assumption that emotions and beliefs are not opposing dimensions, but variously interconnected: emotions are always imbued with beliefs, thus distinguishing themselves from mere sensations (Nussbaum 2001). Moving from symbols to options, the emotional component progressively decreases, and the belief component increases.

In conclusion to this chapter, we can say that political culture, unlike political cultures/theories, can be identified on the basis of the following characteristics: (1) it possesses a low level of reflexivity; (2) individual creativity plays a marginal role inside it; (3) it is characterized by an existential type of coherence, which bears within it the presence of cognitive dissonances; (4) it is in direct connection with the community or social group that developed it; (5) it is not based on basic axioms or assumptions of an immanent type; (6) its contents are mostly opaque and are experienced rather than understood; (7) it is the result of a collective and anonymous construction; and (8) it is subject to processes of change of an intentional type.

In the next chapter, the relationship between political cultures/theories – understood as theoretical traditions – and political culture – understood as that part of the shared common sense that pertains to the political sphere – will be examined. In studying this relationship, the concept of social imaginary will be introduced.

Notes

1 In detail, these attitudes are: interest in the political system and government; feeling of national pride; expectation of fair treatment by authorities; ability to discuss politics freely and frequently; emotional involvement in elections; tolerance of parties opposed to one's own ideas; spirit of civic cooperation and trust; and participation in political associations (Almond, Verba 1963). According to Almond and Verba, the presence of civic culture requires that "all citizens be involved and active in politics, and that their participation be informed, analytical and rational". But "only when combined in some sense with their opposites of passivity, trust, and deference to authority and competence, was a viable, stable democracy possible" (Almond, Verba 1980, p. 16). In this way, "the democratic citizen is called upon to pursue contradictory goals: he must be active, yet passive; involved, yet not too involved; influential, yet deferential" (Almond, Verba 1963, p. 479).

2 According to Pye, "political science was strangely slow to incorporate the concept of political culture. In part the reason no doubt was that political science had long employed cognate concepts which, like culture, promised much for general explanation but proved elusive for pinning down causation in any specific case" (Pye 1972, p. 285).

3 The statement demonstrates that "maximizing benefits" is a prevalent culture in Montegrano. Only a widespread culture can help explain individual behaviour. Rational choice theory would like to explain how individuals behave, but it avoids addressing the question of why the attitude of maximizing interests and nothing else is at the basis of action. It may well be that individuals tend to rationally maximize their own interests, but even if they do it is because they think it is right to do so. All this means that the theory of rational choice needs, in order to be explanatory, to lean on a theory of shared culture. *Ergo*, rational choice theory, does not work.

4 The debate is summarized as follows by Gibbins: "to Marxists political culture was a dependent variable, but to all others it was taken seriously as an independent or at least an interdependent variable" (Gibbins 1989, p. 2).

5 After his historical reconstruction of the different Italian regional territories, Putnam comes to the astonishing conclusion that "economics does not predict civics, but civics does predict economics, better indeed than economics itself" (Putnam 1993, p. 157). In general, the part of the book that tries to explain the differences in institutional performance between the various regions based on their different historical development is perhaps the most questionable and problematic.

6 As Sani writes, "it is possible that the findings of *The Civic Culture* might have painted an excessively dark picture of Italian society", especially because "perhaps the most noticeable change in Italian political life in the last decade concerns the phenomenon of participation" (Sani 1980, pp. 306, 310). The season of the strategy of tension, which began with the massacre in Piazza Fontana on 12 December 1969, marked the definitive challenge which Italian democracy had to face, in a period – that of the 1970s and 1980s – marked by a profound social clash. It should be emphasized that it was precisely the Regions that launched those welfare policies that constituted one of the most important elements of the new Italian democratic season.

7 WD-40 is a multi-purpose lubricant, the exact opposite of a glue.

8 Here are some examples from Putnam: "The black church, for example, brings together people of the same race and religion across class lines. The Knights of Columbus was created to bridge cleavages among different ethnic communities while bonding along religious and gender lines. Internet chat groups may bridge across geography, gender, age, and religion, while being tightly homogeneous in education and ideology" (Putnam 2000, p. 21). Among other things, returning to the Italian case, everything suggests "that because citizens in civic regions enjoy the benefits of community, they can be more liberal. Ironically, it is the amoral individualists of the less civic region who find themselves clamoring for sterner law enforcement" (Putnam 1993, p. 112). Community and freedom are therefore not necessarily antagonistic.

9 Marx can be seen as one of the main exponents of epiphenomenalism. He postulates two distinct dimensions, the mental and the material, one of which is caused, but not causative.

10 Weber, in his study of the spirit of capitalism, highlights the cultural aspects underlying the development of capitalism but also highlights how a specific economic work ethic is influenced by a religious ethic. He connects not only cultural elements with structural elements but also cultural elements from different spheres. Regarding the often overlooked connection between political culture and artistic culture, see Edelman (2007).

11 It is believed that the theorem was also known to the Egyptians and Babylonians. But it was certainly known in China and India as well. Its oldest traces seem to be present in one of the oldest Chinese books on mathematics, dating back to 1500 BC. In addition to the classic demonstration of Euclid, there are many others, including one by Leonardo da Vinci.

12 For example, Mannheim writes that "whereas in mathematics and natural sciences, progress seems to be determined to a large extent by immanent factors, one question leading up to another with a purely logical necessity, with interruptions due only to difficulties not yet solved, the history of cultural sciences shows such an 'immanent' progress only for limited stretches (…). We can probe the secret of this agitated wavelike rhythm of the successive intellectual currents, and discover a meaningful pattern in it, only by trying to understand the evolution of thought as a genetic life process, thus breaking up the pure intellectual immanence of the history of thought" (Mannheim 1997c, p. 135). I emphasize that Mannheim believes he is in total agreement with Weber's sociology of culture (Mannheim 1997e, pp. 60–61). To confirm this, he reports the following Weberian passage concerning law: "In speaking of law (…) it is necessary to pay particularly strict attention to the distinction between juristic and sociological modes of consideration. The former asks: what possesses validity as law in the realm of ideas? (…).The latter mode of consideration asks, in contrast: what *actually takes place* by virtue of the *probability* that persons (…) *subjectively* regard certain regulations as valid and treat them as such, which is to say that they orient their own transactions by reference to them?" (quoted in ivi, p. 60).

13 In fact, "if they were nothing but meaning, one could only *comprehend* them (…). But all these formations can also be *experienced* means that, in addition to their meaning, the experiential contexture from which they arose is more or less given along with them" (ivi, pp. 83–84).

14 Tocqueville is described as "the patron saint of American communitarians" (Putnam 2020, p. 109).

15 The concept of narrative, variously taken up in this text, has to do with the social and narrative character of identities. See, for example, MacIntyre (1981), chapter 15.

16 These nexus, I stress, concern the social location of the thought, not its immanent validity. To give a further example, the connection between Malthus' thought and English industrial development may be true, but the correctness of Malthus' thought is another matter. On the second aspect, the non-immanent analysis can say nothing. It is an expression of humility, entirely in line with the awareness of the limits of any scientific investigation. It is a different attitude from the so-called strong program of sociology of knowledge (Bloor 1991). In keeping with what I believe to be Mannheim's authentic program, I have proposed, on the contrary, a weak program of sociology of knowledge (Santambrogio 1997; 2018).

17 For example, Brint identifies three geographically connoted traditions, the French (Montesquieu, Rousseau, Tocqueville, etc.); German (Kant, Herder, Hegel, Marx, Weber, etc.); and American (the 'scientific' approach inaugurated by Almond and Verba) (Brint 1991). It should be emphasized that the objects studied differ. While the first two are akin, the American approach differs because it concerns political culture as a set of attitudes. It seems important to me what Brint points out about the German approach: these authors, although different, "focus on the cultural and intersubjective symbols and on the *collective meanings* inscribed within political practice. To understand a culture, one must not simply observe the behaviors exhibited by individuals, but one must also learn what might be called the cultural grammar or narrative of polity – the internal coherence of its social, cultural, and discursive practice" (ivi, pp. 5–6, italics mine).

18 As is well known, for Locke private property is based on work and, before that, on the ownership of one's own body. As Locke writes, "though the Earth, and all the inferior Creatures be common to all Men, yet every Man has a *Property* in his own *Person*. This no Body has any Right to but himself. The *Labour* of his Body, and the *Work* of his Hands, we may say, are properly his. Whatsoever then he removes out of the State that nature hath provided, and left it in, he hath mixed his *Labour* with, and joyned to it something that is his own, and thereby makes it his *Property* (...) at least where there is enough, and so good left in common for others" (Locke 1988, § 27, pp. 287–288). Note the last statement, the so-called Lockean clause: if "the labour that was mine, removing them out of that common state they were in, hath fixed may Property in them" (ivi, § 28, p. 289), it is necessary that this "removing" leaves the same possibility for others.

19 This is a conservatism to which Tocqueville's thought is foreign. The conservative Tocqueville criticizes liberal democracy, but in the name of freedom, in support of the individual against the tyrannical principle of the majority.

20 According to Mannheim, "in a word, Germany achieved for the ideology of conservatism what France did for progressive Enlightenment – she worked it out most fully to its logical conclusions" (Mannheim 1997f, p. 47).

21 Mannheim writes: "spiritual realities are not like things, not only by virtue of the fact that only certain realities are present or visible for any given age (...), but also by virtue of the fact that it is in being experienced that they constitute themselves and that, therefore, the attitude of the experiencing subject projects into their inner structure" (Mannheim 1997e, p. 52). In phenomenological language, one could say that there is always a moment of reproduction and a moment of production within the subject of experience.

22 Echoing Durkheim, Moscovici writes that representation "constitutes a social reality *sui generis*" (Moscovici 1984, p. 13).

23 Also for Schütz the change of common sense starts from common sense itself. He writes that "if we encounter in our experience something previously unknown and which therefore stands out of the ordinary order of our knowledge, we begin a process of inquiry. We first define the new fact; we try to catch its meaning; we then transform step by step our general scheme of interpretation of the world in such a way that the strange fact and its meaning become compatible and consistent with all the other facts of our experience and their meanings. If we succeed in this endeavor, then that which formerly was a strange fact and a puzzling problem to our mind is transformed into an additional element of our stock of experiences" (Schütz 1964, p. 105).

24 To give a dramatic example, the Germans who brought Jews to extermination did not think they could be innocent: because they were Jews, they were deemed guilty.

25 Using Schütz's language, the dose of production depends on the way in which the subject grasps an objective sense, bringing it back to a now-and-thus. The objective meaning can thus lose part of its anonymous being, becoming the specific sense of a specific action. The objective sense (we could say, the core) is detached from time and is anonymous and intentional; the subjective meaning is linked to time, to my duration, it is personal and reflexive. Therefore, it is never pure reproduction. It is so only insofar as it necessarily refers to the passive heritage at hand.

26 I take up and generalize here an insight from Moscovici. In his book on psychoanalysis, he studies the way in which representations are made their own by various social subjects within their relationships. In this process, the media play a key role. Therefore, he studies three types of publications – the militant press close to the Communist Party, the Catholic-inspired press, and widely circulated newspapers – each characterized by its own style of communication – propaganda, propagation, and circulation, respectively. The three styles are characterized by a different degree of articulation and structuring, ranging from a minimum (diffusion) to a maximum (propaganda), and reflect conditions that are also different within the social production/reproduction relationship. Moscovici thus concludes that "the three systems of communication retain a remarkable individuality. It is precisely this particularity that authorizes us to approximate, term by term, diffusion, propagation, and propaganda to opinion, attitude, and stereotype" (Moscovici 1961, pp. 630–631, translation mine).

27 I recall that Durkheim distinguishes only between collective and individual representations. There is, however, an interesting passage in which he, speaking of restitutive law, explicitly highlights the role of social groups: "Since the rules where sanctions are restitutive do not involve the common consciousness, the relationships that they determine are not of the sort that affect everyone indiscriminately. This means that they are instituted directly, not between the individual and society, but between limited and particular elements in society, which they link to one another" (Durkheim 1984, p. 91).

28 It should be clear, from what has been said so far, that beliefs and acting are interconnected: the intentions that accompany acting are always interwoven with beliefs.

29 Class consciousness concept can be seen as a set of self-representations. In the same vein, Mannheim introduces the concept of generation (Mannheim 1997c). I have conducted research on the social representations of young people, highlighting

how one can, in a similar way, speak of 'youth consciousness', where young people develop, beyond the merely age-based connotation, their own autonomous social self-representation. This occurs especially for those young people who were protagonists in the season of the protest movements (Santambrogio 2002). Of course, there is a dialectic between self-representations and hetero-representations: just as the latter can heavily affect the ability of various social subjects to have an image of themselves, in the same way self-representations can end up profoundly changing the social image.

30 The naive individual will always be driven to think of his own representations as a product of his individual consciousness. To take a step beyond this ingenuous attribution, the individual must be urged to reflect on his own contents of consciousness. And this happens mostly when he is confronted with a different subject. Then what previously appeared as natural begins to manifest itself as existentially connected to a specific context of experience. On this point the concept of 'surrender-and-catch', introduced by Wolff (1994), is interesting.

31 In my research on the social representations of drug addicts carried out among Umbrian adolescents (Santambrogio 1994), the presence of two different alternative and conflicting central nuclei emerged, that of the 'victim' and the 'guilty' drug addict. The simultaneous presence of these two nuclei, each with its own specific peripheral elements, contributes to producing notable and profound cognitive dissonances (Festinger 1957) in the subjects interviewed.

32 On the symbolic dimension of politics, see Edelman (1976).

3 Social Imaginaries

Science and Common Sense

What is the relationship between theory and political culture, between the reflexivity of the former and the unreflexive intentionality of the latter? We have seen that scholarly scientific culture is relatively independent of any existential link with a community of experience. Its internal development is not directly tied to any community.[1] Consequently, potentially, its universality may be assumed by all and any community. But a collective way of thinking, characterized by the mass of roots that anchor it to an experience, is not transferable in its totality outside its context. Can a bridge span the two dimensions?

To answer the question, it is appropriate to reflect on the diversity between the two ways of thinking. Again, I will use Schütz as the main reference. Firstly, a profound difference between the natural sciences and the social sciences must be postulated. The former select facts and events within a field of observation, but this selection is wholly indifferent to the object; it does not correspond to any criteria of relevance already present within it. On the contrary "the constructs used by the social scientist are, so to speak, constructs of the second degree, namely constructs of the constructs made by the actors on the social scene" (Schütz 1964, p. 6). The reality of the social sciences is made up of constructs, already characterized by their own system of relevance.[2] It is a question of understanding whether a difference between the two types of constructs exists, and what that difference is, starting from the idea that the relationship between social sciences and common sense is based on something profoundly akin, something that is absent in the relationship between science and nature. We too have our own position within the surrounding natural and socio-cultural world, characterized by our role, age, biography, etc. A position implies a whole system of relevance, through which we select, within the infinite heterogeneity of the world, what is significant. Ultimately, if the social sciences are constructs of constructs, it means that they take position upon position, that is, they select upon selections.

A position is the result of the sedimentation of experiences that have adopted a typical connotation, becoming recognizable within a biography.

DOI: 10.4324/9781003229339-4

This process applies to subjective experience: each of us occupies a position characterized by the typical experiences that distinguish it. But it also applies to society, to collective experience, since

> my private world (…) is from the outset an intersubjective world of culture. It is intersubjective because we live in it as men among other men, bound to them through common influence and work, understanding others and being understood by them. It is a world of culture because, from the outset, the world of everyday life is a universe of significance to us (…). This texture of meaning (…) originates in and has been instituted by human action (…). All cultural objects (…) point back by their very origin and meaning to the activities of human subjects.
>
> (ivi, p. 10)

The social world is a world of subjectively attributed meanings, the result of the sedimentation of past actions. Schütz shares with Weber the idea that the task of the social sciences is the interpretation of subjective meanings that are solidified in structures of relevance, in positions within the world, with the awareness that "this world is not my private world but an intersubjective one and that, therefore, my knowledge of it is not my private affair but from the outset intersubjective or socialized" (ivi, p. 11).

Within the world of everyday life, we all wear the natural attitude of commonsense thinking, that is, we take for granted a number of meaningful constructs that make up our world. According to Schütz, I belong to a group when I take two idealizations for granted: that individual differences in perspective are meaningless and that there is congruence in attributions of importance. Ego and alter share a common world if their individual points of view are exchangeable and if they have the same systems of relevance. In short, if they essentially share the same position, what is obvious to one is also obvious to the other. Of course, a position may be common to all those who share the same natural attitude towards the world; an attitude that, once it becomes opaque, may be considered "to be the natural, the good, the right one by the members of the 'in-group'" (ivi, p. 13), based on the socially produced and socially shared knowledge.

The boundaries of rational behaviour within commonsense thinking are therefore defined by the possibility that behaviour can refer to standardized and typified patterns, by both the actor and the interlocutors. Rationality, in essence, means standardization and uniformity: within the common sense of a Hopi Indian, it is utterly rational for the village witch doctor to coax the rains by dancing. Such uniformities exist in our modern world too, so that conversely it would seem strange to write a book on an old typewriter, to go to the office dressed as an ancient Roman; to scream in a library, etc. In all cases, the essential reference is the inter-subjectivity of We and the set of typicalities that this contains, with the related systems of relevance. As Schütz writes, "the more standardized the prevailing action pattern is, the more anonymous it is, the greater is the subjective chance of conformity and, therewith, of the success of intersubjective behavior" (ivi, p. 33). From the point of view of common sense, to return to the example of the rain dance, rationality is not measured by whether it actually rains, but rather by conformity to shared norms, which alone can guarantee the comprehensibility of the action. The understanding of intended meaning is based on sharing within a community of experience. As we have already seen, "a community-wide, conjunctive (historical) concept counts only for those who participate in an experiential space, even if in actuality everyone participates in it" (Mannheim 1997e, p. 203).

Further referring to Mannheim, a general concept of scientific type is instead valid for everyone, even if only one person should think so. Its criteria of validity and rationality are completely different. The question is to understand in what sense the social sciences can produce general concepts with respect to commonsense thinking, that is, starting from subjective interpretation and intended meaning. Are concepts such as role, rite, wages, savings, monopoly, and capital the object of the social sciences thus understood? Do they not refer to aspects that appear independent of social subjects and their subjective ability to make sense of their actions? According to Schütz, two problems arise here: how to make subjective meaning scientifically comprehensible and how to make such knowledge objective, that is, available to all scientists and others. Weber had already posed these questions with the starting point that "the distinctive characteristic of a problem of social policy is indeed the fact that it cannot be resolved merely on the basis of purely technical considerations which assume already settled ends. Normative standards of value can and must be the objects of dispute in a discussion of a problem of social policy because the problem lies in the domain of general cultural values", and at the same time "it has been and remains true that a systematically correct scientific proof in the social sciences, if it is to achieve its purpose, must be acknowledged as correct even by a Chinese" (Weber 1949, pp. 56, 58)[3]

A finalistic theory of action based on the concept of intention must confront a cognitive dimension – beliefs – and that of practice.[4] The social scientist, as mere observer, partially renounces the practical aspect of direct intervention in the world, so as to make a one-sided accentuation of the cognitive aspect. One, as a social scientist, puts in place a different orientation of one's systems of relevance, modifying them with respect to those that belong to one as a subject who lives, through one's biography, within a social world. The world of science is not the world of everyday life, even though it belongs to everyday life.[5] For the social scientist, "the scientific problem is the 'locus' of all possible constructs relevant to its solution" (Schütz 1964, p. 38). For example, the issue of the transformation of values into prices within Marxist economics has enormous social-political implications, but in its purely scientific aspects, is quite independent of them. The doggedness with which a solution has been sought is directly related to the existential involvement of the economists who have tried their hand at the enterprise. Each one of them, however, had to approach the issue from the position of the disinterested observer, who sees the problem in its scientific objectivity. Only a change of scientific perspective – and not of existential location – could reformulate the problematic sphere. One can continue to be a Marxist even without solving that problem. One can coherently continue to be a Marxist economist only by engaging in a scientific solution to the problem, and one remains so even when the question is totally reformulated, erasing the obstacle, provided that this reformulation is scientific in nature.

Rationality implies observation. There is the interested observation of the subject who looks at his own unreflexive intentionality; that of the alter, who looks with a degree of interest at the meaningful interaction between you and me; that of the social scientist, a very particular alter, who looks impartially at selected spheres of the social world. The participants in the interaction and the non-scientific observer both relate to a concrete situation, to a now-and-thus, living it and interpreting it from typical experiences and socially constituted knowledge.[6] The social scientist observes in a disinterested way not from the typical experiences of everyday life, but from selections of relevance that belong to the scientific universe. The observation is disinterested in the part in which it wants to be scientific, and solely in this aspect. Schütz's disinterested observer "does not imply the *naive* neutrality of science but the interest in obtaining scientific knowledge" (Takakusa 2021, p. 64). From this stance, from this specific system of relevance, science acquires its autonomy.

To live meaningfully in the social world is what characterizes everyday life and the commonsense thinking that constitutes it; *to interpret meaningfully the social world* implies the reflexive activity of an observer: the scientific observer, unlike ordinary people, does so in a partially disinterested way. This observer ultimately has a system of relevance that differs from that of everyday life.[7]

Bridging Ideologies

We can now answer the question: what is the relationship between social science and the life-world? And between theories and political cultures? Let us start with the fact that there is no social world external to the life-world. Let us also hold firm to the idea that the social scientist "has to interpret these interaction patterns in terms of their subjective meaning structure lest he abandon any hope of grasping 'social reality'" (Schütz 1964, p. 40, slightly modified). Science, and social science in particular, is thus embedded within the general universe of meaning that constitutes the life-world. This universe of meaning, however, is heterogeneous, depending on the various levels of reflexivity and different systems of relevance within it. The relationships between these various universes of meaning vary according to different historical periods, so that, starting from a sociology of knowledge approach, it is possible to reconstruct them. In pre-modern societies, for example, there is no scientific approach in the strict sense, and the various universes of meaning are variously combined, and sometimes confused.

For the matter that interests us here, I find it particularly valuable to analyse the concept of ideology, reconstructing, through Mannheim, its historical-conceptual evolution, starting from the early Enlightenment period. In keeping with the ideas of the sociology of knowledge, "the history of ideology (…) is not free-floating evolution of spiritual spheres deducible from a purely immanent dialectic. It is, rather, carried by the social process" (Mannheim 1997e, p. 174). It is not, then, a question of analysing the internal, immanent coherence of thought structures, but rather of reconstructing their evolution in relation to that of the social structure, highlighting specific historical-conceptual links.

As is well known, the concept of ideology was introduced by the Enlightenment, through the work of thinkers such as Destutt de Tracy, Cabanis, Condorcet, Volney, Dupuis, and others, belonging to the so-called group of *idéologues.* For all of them, ideology is a new and original science of ideas – as indeed the etymology of the term[8] – capable of direct intervention in social and political practices, with an effect of 'enlightening'. Specifically, it is a study of the genesis of ideas. It constitutes an original way of understanding the relationship between theory and practice, between speculation and action. For the *idéologues*, practical activity represents a direct incarnation of philosophical activity, to the point of thinking of an overlap between philosophy and politics. In extreme synthesis, their main ideas are founded, at a philosophical level, on the faith in the perfectibility of the human being in society; and on a political level, on the aspiration to a constitutional and Republican form of State, liberal-progressive as we would perhaps say today.

In Mannheim's interpretation, that of the *idéologues* is a *particular conception* of ideology. This conception consists in raising doubts about the position of others. It presupposes mutual good faith and the fact that interlocutors are open to rational confrontation with each other. But, even if someone is lying, it holds firm to the idea that there are common criteria of truth, without which comparison would not be possible. These criteria are dictated by reason, by the fact that, regardless of what we think and say, all human beings are rational.[9] There may be a connection between my interlocutor's idea and social position, but it is not thought of as the foundation of their way of thinking and possible errors. It does not become the central explanatory element, and it does not become my core argument against my interlocutor. Other factors may lead that person astray. The level of comparison remains on the psychological plane, that between two or more individuals, and does not systematically involve anyone's social affiliation. Those who err do not do so because they are bourgeois. The approach is not sociological, and the 'social being' of the contenders remains on the side-lines. There is no privileged position: the interlocutors must all be willing to defend their reasons, but also to accept that they are wrong. All are equal because they are all equally rational: this is the basis of confidence in a possible collective enlightenment to which ideology, as the science of ideas, should make an important contribution.

The real breakthrough is the discovery of the social origins of thought, which occurs with Marx under his theory of unmasking. It has its premise in the change of social structure, with the emergence of social groups capable of developing their own autonomous worldviews. The clash between ideologies becomes the expression of that between opposing classes, so that "political discussion (…) seeks not only to be in the right but also to demolish the basis of its opponent's social and intellectual existence", penetrating the "existential foundation" of his thought (Mannheim 1997a, p. 34). It is no longer mere academia, a question of immanent thought. The problem of truth involves the social being of the subject, whether individual or collective, their existential determination, namely, what one really is. Bad faith becomes systematic, because it is an expression of the social situation of the individual, of one's class placement. In a sense, the bourgeois is unable to think correctly, because one's class identity does not allow one to do so. The whole position is wrong, as it is tied to class affiliation. No longer is a single idea unmasked, but an entire worldview, a whole ideology: the term now takes on the meaning of systematically distorted thinking.[10]

In a certain sense, ideologies replace religions, and transcendence is replaced by an immanent, social dimension. As with religions, one cannot be faithful to two ideologies. The total existential involvement of the subject, in their overall identity, produces the radicality of the conflict and is, at the same time, nourished by this radicality. In Weber's words, "worlds struggle against worlds", in a conflict without rules, whose common playing field is nothing other than human history itself. It is no longer a matter of convincing others of their errors, but of destroying the foundations on which one believes one's certainties are based. At this point, Mannheim speaks of a *total conception* of ideology. The enlightened discussion between rational subjects has become a class struggle. Individuals are not all equal, because they belong to different social classes. Among the different classes, there is a privileged position, that of a class whose existential location allows it to think correctly.

The social conflict produces a further evolution of the concept. According to Mannheim,

> At first those parties which possessed the new 'intellectual weapons', the unmasking of the unconscious, had a terrific advantage over their adversaries. It was stupefying for the latter when it was demonstrated that their ideas were merely distorted reflections of their situation in life, anticipations of their unconscious interests.
>
> (ivi, pp. 36–37)

The use of those 'weapons' could only spread, and the unmasking became reciprocal: the discovery of the irrational bases of thought became general. From the standpoint of the bourgeois, from their systems of relevance, the position of the proletarian is also socially, and therefore irrationally, connoted. Even the latter's ideas are connected to specific and determinate class interests. There is not a single particular that, given specific historical characteristics, carries with it the universal. Every particular is unmaskable in its particularity, and every claim to universality – advanced by any social subject – appears ideological. Thus, we move to a *general use of the total conception*. Reciprocal unmasking, in the end, removes confidence in the soundness of the thought not only of some but of all. The steps to total disenchantment are in fact two: the loss of that cultural unity provided by religion and the emergence of the existential and irrational dimension internal to knowledge. The Enlightenment project, the attempt to establish a science of ideas, in its evolution thus seems to vanquish the possibility of certain knowledge and the privileged position that supports it. Enlightenment reason, which wants to free humanity from the irrationality of myths and religions, must paradoxically surrender in the light of its surprising discovery: ineliminable social irrationality.[11]

Mannheim makes a historical reconstruction of some social positions that create the ideological and social history of the nineteenth and twentieth centuries. The three main social classes that make modern history – aristocracy, bourgeoisie, and proletariat – correspond to three major ideologies, understood now as opposing worldviews of subjects in conflict with each other: conservatism, liberalism, and socialism.[12] Social differentiation and cultural differentiation go hand in hand, and the changes within one affect the other. So it is that

> the conservative does not want satisfaction of his interests alone, but also his own world, a world in which his interests are at home. The bourgeois does not want only his demands fulfilled, but also a world shaped by his own mentality. The proletarian is not content to secure his future; he wants a future in keeping with his spirit.
>
> (Mannheim 1997f, p. 55)

Ideologies are therefore mutually irreconcilable epic narratives of identity.[13] I would underline two aspects. The first is that the progressive social conflict between ideologies highlights how the processes of democratization rightfully bring into the social and political arena the ways of thinking of the subordinate classes. These are processes that, in turn, are the result of an awareness on the part of these classes. Secondly, we are on the brink of a new relationship between theory and praxis, of the constitution of new nexus, typical and significant of the relationship between social structures and modes of thought. The latter now need a patina of scientificity: it is no longer enough to enunciate a political creed; it is necessary to argue for it, as rationally as possible, with sound arguments. This fact requires a new and completely original mixture between theoretical reflexivity and everyday life, between theories and political cultures. The latter need to have at their disposal good arguments or arguments that appear as such: they cannot manifest themselves only as mere expressions of identity, irrational in their basic nature.

I believe that this process and this need were at the basis of the development of our democratic systems until the second half of the last century and are still with us today. The protagonists of social and political life, over this long period of time, must be able to refer to a political culture potentially armed with convincing and winning arguments. The unreflexive intentionality of the taken for granted must be nourished by a reflexive dimension that comes from political theory. On the one hand, as we have seen, there are the great theoretical traditions of conservatism, liberalism, and socialism, but also others. On the other hand, there are the political cultures of real social subjects engaged in social and political arenas. I believe that ideologies are particular symbolic structures that allow a mediation between theories and political cultures, and they can do this because they have a degree of reflexivity superior to political cultures but inferior to theories. They are a middle ground between the former and the latter. Their function lies in constituting a bridge between theoretical production and the widespread culture available. Ideologies are the result of the application of specific systems of relevance, through which certain themes of theory are incorporated into political cultures. This does not happen once or uniquely but in response to historical and political needs. Drawing from the reservoir of theoretical production, ideologies make available to various political cultures, contents useful to the arguments of those social subjects directly engaged in social and political conflict. Their function is to translate the logical coherence of theory into the existential coherence of praxis. It is not by chance that a new class of subjects emerges and it is the role of these subjects to produce ideologies. These are the figures of *intellectuals*, especially actively committed intellectuals – be it journalists, politicians, scholars, professors, trade unionists, etc. – whose task is not to produce theory in its strictest sense but to provide content to relevant social subjects that can enter their political culture, giving it that patina of scientificity required to generate arguments.

As we have seen, there is the problem of finding a key to the study of the *production of* political culture, and not only of its *reproduction*: it is a question of understanding, differently from Almond and Verba's approach, how shared symbolic universes are maintained and yet how they change, while they ensure both a relative stability of the political system and still accommodate the production of new horizons. Once ideologies have been assigned the function of mediating between theory and political culture, they must then both produce new symbolic content, which comes from theory, so as to constitute innovation and have the function of maintaining a degree of stability within widespread political cultures. This double function is possible because ideologies, conceived in this way, are the expression of a cognitive dimension that is less reflexive than theory, but more reflexive than political culture.

Mannheim's important contribution lies in having shown that being and thought intertwine in different ways according to different historical contexts. The typically modern need of various social subjects to have their own political culture on which to base their identity requires a specific relationship between the production of theory and life lived. To give an example, Marx's theory must become ideology – in the sense just outlined – so as to be available to the working masses. This availability is realized in the processes of *political socialization*. These processes, by giving voice to social subjectivities, constitute the articulation between the political system and society through the production of complex and articulated cognitive systems such as ideologies. The latter mediate between reflexivity and intentionality, between theory and political culture: a worker on strike can rely on arguments in support of his or her actions without having the onus of cognitively possessing the fascinating mysteries related to the Marxian theory of alienation, or the complex problems posed by the need to transform values into prices.

Ideologies, I insist, have an intermediate character between reflexivity and intentionality. They make possible the translation of theory into everyday language, stepping into play not only in the intellectual arena but also within the necessities of everyday action.[14] At the same time, unlike political culture, they are not a product of unconscious adaptation within common-sense thinking, since behind them operate reflexively clearly identifiable social subjects, who construct their own arena of political confrontation/debate, both within single ideologies and between different ideologies. It is an independent arena, which does not overlap with that of scientific research, but neither with that of common sense. The infinite nuances of Marxist ideology, to remain with the example, reproduce the infinite possible interpretations of Marxist theoretical production, drawing freely from the latter, emphasizing now this or that aspect, depending on the interests and identities of reference. Consider, for example, the Marxian rereading carried out by the intellectuals of the youth movements of the 1960s and 1970s, and how much this differs from the ideological orthodoxy of the official communist parties.

In short, ideologies are a cognitive form that must support collective identities, and that must respond to the specific demands that an identity needs: understandable and expendable ideas, able to be translated into concrete action, and valid emotional support. And they must also give reference subjects that patina of rationality that social conflict requires. These are 'scientific' narratives of identity.

Returning to our workers on strike, they take for granted a whole symbolic universe that underpins their protest, an entire political culture, in the sense outlined above but, when necessary, they must also be able to reasonably argue the reasons that drive them to the streets in the critical moment.[15] Hence, the workers' political culture is nourished by socialist ideology, which in turn can refer to a vast and complex theoretical production. Without excluding, of course, that workers' culture can also draw from other various cognitive influences. Nor that socialist ideology might influence the political cultures of other and different social subjects. Mannheim's reconstruction has not only a historical function in the strict sense but also an ideal typical one: it points to the possible ways in which being and thought influence each other.

To summarize: in a society divided into classes, ideologies play an intermediate role between theories and political culture, mediating between the reflexivity needs of the former and those of opacity of the latter, thus ensuring both the needs of stability (reproduction) and those of change (production) of collective identities. Provided that by ideologies we mean specific and historically determined cognitive systems, produced by the very specific characteristics of a social conflict that expressed itself in the first instance with the weapon of the unmasking of the adversary.

Integration and Solidarity

What has been said so far about ideologies is probably of little use for the interpretation of our current reality. We are experiencing a profound transformation of society, such that social stratification and cultural differentiation seem to take on entirely new characteristics, with resultant changes in the relationship between them.

The possible origins of this transformation may be found in the processes of individualization characteristic of the later decades of the last century and the first decades of this one. The phenomena are widely studied by the social sciences and have generated a vast pool of literature. The process of individualization is probably the key to interpreting the modern world. The classic authors of sociology have extensively shone light on its importance. Tocqueville believes that the central element that characterizes the democracy of the moderns is the disappearance of the principle of hierarchy and the affirmation of the principle of equality among individuals, increasingly free from the shackles of the past. But especially in Durkheim, Weber, and Simmel, the study of the processes of individualization becomes the heart of sociological analysis. Sociology – together with the other social sciences – develops by trying to understand how a *society of individuals* is possible, and how then to reconcile the social order with the autonomy of individuals. The question addressed above of the relationship between individual attitudes and collective political culture is also part of this more general topic. These are processes which, while taking on different forms, maintain a continuity: the autonomy of subjects seems to be gaining, within the history of the processes of modernization, greater territories, and ushering in new problems. With the processes of globalization and the transformations that our world has undergone since the 1980s, some unexpected dimensions have arisen.

Giddens, significantly, has shown how there is a very close relationship between individualization and increased social reflexivity. Within radical modernity, the processes of disembedding are escalating: that the individual can rely on stable points of reference, whether social or cultural, is diminishing and social relations are restructured in increasingly abstract and global space-time spheres. We stand before the separation of time and space, which are unanchored from the concrete experiences of everyday life and are converted into standardized and neutralized forms by the specificity of contexts; and we also stand before a parallel reflexive reorganization of social relations, which starts with the overhaul of all conventions based on shared symbolic systems. These are aspects that urge new forms of re-embedding (Giddens 1990).

According to Beck, ours is a society of *risk*, of a risk produced by new social relations (Beck 1992). The environment is a clear example although the risks are, more generally, within the process whereby individuals become increasingly independent from their forms of life, from those institutions and certainties that early modernity still offered: family, factory, work, profession, science, progress – these are all areas that the current world is increasingly tipping into crisis. Instead of repairing and protecting, society abandons the individual alone to face these new socially produced risks with his own weak forces. They are supra-national and extra-territorial global risks. They impose decisions that it is not clear who can and must take, when faced with alternatives that are challenging to manage. If faced with choosing between eliminating world hunger and advancing standardization of seeds, is it the risk of hunger or the progressive loss of biodiversity that is more pressing? These risks also affect our daily lives: with the evaporation of the certainties enjoyed by previous generations, each one of us is increasingly becoming the sole protagonist of our own biography, abandoning traditional paths, bringing with us the possibility of self-fulfilment, but also, and perhaps more frequently, bearing that of uncertainty, loss, and the subjective inability to deal individually with collective issues. Isolated from social ties, we are driven to think that we can actually be the product of ourselves; that our successes, and especially our failures, can be attributed to ourselves alone, as if it were possible to find individual solutions to systemic problems.

Sennett (1998) dwells notably on the shattering of social ties, especially those linked to work. The rigidity of Fordist biographies is replaced by the *flexibility* of post-Fordist work. Here, too, we see processes of profound individualization of experience. The worker's biography can no longer count on a continuity assured by a stable and guaranteed job. The Fordist worker, typical of the capitalism of early modernity, lives a linear and predictable path, made up of many years spent in repetitive task, within days that are always the same and a daily routine devoid of radical fractures. All this, however, gives meaning to the experience, and gives the feeling of being someone: the bond with colleagues, the after-work experience, the sharing of union life, life in the neighbourhood are beads of the same necklace. Flexibility, on the other hand, crumbles class-based social stratification, replacing it with inconsistent stratification. It is a process of homogenization and standardization, which neo-liberal flexibility and meritocracy translate into an extreme and radical being at the disposal of the needs of the labour market. With the loss of the centre of gravity around which life was organized in class society, namely a relatively stable position in the world of work, all the social coherence that revolved around it vanishes. Everything changes and gains speed. The new capitalism dismantles the factory: the new productive networks do not need rigid bureaucratic hierarchies; they are nourished by a new efficiency, based on flexibility and small dimension, on downsizing; the structuring of rhythms and times – those of work, but also those of everyday life – is liquefied to the advantage of the now and the immediate. The de-structuring of work thus becomes de-structuring of ties and of personality. A total availability to the present inhibits the projection of something stable and lasting into the future, of involving significant ties with significant others.

The metaphor of *liquid modernity* introduced by Bauman sums up all these transformations (Bauman 2000; 2001). It takes up that powerful Marxist notion according to which, within the continuous revolutionization of production and living conditions introduced by modern capitalism, everything solid is not only liquefied but even 'melts into air' (Marx, Engels 2014; Berman 2010). For Bauman, fluidity becomes the metaphor for our current social condition. It takes shape in many ways: deregulation, liberalization, flexibility, mobility, total opening up of markets (financial, real estate, and labour), decreasing the tax burden are processes before our eyes. All this accelerates the processes of individualization, in step with the demands of the neo-liberal capitalism. Bauman distinguishes between de jure and de facto individualism: in principle, society promises us possible fulfilment and emancipation; in truth, it does not allow us to realize what it promises. On the one hand, there is the abstract individual, totally dispossessed of his real characteristics; on the other, the concrete individual, who can never find himself in the abstraction into which he is forced. The liquid society denies – in a certain sense 'liquidates' – without opposing resistance. The promise becomes the form of negation. For the disadvantaged classes of early modernity, emancipation was the expression of a revolt against something that resisted, that had its own solidity. But how is it possible to break down a system based on the idea that the subject has potentially all the ways to self-fulfilment, which totally privatizes the idea of emancipation?

The radicality of these processes has led to talk of radical modernity, end of modernity, liquid modernity, reflexive modernity, post-modernity, etc., in an attempt to give a name to a profound change. However, I believe that these are new forms of older processes, which concern the nature of the modern world, and primarily the affirmation of the concept of the individual. In any case, as has been said, radical change in the structure of social stratification prevails. Individualization proceeds by disembedding the subject from the strong bonds in which he was embedded, dissolving – or diminishing – their importance. The opportunities that this individualization seems to offer dissolve in the critical interpretations above with the loss of the characteristics that make each of us something unique and special. Globalized individualization liquidates the individual: the worker – but also the consumer – in New Delhi is a worker just like the one in Detroit, because the roots of both – what makes them two significantly different people – become insignificant. Distance and time seem to no longer matter; globalization erases our space of experience, making it increasingly homogeneous and meaningless through a process of standardization, which affects material structures, experiences, and emotions. The idea that one can be anywhere at any time, that 'anywhere' can replace 'place', is one of the ways in which every firm, real relationship is erased – think, for example, of the relationships of friendship – which, as such, needs to be set in a time and a space, needs attention and cherishing.

The new fact is that the system of interests and identities cannot be traced back to simple aggregative nuclei – classes, territories, generations, just to mention some dimensions around which conflict has traditionally developed – because these aggregative nuclei have mostly dissolved.[16] Ideologies constitute the worldviews of the different social classes, in a model of society whose social stratification is made up of a pluralism of clearly identifiable social subjects, each one the bearer of his own position. Individual identities mostly coincide with social identities, in a reality in which being a labourer or a farmer or an office worker or an entrepreneur implies a precise position within the general social structure, in terms of disposable income, consumption, social circles, lifestyles, political representation, generational mobility, access to education, etc. Today all these distinctions are far more fluid and unstable. Certainly, inequalities have not disappeared. Globalization and the neo-liberal capitalism create new forms of poverty, new modes of exclusion, new social barriers. The theme of redistribution of resources, after the crisis of welfare policies, continues to be central. And while the development of new productive strategies, more sustainable from both an environmental and, above all, human point of view, is becoming increasingly central, these issues must now be expressed with a new language that is closer to the new social reality and its dynamics.

We are witnessing that individual and social identities tend to coincide less and less. The worker is no longer only and above all a worker: in general, the identity of each of us is nourished and composed of a plurality of social affiliations, so that the ties and interests that bind us to others are also heterogeneous, complex, and not so coherently organized. Each of us can refer to a multiplicity of spheres of belonging, some narrower and more binding, others broader and looser, including family, neighbourhood, profession, politics, associationism, religious sphere, etc. There is rarely one thread that binds together this multiplicity, capable of constituting relatively coherent and well-structured identities. Increasingly, each of us finds ourselves having to manage this heterogeneity, which at times produces contradictions between the symbolic universes available. And, at the same time, an increasingly greater number of possible experiences, in the past inaccessible to one's own identity, become potentially common.

In short, we are faced with a new form of pluralism. It does not envisage the simple presence of a multiplicity of social subjectivities that are clearly identifiable and separable from one another, as classes are, for example. Rather, it implies their intertwining, their not being mutually exclusive, their contamination and overlapping. No longer are worlds fighting worlds, but social conflict crossing social identities and individual identities: one can end up at odds with oneself. Ideologies are part of a world characterized by a *first-level pluralism*, whose exemplary model is the class society; today we live in a different world characterized by a *second-level pluralism*, in which division no longer reigns but differentiation. At the social level, *solidarity* no longer coincides with *integration*; at the individual level, *identity* no longer coincides with *belonging*. It is necessary to hold together, in social solidarity and in individual identities, a complex and connected number of different spheres of integration and different belongings.[17]

The end of ideologies, already predicted by Mannheim and variously taken up by others a number of times during last century, coincides with the transformations briefly described above, and expresses them. Ideologies are great narratives (Lyotard 1984). With the world's religious unity gone, they express a social reality that seems to have lost every common denominator, torn by an irreconcilable conflict between subjects each of whom has his own irreducible vision of things and non-negotiable interests. After the ideologies, the new narratives no longer have 'mentality bearers', to use the Weberian expression; they no longer have cohesive social subjects of reference. Which social subject, for example, is environmentalism an expression of? A new term is needed to identify a new form of symbolic production. I propose to use the concept of social imaginary. Before going into the details of this proposal, it is useful to dwell on the meanings that the term imaginary has recently assumed, particularly through the work of Taylor.

Modern Social Imaginaries

The term imaginary has an almost infinite semantic capacity. We can think that there is a social imaginary of practically anything. I would like to give the term a circumscribed and precise meaning, to use it in reference to the processes described above. A first step in this direction may be Taylor's use of the concept of imaginary in reference to the modern world.[18]

Being modern is not simply a chronological placement. For Taylor, it has to do with a new capacity of individuals to "imagine their social existence" (Costa 2005, p. 9, translation mine). Consequently, modernity – beyond its structural characteristics, the changes that affect the economic, legal, and political spheres –

> is a new conception of the moral order of society. This was at first just an idea in the minds of some influential thinkers, but it later came to shape the social imaginary of large strata, and then eventually whole societies (…). The mutation of this view of moral order into our social imaginary is the coming to be of certain social forms, which are those essentially characterizing Western modernity: the market economy, the public sphere, and the self-governing people, among others.
>
> (Taylor 2004, p. 2)

Taylor also considers fundamental the process through which some symbolic content produced by theory, that is, by a small group of experts, gradually becomes part of a shared vision of being in society. How does theory become imaginary? Taylor leaves this question open[19] while focusing on the forms that the modern imaginary takes, beginning with content – primarily Grotius's theory of natural law – produced by theory. As elements of theory, they respond to the demands of interpretative correctness: they become imaginary when they are transformed into a prescriptive dimension, involving praxis, thus creating moral and social order. We move from the question 'is this concept correct?' to the question 'does this idea tell me how to act?' Starting from the modern theory of natural law and the state of nature, a new *moral order of society* is built, the modern one, and to the definition of how it is right to act within it.

Let's look at what, according to Taylor, are the background contents of modern social imaginary, meaning the fundamental characteristics of its moral order. The pre-modern imaginary is characterized by a strong harmony between human order and natural order: there is an ontological dimension at the basis of everything which concerns God and the cosmos. From this order, the human order descends, organized in a hierarchy of positions, on a scale of decreasing dignity: those who pray (the clergy), those who fight (the nobles), and those who work (all the others). This order becomes modern when, the hierarchies and their reference to a cosmic dimension cancelled, it becomes the expression of relationships between individuals who cooperate for the common good: morality sheds being part of, and the expression of, an objective natural order. Everything is now based on reciprocal relationships between equals, who freely pursue the security and prosperity of all. The process that transforms the pre-modern order does not dissolve the principle of sociality: for Taylor, in fact, modern individualism brings with it a new form of sociality. It is not what remains after abandoning the religions and metaphysics of the past: it represents something new and original, which has been haphazardly constructed, and not through a process "by subtraction" (ivi, p. 18). Significantly, an important part of this new principle of sociality are the new narratives contained in imaginaries.

Within these premises, four essential elements can be identified. (1) Society is a structure made up of free and equal individuals, understood as moral agents independent of any pre-defined hierarchy, which comes before the political sphere and becomes independent of the latter. (2) In this framework, politics "appears as an instrument for something pre-political" (Ibidem), it is the place that makes possible the achievement of mutual well-being, based on the needs that come from society. (3) Politics is, therefore, at the service of citizens and must guarantee their freedoms, understood as rights. (4) All this must be guaranteed to all: as Tocqueville would say, the principle of equality replaces that of hierarchy.

Modern social imaginaries, from a phenomenological point of view, appear as a kind of common sense of modernity. Taylor writes:

> By social imaginary, I mean something much broader and deeper than the intellectual schemes people may entertain when they think about social reality in a disengaged mode. I am thinking, rather, of the ways people imagine their social existence, how they fit together with others, how things go on between them and their fellows, the expectations that are normally met, and the deeper normative notions and images that underlie these expectations.
>
> (ivi, p. 23)

This 'disengaged mode' closely recalls the idea of pre-reflexive intentionality, while the rest of the quotation echoes that dimension of opacity and taken for granted typical of common-sense thinking. The phenomenological approach allows us to root these modern imaginaries in everyday life, in an attempt to explain the social actions that we perform every day. The affinities become even more evident when Taylor, a few lines later, writes that "the social imaginary is that common understanding that makes possible common practices and a widely shared sense of legitimacy" (Ibidem). Without exaggerating, I think it is possible to say that the contents described by Taylor can be seen as typifications now embedded in our modern being, typifications that belong to our deep common sense.[20]

Three other ideas that Taylor believes characterize the modern imaginary also resonate with the general approach advocated here. The first concerns his conception of the relationship between ideas and praxis, between cultural and material structure. Taylor rejects both an idealistic and a materialistic approach. This, according to Taylor, "because human practices are the kind of thing that makes sense, certain ideas are internal to them; one cannot distinguish the two in order to ask the question Which causes which?" just as "ideas always come *in history* wrapped up in certain practices" (ivi, pp. 32, 33, italics mine). I find fundamental the reference to history: the theoretical approach, as mentioned above, abstracts from every now-and-thus, from the practical dimension within the social action. Of course, to practise science is also a praxis: but the characteristic that distinguishes it is that of using a systematically reflexive approach. The second idea, already mentioned above, implies a new conception of sociality, which becomes independent of any sacred or natural dimension: "This is what underlies the, to us, striking ethnocentricity of our ancestors. They didn't see their difference from, say, Amerindians as that between two cultures, as we would say today, but as that between culture and nature" (ivi, p. 38), between the civil and the uncivil. The third idea moves from the interrelated concepts of disembedding and disenchantment. They "involved the growth and entrenchment of a new self-understanding of our social existence, one that gave an unprecedented primacy to the individual" (ivi, p. 50). Now we no longer relate to the sacred as a society but increasingly as individuals.[21]

What has been said so far, according to Taylor, is realized in three dimensions of 'social self-understanding': the *economy*, the *public sphere*, and *democratic self-government*. The first replaces the cosmic order, governed by divine benevolence, with a material order, within which it is possible to achieve the benefit of all through mutual benevolence. While "God's design is one of interlocking causes", that of humankind concerns "harmonized meanings" (ivi, p. 71): we may think, for example, of Smith's theory of the 'invisible hand' and of his theory of moral sentiments, in particular, of sympathy. Now benevolence is exercised to a new end, which is materialistic: to ensure economic well-being, no longer spiritual well-being. Consequently, "for moderns, organized society is no longer equivalent to the polity" (ivi, p. 79), nor, a fortiori, to religion.

The public sphere constitutes a common space of encounter between subjects, which can take advantage of the media. It is a set of real spaces that constitute an imagined, meta-topical space, as Taylor calls it. Its main characteristic is that it is not immediately political, although it can become so. In keeping with the ideas of Habermas (1992), it is a space of reflexive discussion that potentially involves everyone, because everyone can develop an interest in all public issues.[22] In this way, the public sphere acquires a normative status. Despite conflict and difference, indeed through them, it makes agreement possible because it is based on rational discussion. The sense of belonging to a political community is now replaced by that produced in a sphere independent of politics, within which there is room for the maintenance of pluralism. Social heterogeneity, in fact, can be recomposed through a process that is also pre-political. A political unity is replaced by a social unity, of which the former is only an expression. This new social unity – just like the economy – is also wholly secular: "the public sphere is an association that is constituted by nothing outside of the common action we carry out in it". In short, the public sphere is "an extra-political, secular, meta-topical space" (ivi, pp. 94, 99).

The third extra-political dimension – after the economy and the public sphere – is civil society organized around the idea of the people, understood as a new collective actor. 'The people' constitutes the normative fiction on which to base the polity, independently of any previous legitimation, whether it comes from religion or is formed from a pre-existing state of nature. This is possible by thinking of people as a subject capable of acting, and therefore of constituting a political unit. Taylor recalls, as a paradigmatic example, the American Constitution, whose proclamation is made in the name of "We, the people" (ivi, p. 156).[23]

In all three new realities, the idea of the imaginary is at work: all three exist insofar as it is possible to imagine them as autonomous realities. Modernity brings with it, beyond structural transformations, and perhaps even deeper than these latter, a new collective imaginary, a new collective vision of reality that informs our common sense. Within this imaginary, "the society in which we live is not just the politically structured order; we also belong to civil society. We are linked in an economy, can seek access to a public sphere, and move in a world of independent associations" (ivi, p. 143). It is precisely on these characteristics of modern common sense that my analysis will proceed.

Social Imaginaries

Modern social imaginaries, as defined by Taylor, act within modernity; they are active and dynamic forces. Modernity makes change one of its fundamental characteristics. Whereas in pre-modern societies stability is the norm and change the exception, the opposite is now true. The ideas contained in modern social imaginaries are among the main drivers of change, in keeping with the concomitant internal transformations in the structure of social stratification. There has been an increase in the importance that our memberships within civil society have for our overall identity, to the detriment of political identities. This process unfolds before our eyes, despite its erratic course. Modernity brings with it the development of a pre-political sphere, that of civil society, to which politics should put itself at the service. The affirmation of modern social imaginaries has therefore directly to do with the reflections upon democracy and its quality, reflections at the heart of which are the questions of rights and equality.

Through the push for the inclusion of marginalized social strata, and not only of the working class, the new moral order, both individualistic and based on rights, tends to penetrate all social niches. We can think for example of the family.[24] My idea is that this penetration occurs through the autonomous production, by variously interconnected subjectivities within civil society, of new worldviews. These worldviews are different from previous ideologies and which I would like to call *social imaginaries*.[25] It is a process that increases the horizontalization of society, the affirmation of the modern egalitarian principle against the pre-modern hierarchical one. These are social imaginaries internal to the modern social imaginary described by Taylor, and they express its most recent development. The affirmation of these new social imaginaries involves a model of society within which each member "is 'immediate to the whole'" (ivi, p. 157). The individual is decreasingly confined, and confinable, to isolated, circumscribed and hierarchically organized niches, and increasingly feels a subject who, in his individuality, freely belongs to the whole society, which he can see as a whole. Let's proceed step by step.

We must start from the twofold ending of ideologies. According to Mannheim's reconstruction, they end a first time through a conflict between social classes that renders the technique of unmasking useless. The general use of the total conception of ideology undermines the possibility of identifying a non-ideological thought: the proletarian thought, like all the others, is in unison with certain interests. All ways of thinking become different and opposing worldviews, all placed on the same plane: there is no privileged position, and it is only a matter of choosing which side to be on. The second sense in which we can speak of the end of ideologies – also predicted by Mannheim in his theory of the masses and totalitarianism (Mannheim 1997b) – appears fully only to us contemporaries. It coincides with the end of social classes, of positions that bear overall worldviews, in practice with the transformation of the structure of social stratification typical of our present world.

For the social subjects that populate our contemporary reality, it is very difficult to gain access to complex and general worldviews like the ideological ones typical of the social classes. An identity that refers primarily to a single belonging requires that the latter be relatively inclusive of all aspects that concern the experience. Being a worker was an identity that thereabouts covered the overall experience of these subjects. In a world in which the worker is no longer just a worker, in which identities can no longer rely on a single, all-embracing belonging, but are propelled to build their own autonomous coherence from a multiplicity of belongings, the latter can only be pieces of the world and be experienced by the subject as such. Identity becomes an open process, with aspects both of stability and of change, which intersect in an often fragile and precarious balance. The symbolic and structural dimensions push in the same direction: social identity and imaginary identity, and structure and culture become parts of a whole that is not immediately recognizable. Not even for the social scientist.

The modern imaginary – even in Taylor's conception – produces disembedding and must cope with it. In fact, we are once again faced with the problem of identity. In traditional societies, "the most important actions were the doings of whole groups (tribe, clan, subtribe, lineage)", to such a degree that human beings "couldn't conceive themselves as potentially disconnected from this social matrix" and "it would probably never even occur to them to try" (Taylor 2004, p. 54). Think of Socrates, to whom it does not occur that there might be a place for him other than his polis, than the law that has – unjustly – condemned him. Disembedding produces the autonomy of the individual and, at the same time, his solitude. The embedded subject is transformed into an abstract and bedless individual. Class placement constitutes the ideological solution to this solitude, to this process of abstraction.[26] Now that this too has vanished, how is it possible to reconstruct a relatively reliable identity for disembedded and disenchanted individuals?

The conception of the imaginary that I want to propose stands within Taylor's modern imaginary as an attempt at a new embedding, in the face of the transformations that modernity has undergone in recent decades. Its inspiration, consequently, is more circumscribed, actual, and with greater pertinence to our collective contexts. New social subjects build significant pieces of their identity when taking up memberships that produce new partial visions of the world. It is a question of developing roots that can no longer count on a fundamental central root. I am thinking, for example, of young people, women, the weak and excluded; of ecological and pacifist movements;

of new territorial identities and sexual identities; and so on. These are collective subjects that autonomously produce what I believe to be the new social imaginaries: youth, feminist, ecologist, pacifist, vegetarian, animalist, no-global, etc.[27] Making one of these imaginaries one's own does not necessarily mean belonging to a specific social group. It does not follow that an environmentalist is also a vegetarian, pacifist, etc., even though it may well be that that person, to continue giving examples, might also protest together with vegetarians and pacifists against violence against women or in support of migrant welcome policies.

In keeping with Taylor's hypothesis, civil society has acquired a new centrality today. While at the time of ideologies, cultural models were imposed from above, dictating specific modes of action, now autonomous social contexts develop their own autonomous visions of reality from below. The relationship between politics and society has changed. Ideologies, through the *political socialization* of substantially non-political masses, built – through parties, trade unions, the Church, etc. – identities that were both social and political. Now politics, and the parties, have lost this ability and observe, generally with little attention or understanding, what is happening in an increasingly tumultuous society. In recent decades, politics has produced nothing new, in terms of values and worldviews. The production of values, and of identity, no longer has a political centrality – whose subjects of reference were the State, the parties, the institutions, the trade union, etc. – but a social centrality which sees movements, associations, communities, etc. as the protagonists.

Starting with the protest movements of the 1960s and 1970s, women and young people were the first collective subjects to change course. Their ideas do not constitute ideologies because the 'mentality bearers' are not social classes that clash with each other in an unmediated conflict. Conflicts now involve identities because they touch the various belongings that constitute those identities. A young '68er is in conflict with parents, with an employer or teachers or professors, with a partner: generational, class, and gender conflicts – just to name a few – are difficult to reconcile in a single clear and general overall vision of the world. Sexual liberation and the value of peace – just two examples – are difficult to reconcile with traditional working-class ideology. And with which, even less, environmentalism will later be reconciled.

Within these processes, we must not forget the relationship between modernity and democracy, a relationship that is not without alternatives, but that little by little builds significant links. Even a democracy has its own non-derogable values, which have been affirmed, especially after World War II.[28] The progressive sharing of these values, produced also through class conflict, has resulted in depowering the radicality of the conflict contained in the ideologies. The European working class, through suffered and complex paths, ended up embedding its political and social position within the model of European democracy, abandoning deferral to Soviet communism. As an Italian, I can only emphasize the decisive role for the defence of democracy that the working class of my country played in extremely difficult moments of recent Italian history. Even the young revolutionaries of 1968 eventually contributed to the development of a freer and more democratic civil society: their anti-systemic potential dissolved and depleted.

If on the one hand, democracy needs to rely on some shared values, on the other, it does not seem to be capable as such of producing values and probably does not even need to do so. As a legitimate political system and starting from the values at the basis of its legitimacy, it leaves the subjects that animate civil society free to produce their own perspectives of emancipation, which they can adopt when they are compatible with the common basic values. All this could explain the progressive social protagonism and the decline of the political one in the strict sense. To return to the question of democratic political culture, it would be a mistake to see it as the sole result of socialization processes that originate from above. There is a need for democratic socialization in the system itself, but it no longer constitutes – as it did in the scheme of Almond and Verba – the whole of the political culture, now increasingly civic, that citizens have at their disposal. A civic culture today is also nourished, according to my hypothesis, by these new social imaginaries, which are being produced independent of the political system and the subjects who inhabit it.

This process has been implemented by the course of globalization brings with it an acceleration of the processes of disembedding, in terms of consumption, daily rhythms, our vision of space, our relationships. And this produces a new need for roots, for identity. Thus, alongside the global that depersonalizes, a local identity is generated, made up of slowed-down time, real spaces, local consumption, and rewarding relationships. Society sets itself in motion in order to offer its members these opportunities. And individuals act autonomously to make sense of relationships that would otherwise remain anonymous and impersonal. In this way, associative micro-contexts flourish – based on volunteering, on associationism, on local identities, on gender, local affiliations, etc. – that are capable of regenerating social solidarity and new ties. The micro seems to prevail over the macro: effective and concrete cooperative and solidarity logics become predominant over the abstract ones associated, for example with the sharing of social class. A centrality of social issues is often linked to a de-politicization of one's own horizons of action. Traditional forms of political representation are increasingly lacking: the world of institutions is receding, not only because it appears blind to real needs, but, at times, is explicitly and deliberately ignored.[29]

These are subjectivities that do not look directly to the old ideologies, even if traces of the past can be found in their ways of thinking. New problems unfold, related to the new way of looking at consumption and development; to new forms of critical solidarity; to new forms of life in common; to new relationships with cities and territories. Organizational methods are used that, in part, take up those of historical associations (associations concerned with promoting culture, assisting the poor and sick, blood banks, saving the environment – in Italy namely: ARCI, Caritas, AVIS, Legambiente, etc.); but also in part, take on new, freer and improvised forms, with an accentuated use of social media. Beyond the specific topic of concern, the moment of relationship, the fact of being together, the strong experience of meaningful ties, whose forms are not pre-defined, but are woven as we go along, as an expression of an inescapable desire for sociality, takes on significant importance. As Bruni writes, the valourization of subjectivity "is therefore neither the reflection of a self-constituted and atomized individuality, nor the expression of strictly codified collective identifications, such as those that have characterized political participation as traditionally understood and in which collective commitment was seen as a dimension that was at times totalizing, which went on to define large portions of personal identity". In this way, "participatory action is no longer the consequence of a strong identification. That is, acting is no longer the reflection of given and codified social identities, such as class membership, but rather the very redefinition of identity is entrusted to highly performative social relations, which produce and reproduce open processes of identification " (Bruni 2021, pp. 229, 230, translation mine).

These are partly different phenomena from those Putnam observes in the USA. They share however the increase in the distance between society and politics, with the potential risks that this entails. But this increase seems to take different forms: in USA through the loss of associationism; in Europe with an associationism without voice in politics. To better understand this phenomenon, we should dwell on other characteristics that, in my opinion, the new social imaginaries assume.

Common sense, as we have seen above, is unreflexive intentionality. These social imaginaries are, like ideologies, universes of meaning that lie between reflexivity and intentionality.[30] As in ideologies, there is here a dimension of conscious production that brings with it a degree of reflexivity. They constitute models of spontaneously produced collective self-representation.[31] Their product feature is evident: for example, many in Italy are aware of the food revolution proposed by *Slow Food*, of the individuals that initiated and made it their own. The reflexivity that characterizes them makes them visible, in contrast to the typifications of common sense. The values that shape them, and the images that nurture them, are there for all to see and are subject to actual choice.

In the social imaginary there is a creative dimension absent in common sense. The imaginary is the product of a desire that materializes reflexively in values, world images, aspirations (Appadurai 2011; 2013). It is an extremely creative and mobile symbolic universe, characterized by far more evident and continuous change than the invisible and unreflexive one that characterizes common sense. Sometimes it resembles a bubbling magma, yet to solidify. Unlike common sense, it does not function as the cement of everyday life, or as the invisible and hidden basic software that is taken for granted: on the contrary, it is visible and partially reflexive. Partially, because, at the same time, it does not have the characteristics of reflexivity typical of theory. Behind the imaginary, the creative fantasy of the desire to correct a world that is wrong is buzzing. While common sense reduces uncertainty, the imaginary tries to tackle it, but, inevitably, produces it. In general, just as Sartre thought, it is an expression of human freedom to transcend reality.[32] It points to an unidentified place beyond.

Unlike ideologies, however, it is difficult to find specific social subjects at the basis of their formation. In the construction of these new social imaginaries, the role of certain intellectuals, men of action, politicians, etc. can be identified: but their contribution is mixed with that of other anonymous subjects who, consciously and reflexively, contribute to their formation.[33] Moreover, it is always a contribution that does not constitute their identities, as was the case with the traditional figure of the intellectual. All this affects the internal coherence of the imaginaries. They inevitably are less coherent. For two reasons: they are not the product of a recognizable subject, as were the intellectuals who produced ideologies; they are not addressed to a single reference subject.

Imaginaries propose, like any symbolic universe, both a closure – in this they are recognizable – and an aperture – in this they are inconsistent. With the former, they identify an area of belonging that is available to support individual and collective choices: am I for or against same-sex marriages, euthanasia, a new highway that will destroy the landscape, and so on? With the latter, they bestow this area with a perpetually uncertain and provisional character. They provide individuals of different social backgrounds, of different generations and genders, of heterogeneous cultural and professional backgrounds with the opportunity to meet in the same plazas and to share common choices. These people are able to recognize – almost always but in any case, significantly – the imaginaries to which they turn. The relative incoherence within imaginaries offers a space of expression for collective action that is infinitely more open and available to subjectivity than ideology. The system of ends within an imaginary rarely has a defined structure and articulation. The sense in which, by pursuing a certain end (e.g., better management of the environment), another end (e.g., greater equality) is also pursued, remains completely undetermined. An idea of impracticability, utopia, and scant realism hovers over social imaginaries. Creative moments are always naive. Social imaginaries preserve within themselves this naivety, which holds open a door to creative change. At the same time, they are able to support concrete and real actions, which may invade everyday life, sometimes even thoroughly transforming it.

To summarize: the processes of modernization and rationalization do not seem to have reduced the imaginative dimension of social subjects and their ability to produce new narratives. On the contrary, they dilate and expand it. It seems to become a direct competence of many social subjects, who, to assert their autonomy, produce original cultural models. These are certainly new forms of enchantment.[34] Through the work of many – and potentially made available to all, unlike the ideologies that had their own specific subject of reference – sets of ideas are being assembled that, so to speak, float above the heads of individuals, who freely draw inspiration from them to give meaning to concrete actions, without necessarily having to commit their entire identity. These new social imaginaries are not, however, unrecognizable symbolic universes[35]: the different aspects that constitute an imaginary, despite the inconsistencies and often internal contradictions, have some common denominator, capable of giving rise to a belonging, which can then freely combine with others.

In conclusion, the main characteristics of social imaginaries can be summarized in the following points. (1) They are a product of civil society, which through them amplifies its autonomy from politics, and not of a specific and identifiable subject, such as the intellectual. (2) They are visions that concern and involve parts of the world, and they are not interpretative *Weltanschauungen.* (3) They help to provide models of belonging to individuals, who can autonomously use them to compose, even in complementary ways, their identities. (4) They are characterized by a degree of reflexivity intermediate between that of theory and that of common sense. (5) They have a powerful capacity for change and projection into the future, also because of a relatively low level of internal coherence. (6) They trigger a great deal of conflict, possibly radical, but hardly anti-system. Rather than undermining democracy, they seem to promote further development of the democratic quality of the societies within which they proliferate.

Identity without Politics

We have seen that social imaginaries promote great and important goals, bringing into play values such as the environment, sexual identity, new models of development, equality, new forms of social ties, and solidarity. But while they materialize in important and clear aims, they are often short-lived – city gardens, solidarity actions, alternative living and consumption spaces, purchasing groups, etc. When they try to flee the rather restricted social circles in which they are activated, they seem to constitute a voice incapable of acting on wider and more general stages. In short, it seems that social imaginaries are both too big and too small. A hiatus exists between the breadth of values and the daily realization of goals. What is missing is that significantly political expression that can lead from narrow goals to broader and more general goals, within common values.

Ideologies provided a bridge between political and social spheres. Political identities tended to coincide with social ones: class identity also provided a political identity and a party of reference. The striking worker knew that the picket in front of the factory gates was a part of a wider vision, politically expressed in a greater project. What was at stake was not only an increase in salary but also, hopefully, a new model of society, which would involve future generations. In that context, the deferment of happiness played a central role: the suffering of today made sense because on it was based the promise of a better future. This allowed harmony between the social and the political, but also the unity of theory and practice. Ideology guaranteed this unity, a unity that was embodied in the figure of the engagé intellectual, who guaranteed that ideas were in unison with the real transformation of the world carried out by a social subject.

It is about a vanished world. But one that leaves an important question entirely unresolved. New social imaginaries help build social identities, but rarely have an institutionalized political voice. The autonomy of civil society – the development of a pre-political dimension, one of the key features of the modern social imaginary, as depicted by Taylor – could thus contribute to the eventual construction of a separate world, which sometimes even claims that separateness, legitimizing it. We would have, and in part already have, *identities without politics*. To which, respectively, we would counterpose *politics without identity*. On the side of politics, the end of the so-called mass parties has left party structures without a soul, dominated by processes of personalization of politics, which see more or less authoritative leaders try to impose their personalities – but rarely original ideas – on narrow oligarchic groups and malfunctioning bureaucratic machines.

The bridge has toppled: politics and society seem to be in a state of almost total incommunicability. A vital issue for our democracies is precisely that of rebuilding meaningful connections between society and politics. It is a question of being able to give a wider-ranging expression to the actions that parts of civil society set in motion with reference to the values present in their collective imaginaries. In the past, ideologies, through processes of *political socialization*, provided a bridge between the top of politics and the bottom of society, in what was almost entirely a one-way process. Today, the opposite process seems necessary, that of *politicization of the social*. These issues will be addressed in the next chapter.

Notes

1 The community of scientists, in fact, is an atypical community, with quite specific characteristics.

2 On the concept of relevance, see Schütz (1970) and Nasu (2021). The problem of relevance "concerns the question of why these facts and precisely these are selected by thought from the totality of lived experience and regarded as relevant" (Nasu 2021, p. 28). For Schütz, "the problem of relevance is the fundamental problem of sociology" (Schütz 1996, p. 76), since it is the result of the selective and interpretative activity of the subject within the stock of knowledge at his disposal. It is possible to select something, giving it relevance, only because it is already constituted as typical.

3 In Schütz, the relevance system seems to replace Weber's concept of value-rational action. On this aspect, the literature is divided. Personally, I believe that giving relevance to one aspect rather than another within the totality of the world (social, but also natural) involves the same process of valourization that concerns the concept of value, as understood by Weber. Relevant is something that has been the object of valourization, of attention: in this direction, affinities seem to me more significant than divergences.

4 This complementarity applies to all the dimensions analysed: to political culture, to imaginaries, to the theory of ideology, and to utopia. For example, with regard to the imaginary, Taylor writes that "the modern social imaginary is thus both active and contemplative. It expands the repertory of collective action, and also that of objective analysis" (Taylor 2004, p. 167).

5 I underline the fact that, for Schütz, the world of everyday life is "the whole universe of life" (Schütz 1964, p. 246).

6 In reality, there is an important difference between the participants and the observer. The latter is not in a position to acquire the totality of the sense connections internal to the interaction, but only fragments of it. Someone observing me now, as I write, is not aware of the complex project of action in its entirety, involving past and future, within which what I am now doing is embedded.

7 From the Weberian point of view, one can say that the scientist uses his own reference to value, which does not imply a value judgement at all.

8 The term is used for the first time by Destutt de Tracy, who, contrasting ideology and psychology, writes: "I would much prefer that the term ideology, or science of ideas, be adopted" in an attempt "to give an exact and circumstantial description of our intellectual faculties, of their principal phenomena, of their most remarkable circumstances: in a word, of the true elements of ideology" (Destutt de Tracy 1970, p. XV, translation mine).

9 I bring to attention that the Habermasian theory of communicative action is also based on similar assumptions. For Habermas, however, the criteria for validity are internal to language and are not a pre-requisite of reason (Habermas 1984). The idea is that, beyond irrational factors – including lies and bad faith – a set of transcendental truth conditions is identifiable without which mutual comparison would not even be possible.

10 With Mannheim's words,

> the essential difference between the unmasking of a lie and that of an ideology consists in the fact that the former aims at the moral personality of a subject and seeks to destroy him morally by unmasking him as a liar, whereas the unmasking of an ideology in its pure form attacks, as it were, merely an impersonal socio-intellectual force. In unmasking ideologies, we seek to bring to light an unconscious process, not in order to annihilate the moral existence of persons making certain statements, but in order to destroy the social efficacy of certain ideas by unmasking the function they serve. Unmasking of lies has always been practised; the unmasking of ideologies (…) seems to be an exclusively modern phenomenon.
>
> (Mannheim 1997f, p. 141)

11 Mannheim speaks of the end of ideologies. It coincides with the impossibility of imputing to any worldview the charge of being ideological, and to impute it to this alone. It coincides with the futility of the technique of unmasking: once all positions are unmasked, since their existential roots have been shown, none can have a privileged point of view. If they are all ideological, none of them is. All this produces an obvious relativism: we are now faced, simply, with different *worldviews* that correspond to different social subjects. Mannheim believes that his sociology of knowledge can be a solution to the problem of relativism. In this context, the figure of the relatively free-floating intellectual takes on a decisive role in him. The issue can be briefly summarized as follows. If all positions are socially

anchored, how is it possible to have a social science? For Marx, it is possible when science takes on the position of the social subject who is on the side of history, and the latter accepts the idea of history that social science proposes, thus creating the short circuit between determinism and voluntarism, typical of Marxism. For Mannheim, on the other hand, it is possible as a product of a subject not entirely anchored to a specific social position. The modern intellectual conquers this position because he becomes an autonomous social figure, acquirable – as a consequence of the processes of democratization of education and the increase of social mobility – even by individuals coming from the less wealthy classes. To be an intellectual, unlike in the past, no longer means belonging to a well-identified social class, but constitutes an autonomous, independent, and therefore relatively detached social position. This idea has been deeply criticized, for some of its obvious internal problems: how autonomous is the figure of the intellectual? If the social structure changes, can this figure of the intellectual also disappear and so end the autonomy of science? Schütz's position seems more consistent to me. Social science is possible not through the unity of theory and praxis, not because of a historically produced class of intellectuals, but from a specific attitude, available to anyone who practices it: the attitude of the disinterested observer, with his own specific systems of relevance.

12 Minkenberg and Inglehart write:

> Karl Mannheim has emphasized that conservative and progressive thought have been established as the two socially based and mutually related *Weltanschauungen* in the modern world as a result of the differentiation of the traditional feudal order into diverse classes, interests and ideologies and through the coming of bourgeois society.
>
> (Minkenberg, Inglehart 1989, p. 86)

13 Through conflict, however, a set of experiences and common thinking can be produced. This is an important point, which will be taken up later. I would like to give an example here. About Romanticism, Mannheim writes:

> The sociological significance of Romanticism lies in its achievement, as experiential reaction against Enlightenment thinking (the philosophical proponent of bourgeois capitalism) (…). "Community"-bound experience is pitted, in various forms, against manifestations of the turn to "society" (…): family against contract, intuitive certainty against rationality, inner experience as a source of knowledge against the mechanistic.

In doing so,

> Romanticism wanted to rescue these displaced irrational life-forces by taking them up, but it failed to notice that paying attention to them *consciously* in and of itself served to rationalise them. Romanticism achieved a rationalisation which the bourgeois, rational Enlightenment could never have carried through.
>
> (Mannheim 1997f, p. 65)

14 We can think, among other things, of the role played by party newspapers and, more generally, the mass media. Nor should we underestimate, as a place of continuous production/reproduction of ideologies, the function that party schools have had, precisely in the direction indicated by Weber.

15 It is a matter, to use Schütz's language, of the varied articulation with which, within a project of action, one can identify intermediate ends (the success of the strike, to remain with the example), more far-reaching ends (the success of the labour dispute), up to the conception of real final ends (the socialist revolution?) (Schütz 1972; the examples are mine).

16 We can consider the concept of generation. When does a new generation begins and ends? When exactly is one no longer young? The generation of 1968 could count on a certain 'unity of generation' – I use Mannheim's concept – representing itself, starting from this unity, as an autonomous social subject. I'm afraid it's more difficult to do that for today's youth.

17 All this raises the important question, which cannot be fully addressed here, of a new model of universalism, which I like to call *welcoming universalism*. I find that the best point of reference still resides in the Durkhemian proposal of moral individualism, understood as the only 'religion' possible after the end of religions, and ideologies. All that modernity can believe in, and cannot renounce believing in, is the idea of the individual as a bearer of rights, which society must in some way feel committed to guaranteeing and developing. In this perspective, that second level pluralism I mentioned above can flourish.

18 An interesting reading of Taylor can be found in the first part of Alma, Vanheeswijck (2018). James (2019) rightly highlights how the historical character of social imaginaries is central in Taylor. An important point is to distinguish between imagination and imaginary. According to Bottici, these are alternative concepts. The former is a faculty of the individual; the latter pertains to the social context and is anticipated by the individual. Bottici, in order to overcome the dichotomy, proposes the concept of 'imaginal' (Bottici 2014; 2019). An excellent discussion of the relationship between imagination and imaginal is in Lennon 2017. For an in-depth discussion of the historical and open-ended character of the development process of modern imaginaries, which does not follow a predetermined evolutionary line, see Rundell (2020). This character of openness produces, according to Rundell, different modernities.

19 According to Taylor, theories at first shared by a minority, such as the ideas of Grotius and Locke, pass into the social imagination first of the elite and then, eventually, of the entire society. As we have seen, this is not just any minority, but a special one, made up of experts capable of exercising theory. In my opinion, the process by which, at an early stage of modernity, their ideas creep into the imagination is made possible, in a society stratified into social classes, by ideologies. The transformations of common sense activated by anchoring processes, on the contrary, are promoted by non-expert subjects, whose names are not even known.

20 In keeping with this, Adams, Blokker, Doyle, Krummel, and Smith argue that

> his long interest in the phenomenological themes of practical know-how and implicit knowledge influences his understanding of social imaginary. Although Taylor traces the advent of social imaginaries through key philosophical-theoretical articulations by such thinkers as Locke, Grotius, Rousseau and Tocqueville, his aim is rather to assert their common bedrock in everyday life as well as what underlies an (admittedly fragile) sense of unity dispersed across geographical space.
>
> (Adams, Blokker, Doyle, Krummel, and Smith 2015, pp. 24–25)

21 It is striking, in this regard, that Taylor makes no reference to Durkheim, to his idea of religion as a social fact (Durkheim 1995).

22 Taylor cites a passage from Burke, quoted by Habermas, that "in a free country, every man thinks he has a concern in all public matters" (Taylor 2004, p. 89).

23 To take another important example, not recalled by Taylor, we can consider Marx's critique of Hegel's philosophy of law. According to Marx, it is not the constitution that constitutes the people, as Hegel thinks, but the people that give themselves the constitution (Marx 1970). I emphasize the fact that for Taylor, in line with the position held in this book, all the imaginaries we are talking about, which articulate in various ways the modern social imaginary, start from a theory, which then "gradually infiltrates and transmutes social imaginaries" (Taylor 2004, p. 109; see pp. 109 ff.). The phenomenological approach – but also that of social representations – allow us to interpret these transformations as a passage from the reflexive sense of theory to the shared sense of common sense.

24 Of course, there may be a tension between the normative content of modern imaginaries and concrete social practices. According to Diehl, these are two different models of temporality: the affirmation of the former may have different timescales than their realization within various social contexts, some of which may be more refractory than others (Diehl 2019).

25 Taylor reconstructs the different ways in which modern social imaginaries have become established in different countries. In particular, he shows the difference between the USA and Europe. In the old continent, the processes of universalization of the new moral order were also realized through the development of what Taylor calls "class imaginary" (ivi, p. 153), which I, following Mannheim's approach, call ideologies instead. Beyond the names, what is important is the idea that, once ideologies have ended, or class imaginaries have ended, we are faced with the production of new imaginaries, connected to a different social stratification, but always triggered by that more general process which for Taylor is the progressive affirmation of the modern social imaginary. From now on, I will use *social imaginaries*, in the plural, in reference to my proposal; *modern social imaginary,* in the singular, in reference to Taylor, since I believe that his imaginaries constitute a kind of 'modern common sense'.

26 For example, according to Marx, capitalist exploitation is realized precisely through the cancellation of the concrete characteristics of the workers, transforming the real subject into the abstract subject, and its concrete work into abstract work. The consciousness-raising of the working class not coincidentally coincides with the consciousness-raising of its own concrete existence as a real subject.

27 I cannot dwell in this text on the contents of each of these imaginaries, on their specific characteristics, on the subjects who have reference to them. To address all these issues, empirical research must be done. From here on, I set myself only the task of outlining some general characteristics of these new social imaginaries, starting also from the empirical research I have done in recent years.

28 According to Gauchet, there are two alternative models on the genesis of democratic societies. The first considers the characteristics of their starting point; the second begins from social conflict. The first concerns mainly the American experience, of a society that is born democratic; the second concerns the European experience, especially continental, of societies that become democratic, in a path within which democracy is itself the object of conflict (Gauchet 2016). In post-war

Italy, to give an example, the acceptance of the democratic model, of its liberal and representative bases, was not at all taken for granted.

29 On these phenomena, there is an extremely vast and articulated research literature, which deals with various and heterogeneous models of associations and/or movements. I list some texts haphazardly and by way of example, in the Italian context: Rebughini (2008); Graziano (2010); Anitori (2012); Guidotti (2013); Santambrogio (2015); Gili, Ferrucci, Pece (2017); Pasqualini (2018); Federici, Conti (2020); Bruni (2021). These are associations that deal with critical consumption, co-housing, land management, urban redevelopment, the vulnerable and/or excluded, gender issues and/or related to sexuality, recycling, environment, eco-villages, Km 0 agricultural production, urban gardens, etc.

30 On the topic of imaginaries Costa declares that, "we are faced with a form of true collective intentionality" (Costa 2005, p. 11, translation mine): an utterly correct statement, since all symbolic universes are intentional. I believe that in the social imaginaries I am discussing there is also a certain dose of reflexivity.

31 The product character of the imaginary is also emphasized by Castoriadis. He writes:

> Those who speak of "imaginary", understanding by this the "specular", the reflection of the "fictive", do no more than repeat, usually without realizing it, the affirmation which has for all time chained them to the underground of the famous cave: it is necessary that this world be an image of something. The imaginary of which I am speaking is not an image *of*. It is the unceasing and essentially *undetermined* (social-historical and psychical) creation of figures/forms/images, on the basis of which alone there can ever be a question *of* "something".
>
> (Castoriadis 1987, p. 3)

Ricœur, starting precisely from a phenomenological approach, emphasizes the productive and not merely reproductive character of imagination: the imaginary is not a copy of the existing, its fictitious reflection, but it is the expression of a faculty that can dare beyond the existing social and political structures (Ricœur 1986; see also Taylor G. H. 2015). This is a central point: according to MacIntyre, "the agent is not only an actor, but an author", and all of us are "the co-authors of our own narratives" (MacIntyre 1981, p. 230). On the usefulness of the concept of the imaginary for a phenomenological theory of action, beginning with Castoriadis and Ricœur, see Sarantoulias (2019); Adams (2017). According to Diehl, the imaginary is not only a set of elements, "but also the capacity to produce this set" (Diehl 2019, p. 414).

32 For Sartre, following a reflection on Husserl, imagination is always something more than perception, because it is an expression of the active nature of the consciousness that imagines (Sartre 2004).

33 As Castoriadis writes,

> we cannot conceive such creation as the work of one or a few individuals who might be designated by name, but only as that of the collective-anonymous imaginary, of the *instituting imaginary*, to which, in this regard, we will give the name "instituting power". Such power can never be rendered fully explicit.
>
> (Castoriadis 1993, p. 103, italics mine)

34 The idea of the imaginary that I want to propose is not the only possible response to modernization and disenchantment. In our world, new forms of more or less irrational narratives are appearing, which take up memberships of a religious kind – think of the flourishing of sects or fundamentalism, within all the traditional religions; of a political kind – the new forms of nationalism; up to even more radically irrational forms, based on race or gender. But surely, it is a possible response. Which involves the development of narratives. Of all the possible responses, social imaginaries are those most in unison with the developments that the processes of individualization have undergone in recent decades, and with the modern social imaginary outlined by Taylor, avoiding dangerous returns to the past.

35 I find it interesting that the same individuals can participate in initiatives that refer to more than a single field, to more than a single imaginary, without feeling the need to share in toto the ideas of all. Whoever had participated in a manifestation of the 'sardine movement' in Italy would surely have noticed the extreme heterogeneity of the subjects present: there is an air of familiarity among them, but no real common identity. A sensation even more evident, to give another example, to those who have participated at least once in a Perugia-Assisi peace march.

4 Ideology

Ideology and Unmasking

The relationship between society and politics is in need of repair. The issues at stake are broad and general, and they concern the quality of democracy. A whole world has ended, and the new one does not yet have clear boundaries. Class society, Fordism, ideologies, mass parties, trade unions, engagés intellectuals, etc., were elements mutually linked by significant nexus so that they constituted a constellation, a relatively coherent world with its own identity. Most of these elements are in profound crisis, leaving many with regret and a lingering nostalgia. Regret and nostalgia, however, distance us from an understanding of reality, which is vital for the reconstruction of new meaningful nexus that can restore a sense of unity and coherence to our experience.

A good starting point may be the concept of ideology, which, in my hypothesis, provided a bridge between society and politics until recent times. And yet, while ideologies are gone, it is not necessarily the case that the theory of ideology must also be shelved. I set myself the task here of resuming an interrupted thread, returning to the question of what sense a theory of ideology can have today, understood as it was at the time of its founding during the Enlightenment as an analysis of the relationship between theory and praxis. To introduce this perspective, it may be useful to reflect again on ideologies, and the concept of unmasking, which made it possible to distinguish what is ideological from what is not. According to Eagleton, "no one would claim that their own thinking was ideological, just as no one would habitually refer to themselves as Fatso. Ideology, like halitosis, is in this sense what the other person has" (Eagleton 1991, p. 2). What exactly do other people have when their thinking is ideological? Can one be, or become, aware of having ideological halitosis? Can it be healed? The answers to the three questions raise the following reflections, beginning with Marx.

Marx's theory raises complex questions, addressed, and never fully clarified, by an endless literature. His most sociologically important contribution consists in the idea that consciousness is social consciousness and that man, consequently, is a social being. There is no abstract individual consciousness. Our thinking is socially determined by the social conditions underlying our

DOI: 10.4324/9781003229339-5

identity. Marx is, as it were, a one-sided sociologist of knowledge, who places at the centre of his analysis the ways through which a certain form of existence produces a certain form of consciousness, underestimating the influence the latter can independently have. His sociology of knowledge coincides with a critique of ideologies, which intervenes in the gap between existence and consciousness. Starting from the idea that the latter produces a representation of the former, it is possible to think of four different alternatives: (1) to a true existence corresponds a true representation of that existence; (2) to a false existence corresponds a false representation; (3) to a true existence corresponds a false representation; (4) to a false existence corresponds a true representation. All this provided that the protagonist is a consciousness that produces representations in a manner connected to existence, and not a consciousness independent of the same.

For Marx, the nexus that link ideas to the economic material structure, to existence, in addition to being in tune with a specific philosophical anthropology,[1] is the answer to an intellectual need: to anchor the cognitive process in an evident, concrete, objective reality. If there can be social science, it must be the science of empirically recognizable objects. In Marx, there is a need for scientificity, from which to address an ethical question: the liberation of alienated labour and the end of exploitation. The young revolutionary Marx and the mature scholar Marx are complementary: the latter scientifically answers the questions posed by the former. Marx feels himself a social scientist of capitalism, the real underlying mechanisms of which he wants to show (Aron 2019). For him, capitalism is a complex mix of economic structures and social relations, the most hidden configurations of which should be brought to light, based on the idea that this emergence would serve the progress of humanity. A scientist then, and a science, at the service of all. And, for this very reason, compelled to produce the radical critique of those social subjects who, for their special interests, would like to freeze reality and block change.

The latter, in addition to being against the progress of humanity, end up opposing the progress of science, primarily the social sciences. The social clash is thus also a clash between science and ideology: the bourgeoisie, and their thinking, are anti-scientific. Science has the task, from an Enlightenment/positivist perspective, to unmask those socially produced forms of thought that aim to conceal their social genesis for merely instrumental purposes and to show the true reality of which they are an expression. This is because consciousness can become false consciousness, and thought ideology, distorted thought. However, the reality of capitalism itself contains irremediable contradictions. The issues are complex and, in some ways, obscure. Let us return to the questions posed above: in what sense can we distinguish between consciousness and false consciousness (and, correspondingly, between a true and a false existence)? And is the latter conscious of being so? Is there bad faith in the bourgeois deceiving the proletarian, or is his worldview naturally distorted, being the result of an internally contradictory reality against which he can do nothing?

Of the four hypotheses formulated above, the first two can be expunged from the analysis. A true existence of which it is possible to have an undistorted representation would constitute the end point of history, realized communism, within which, having overcome the contradictions of class society, there would perhaps no longer even be a need for a superstructure. Only exploitative relations require regulation and disguise through legal, political, and ideological artifices. Without exploitation, our social relations would become transparent to ourselves. This is a universal process, to which capitalism also makes its contribution. Marx and Engels write that, in the new capitalist social order, "all that is solid melts into air, all that is holy is profaned, and man is at last forced with sober senses to face his real conditions of life and his true relations with his kind" (Marx, Engels 2014, p. 13). Obviously, this path of collective self-clarification is very long, conflictual, and perilous. The second hypothesis is unrealistic and hopeless: what would be a science for which it is impossible to have a minimally true representation of a world about which nothing can be known? More importantly, to what kind of consciousness would it be accessible? This position approaches radical relativism: everything is false except the statement that supports it. It is not an option espoused by Marx. It is then worth dwelling on the other two possibilities, and reasoning upon the gaps between existence and consciousness, and upon the deceptions and distortions that can be produced between one and the other.

Let us start with hypothesis number 3, the one that coincides with the idea of false consciousness, of a – conscious? – false representation of reality. Simplifying, consciousness can be false in three ways: because it has false beliefs within it, because it supports an unjust power, and because the origin of its ideas is as such false (Geuss 1981). These three aspects are intertwined in Marx, and this intertwining constitutes a large part of the problem. They are aspects that move on different planes, epistemological, political, and ontological. The first meaning and the second are broader than the concept of ideology. Indeed, false claims can exist without being ideological. Defending the idea that the earth is flat is not, properly speaking, an ideology. Nor is claiming that 2 + 2 = 5. Lies are also not necessarily ideological. There may be unjust powers whose justification does not lie in ideology, unless, for example, one also deems medieval religious thought as ideological, using a dogmatically Marxist historiography. Therefore, ideological error and ideological power must be a specific kind of error and power. The falsehood of ideological consciousness, following Marx's historicist approach, is an expression of a particular historical context, the modern context. The falsity of false bourgeois consciousness – of a subject therefore collective – derives from the origin of the ideas that constitute it, from their social genesis. This is Marx's sociological discovery: his sociology of knowledge, as a study of the social genesis of thought, coincides with a theory of unmasking, with a critique of ideology.

Bourgeois thought is false because it is bourgeois. This kind of falsity can only appear in the world of bourgeois relations, in capitalism. Only at this stage of human history does reflection, which can show the falsity of ideology, develop, a task inaccessible to classical and medieval thought. There is a link between the development of capitalism and the establishment of a science capable of radical criticism of the same. Now a nexus, that between existence and consciousness, which runs through all of human history, but which only capitalism and its social relations allow to be brought to light, becomes evident. As Marx and Engels write,

> Each new class which puts itself in the place of one ruling before it, *is compelled*, merely in order to carry through its aim, to represent its interest as the common interest of all the members of society, that is, expressed in ideal form: it has to give its ideas the form of universality, and represent them as the only rational, universally valid ones.
>
> (Marx, Engels 1974, pp. 65–66, italics mine)

Each ruling class is forced to give an altered and inverted image of reality so as to justify its domination. But only in capitalism does it become possible to unmask this distortion.

Masking coincides with a process of reversal, described by Marx with the metaphor of the camera obscura: the raw truth of reality is reversed to make it acceptable to the dominated. Real social relations now appear upside down[2] and human praxis is distorted. The task of critical thinking is to overthrow this reversal, to allow things to be put back where they belong. Bourgeois idealism, particularly that of German ideology, gives predominance to ideas in order to conceal the truth of material exploitation. On the contrary, "life is not determined by consciousness, but consciousness by life" (ivi, p. 47).[3] In its materiality, capitalist enterprise, with its combination of economic and social relations, has a concreteness to which criticism can refer in order to expose the false representation that ideology gives it. There is a materiality to refer to in order to unmask the false universality. The capitalist is 'compelled' to represent his particular interest as universal, but the relations of production continue to be, despite ideology, what they are. In this sense, alienated labour for Marx is real; and ideology is masquerade, an expression of false consciousness. Ideology is opposed to reality, to the praxis of solid social relations.

If the bourgeoisie is 'compelled' to present itself as the embodiment of the universal, this may mean that its ideological construction is inevitable and justified. More importantly, is the bourgeoisie aware of the falsity of its ideological consciousness? The Marxian formulation poses several problems.[4] If the universalization of special interests is indispensable for any social group that desires to forward its candidacy on the social scene, does such universalization necessarily produce ideology? Two different aspects overlap here: an idea of truth as adaptation to the social structure (being determines consciousness) and an idea of truth as the unmasking of a concealment (the reversal of the reversal produced in the camera obscura).

In the first case, the thought is first true, when the class of reference is attuned to the forces of development present in society and represents the change taking place; and then false, when the interests of that same class slow down the change and attunement fails. This is the Marxian materialist approach, embodied in historical materialism. It does not see in the ruling class a subject capable of truly autonomous thought, independent of the material structure. Its ideas must be in tune with its material interests. Think, for example, of the ideas of private property, subjective rights, division of powers, etc., all bourgeois ideas.[5] But also the development of scientific knowledge, or artistic products: are Volta's battery or Chopin's music bourgeois?[6] Do all these ideas and products of thought, if they are the expression of a certain material structure, all automatically become false when economic forces develop further? Are they merely the expression of special interests?

In the second case, the thought is false because it conceals its social origins. Now it is necessary to presuppose a subjectivity that becomes active, that is able, first, to become aware of the social origins of its thought, then to conceal them. There is no materialistic determinism at work, but rather a free collective subjectivity that becomes the protagonist of its own history, and that of others. It is also necessary to presuppose the awareness of some, the bourgeoisie, and the blindness of others, the proletarians. Therefore, what is the point of observation from which the bourgeoisie gains awareness of the partiality of its ideas? Could it not be in good faith? Either the bourgeois is self-deceiving and is a victim of the same concealment that he imposes on the proletarian, and is therefore not aware of, and responsible for, the partial character of his ideas. Or, if he sees that limitation, and is aware of the social origins of his worldview, if he realizes that "our conceptions are internal to our practice" (Eagleton 1991, p. 75), he is no longer a bourgeois, he has access to a position external to his class position. If ideology is able to completely rework reality so that it appears entirely different from what it is, concealment or criticism of that concealment is no longer possible; if however, it is possible to use ideology for one's own ends, there is a perspective that is not determined by one's social position.

Other problems arise in discussion of the last possibility, the fourth, the one for which ideology is the true representation of a distorted reality. This is the position found in the first book of *Capital* (Marx 1992). Here the analysis aims to unmask alienation as an expression of an internal contradiction within the reality of capitalism. It is no longer ideas that distort reality, as the camera obscura of bourgeois ideology and German idealism do, but it is reality that is upside down. In capitalism, what is means becomes ends; what is ends become means. Money, which is the means of exchange, becomes the end of economic activity; it becomes capital. In this way, the product of human activity, by becoming a commodity, acquires a reality and a force independent of its producer and is imposed upon him, without his being able to realize it anymore. Human labour also becomes a commodity. Reality is itself false because social relations are dominated by forces that distort them. And bourgeois consciousness only represents this falsity, presenting itself attuned to the times, with the stage of development of the forces of production.[7]

In Marx's early writings, especially in *The German Ideology*, influenced by the philosophy of Feuerbach and his critique of religion, the question of ideology concerns the false representation of reality, used instrumentally to defend special interests. The exploitation and alienation of the proletariat are masked before the eyes of the latter to make them acceptable, just as religion is the opium of the people.[8] In contrast, in *Capital*, it is bourgeois and capitalist reality that is false.[9] What the two positions (3 and 4) have in common is the theory of alienation: in the third, alienation affects only the exploited classes; in the fourth, it becomes internal to reality itself, affecting everyone, even the bourgeoisie. The latter, if it thinks that capitalist reality attunes to its own interests, makes a mistake to its own detriment; it does not recognize that it itself is alienated. The bourgeois subject that knows and keeps silent is simply masochist. Inside an alienated world there is no truth for anyone. This is the conclusion reached by the thinkers of the Frankfurt School: the Americanized consumer society no longer grants any space for authenticity, not even to the bourgeois.

Conceptions 3 and 4, which think of ideology as the product of a gap between existence and consciousness, imply two different notions of false consciousness. For 3, the thought is ideological, and therefore false, either because it is an expression of material class relations, of social structure, or because it conceals its social roots. For 4, it is so because it is incapable of becoming aware of the internal alienation of capitalist society. Essentially, the thought is ideological because – more or less deliberately – it distorts reality, painting a different picture to what it is; or because it faithfully reflects an upside-down reality. In the former case, ideology is opposed to the praxis of real social relations, to existence; in the latter, it is opposed to science.[10] Either it is the false representation of a true reality, or it is the true representation of a false reality.[11]

It may be useful to recall an important attempt to dissolve this dilemma. In Lukács' *History and Class Consciousness*, the relationship between being and thought is no longer seen in the form of false consciousness, of a distortion to be unmasked but as expression of "one and the same real historical and dialectical process" (Lukács 1971, p. 204), which entrusts the proletariat, its being and its thought, with a privileged point of observation. For Lukács, in fact, "the self-understanding of the proletariat is therefore simultaneously the objective understanding of the nature of society" (ivi, p. 149): it is true because it is objective. Rightly, Lukács speaks of 'self-understanding'. How and why that of the proletariat is true, that is, it is 'objective knowledge' of society and does not also have social origins, however, is difficult to argue. The dialectical process of being coincides with that of thought: therefore, a true thought is an expression of a true being, both of which are those of the proletariat. Lukács' position, not surprisingly, is an attempt to answer the first question raised above: What is the subject that is capable of producing science and not ideology? What is the subject that is capable of escaping the mechanism of the social genesis of thought, and thus the trap of false consciousness? That it is only the proletariat who does not suffer from halitosis, and not some other social class, is obviously an answer in need of justification.[12]

At the heart of the problem, and beyond false consciousness and ideology, the question of bad faith remains. A subject who knows could conceal what he knows out of bad faith. The question is to see if and how bad faith can be connected to a class position, may be socially determined and thus become a collective feature. Could bourgeois false consciousness become bourgeois bad faith? It is difficult to avoid briefly recalling Sartre's analysis. While the lie consists in the fact that "the liar actually is in complete possession of the truth which he is hiding" from someone else, bad faith on the other hand is a situation in which "it is from myself that I am hiding the truth. Thus the duality of the deceiver and the deceived does not exist here". In this way, "that which affects itself with bad faith must be conscious (of) its bad faith since the being of consciousness is consciousness of being. It appears then that I must be in good faith, at least to the extent that I am conscious of my bad faith" (Sartre 1966, pp. 87, 89).

Bad faith refers back to the structure of consciousness: "consciousness has to be its own being, it is never sustained by being; it sustains being in the hearth of subjectivity, which means once again that it is inhabited by being but that it is not being: *consciousness is not what it is*" (ivi, p. 105). The theme of ideology – that is, of the more or less conscious gap between the particular and the universal – is transformed by Sartre into the ontological condition of human existence, which takes on different social connotations but is not determined by them. This is a conception taken up by Goffman. Consider the lengthy quotation in *The Presentation of Self in Everyday Life* of Sartre's famous example of the waiter (ivi, pp. 101–103; Goffman 1959). The waiter is what he does, since consciousness can only 'represent' itself: "it is necessary that we *make ourselves what we are*. But what *are we* then if we have the constant obligation to make ourselves what we are, if our mode of being is having the obligation to be what we are?" (Sartre 1966, p. 101). For Sartre, making 'sustains' but does not determine being, and there is no way out of bad faith. If bad faith is internal to the mode of being of consciousness, social conditioning disappears and Marxian materialism disappears.

In conclusion, we are probably all exposed to the risk of halitosis, because, fortunately, it is impossible to think that existence and consciousness coincide. Therefore, an end treatment is not thinkable, and perhaps not even desirable. How to become aware of this inevitable risk and how it can be managed are questions that concern the relationship between theory and praxis, starting with the recognition of the limits of one and the other. We can take it for granted that interpreting reality and transforming it are two separate and distinct, and therefore related, processes that cannot rely on scientific knowledge, at least as Marx understood it.[13] These are issues that must be addressed today, unlike in the past, starting with the end of the concept of ideology, the unusability of the concepts of unmasking, and false consciousness. And from the ultimate realization that it is impossible to acquire a privileged viewpoint of history. Reflection on the end of ideologies has spanned the entire intellectual history of the twentieth century. In the next section, this history will be reconstructed along its principal lines.

End of Ideology

The concepts of unmasking and false consciousness, foundations of ideological thinking, carry with them a complex set of problems, which ran through Marxist thought for much of the twentieth century. More generally, the concept of ideology, and the debate around the end of ideologies, characterized cultural history throughout the century. This debate is concentrated on three particularly critical and problematic historical moments: the 1920s, after the Great War; the 1950s, after the end of World War II; and the 1960s and 1970s, coinciding with the season of movements. Talking about ideologies, and their end, is thus a way to reflect on the contradictions of particularly complex times. It is not possible to make an exhaustive presentation of the twentieth-century debate on ideologies, but a brief review focusing on a few significant aspects will suffice.

Marx's contribution to the sociology of knowledge is to reinsert human beings and their consciousness within the social context of which they are an expression. According to Mannheim, progressive awareness of this reality transforms the concept of ideology into that of a worldview. Through social conflict, by unmasking each other – not in a purely doctrinaire way – all social subjects are led to recognize the partial character of their own ideas and social location. As we saw in the previous chapter, this is a long process, which, according to Mannheim, takes the concept of ideology from a particular conception – of Enlightenment origin – to a total one, up to a general use of the latter. At this point, when all social subjects are unmasked, and all recognize the equal existential locus of their own thinking, the concept of ideology no longer makes sense. This is a reflection that engages Mannheim in the second half of the 1920s and finds its culmination in *Ideology and Utopia*.

The strength of Mannheim's reflection is to take Marx's discovery seriously, radicalizing it. Our thinking cannot be separated from our social existence, to which it is bound in a relationship of mutual influence. The end of the war leaves European society in dire economic and social circumstances, characterized by the disintegration of traditional collective identities. The structure of social stratification changes radically, and a new social subject with characteristics of its own emerges from the crowd. Mannheim believes that the work of reorganizing a fragmented and undone society is in fact taking two alternative and radically conflicting paths: the totalitarian one, which can be glimpsed with the gradual establishment of Fascism and Nazism[14] and the development of Soviet communism, and the democratic one, which must take new shape from an awareness of the social transformations taking place. These are issues that will be developed in his later books (Mannheim 1997a). Already present, however, is the effort to devise a new way of dealing with social questions – his sociology of knowledge – capable of avoiding both the dangerous swamp of relativism and the presumption, also ideological, of being able to acquire an exhaustive point of view.

The end of ideologies can be seen in two senses: end of the possibility of a *true* worldview and end of the possibility of a *comprehensive* worldview. There is truth in arguing that ideologies are a new form of religion; they are modern religions. Like religions, they trigger conflict between alternative conceptions of truth; they can do so because they present themselves as true and comprehensive worldviews. They are produced by social subjects capable of self-representation as such, able to constitute recognizable positions within society from which the identity and destiny of the individuals belonging to them are determined. For Mannheim, on the contrary, the truth that each position carries with it is only existential, an expression of concrete historical existence, of partiality. The step backwards is remarkable: no longer at issue, as in Marx, is the opposition between truth and falsehood, between being in tune with historical development or obstructing it to one's own advantage. All positions are true because they are expressions of a socially existing reality. None has the universal with it, as the proletariat could think it had. Totality and universality no longer belong to anyone but are potentially available to a class, that of intellectuals, which engages in the difficult and relentless task of recomposing the various positions, which Mannheim calls a dynamic synthesis. Beyond the correctness of the proposal, there remains the acknowledgement of the end of a possibility, the one whereby a single social subject can bring with it the correct point of view for all. I insist on the point: the end of ideologies is a historical fact, empirically reconstructable, through the dynamics of class conflict; and it is also the intellectual realization that a new world brings with it new social subjects and new representations. Of course, the end of ideologies does not mean the end of narratives, but only the fact that they take a new form.

The discussion of the 1950s also delves into the issues of the time. The literature is quite extensive.[15] I would like to dwell on Bell's book, *The End of Ideology*, published in 1960. The book makes explicit a widespread sentiment among a significant number of intellectuals – Aron, Lipset, Shils, and others – tending to stigmatize the role that dogmatic ideologies, with their exclusive and totalizing apparatus, can play in public life. According to Bell, a totalizing ideology is"an all-inclusive system of comprehensive reality, it is a set of beliefs, infused with passion, and seeks to transform the whole of a way of life. This commitment to ideology – the yearning for a 'cause', or the satisfaction of deep moral feelings – is not necessarily the reflection of interests in the shape of ideas. Ideology, in this sense (…) is a secular religion". It is "a hardening of commitment, a freezing of opinion" (Bell 1988, pp. 112, 350). It is a secular religion lived not with a Franciscan spirit, but with that of the Inquisition. The reference is to Soviet communism. After Stalin's death and

Khrushchev's revelations, after the Poznań uprising in Poland in June 1956 and the Hungarian revolution in October of the same year, it was credible to think of the end of the infatuation of Western intellectuals – and working classes – with the Soviet regime. The announcement of the end of ideology seemed to mark the end of a collective nightmare. In this context, ideology is not just any system of thought: it qualifies as a totalizing ideology.[16]

For Bell, "socialism was an unbounded dream" (ivi, p. 275). One of its characteristics is simplification: the complexity of reality is compressed into a few affirmations that do not tolerate contradiction. According to Bell, "how does the proletariat see through the veils of obscurity and come to self-awareness? Marx could say with Jesus, 'I have come to end all mysteries, not to perpetuate them'" (ivi, p. 282). In this way, history is forced into a reading that is all too effective in its linearity: the future is all inscribed in the potentialities of the present, with no room for the unexpected. Again, in Bell's words,

> The twentieth-century Communist (…) is the perpetual alien living in the hostile enemy land. Any gestures of support, any pressure for social reforms, are simply tactics (…). His is the ethic of 'ultimate ends'; only the goal counts, the means are inconsequential.
>
> (ivi, p. 292)

What remains after the end of total ideology? The question is left open. The author suggests a neutral position may be possible, based on openness rather than closure. His is not a conservative position, nor is it a progressive one. The task of the kind of critique proposed in the book is to unmask those ideological simplifications that, fed by fanaticism and blindness, think they possess the truth about the world. The defense of openness is the defense of freedom, even to err, but in one's own way. In this sense, the book – and the debate surrounding it – mark a new approach to the debate on ideology: regardless of its social roots, it characterizes a simple and dogmatic thinking, incapable of understanding the complexity of the world. If this ideology, thankfully, ends, ideology can be any belief or belief system that imposes obligations on those who adhere to it. Thus defined, the term loses all specific meaning, going on to characterize another, and perhaps more definitive, end.[17]

The third period is perhaps the most culturally dense and rich. There are many approaches that, more or less explicitly, stem from the idea that ideologies have waned. All of post-structuralism, hermeneutics, post-metaphysical thought, but also the thought of Foucault – who replaces the term ideology with the broader term, discourse (Foucault 1981; 1989; 2020) – start from the idea that ideologies are over. Some go so far as to think that reality itself has waned: for Baudrillard, "it is no longer a question of a false representation of reality (ideology), but of concealing the fact that the real is no longer real" (quoted in Eagleton 1993, p. 63). To get Marxianly back on the ground, I would like to present *a text* and *a debate*, which I find particularly significant.

The text is Lyotard's *The Postmodern Condition*, published in 1979. The basic idea of the book is the end of meta-narratives, which coincides with the end of modernity. Ideologies would be the last great narratives – of history, society, and politics – produced in the modern world: after their demise, there remains a shattered world, dominated by a science that simultaneously imposes its techno-cognitive dominance and its inability to offer a finalistic worldview. The term post-modernity opens a discussion that will feed into the following decades. The fundamental question, ignited after the fall of the Berlin Wall, is: are we facing the end of the modern project or its further internal development? The various answers will take the names of accomplished modernity, reflexive modernity, second modernity, liquid modernity, etc., up to the questioning of the idea of a single modernity, as occurs within post-colonial studies. For the latter, if there is an ideology it is precisely the modern Eurocentric narrative.

Lyotard writes: "I define postmodern as incredulity toward meta-narratives (…). The postmodern condition is as much a stranger to disenchantment as it is to the blind positivity of delegitimation. Where, after the meta-narratives the legitimacy reside?" (Lyotard 1984, pp. XXIV–XXV). We see that the problem of truth has disappeared: ideologies are seen as meta-narratives because their specificity is that they are comprehensive worldviews, regardless of their truth. Emphasis is placed on their effectiveness in building social bonds and containing a vision of a just society. Science, on the contrary, may be true but is incapable, especially in a world dominated by its technical consequences, of providing an answer to these two questions, which are central to social life. The end of the modern narrative is thus the end of all meta-narratives: they had been first religious, in the pre-modern world, then ideological, in modernity. The latter is configured as a great meta-narrative, which contains within it, nourished by the progressive development of techno-scientific rationality, the germ of its end. Now, "we no longer have recourse to the grand narratives (…); the little narratives (*petit recit*) remain the quintessential form of imaginative invention, most particularly in science" (ivi, p. 60). Science informs the fate of narratives with itself: they, too, take on its same form, becoming incapable of constructing grand overviews, of offering the subject a world endowed with meaning.

Extremely dense and rich is the debate between hermeneutics and the critique of ideologies, featuring Gadamer and Habermas. Triggered by the latter's lengthy critique of the former, this debate is fed by the reciprocal rebuttals and many other important interventions, including those of Apel, Bubner, Ricœur, and others.[18] While Gadamerian hermeneutics tends to eliminate the concept of ideology, dissolving it into that of interpretation, Habermas wishes to maintain the possibility of a critique of what may continue to be seen as ideologies. In general, the question is whether with the end of ideologies the possibility of critique also ends. Within this confrontation, the relationship between genesis and validity of thought, that is, the issue of ideological critique, is reread as a problem of the relationship between truth and history.

For Gadamer, hermeneutics is not simply the art of understanding that relies on technical skills. Recalling Aristotle, it is not only *techne* but also *phronesis*.[19] As philosophical hermeneutics, it "no longer serves to overcome certain difficulties of understanding" but "what it tends toward is (…) a critical reflexive knowledge" (Gadamer 1979, p. 288, translation mine). As critical practical knowledge, it seeks to shed light on the pre-judgements implicit in all understanding and generalizes this attitude by addressing it to the social life of man as a whole, understood as a dialogical community: "from this dialogical community nothing is excluded, no experience of the world (…) the *communicability of understanding* thus constitutes the theme of hermeneutics" (ivi, p. 291, italics mine, translation mine).

The universalistic aspect of hermeneutics thus lies in the dialogical nature of human experience: invoking Heidegger, for Gadamer, understanding is the mode of being of existing. The understanding of the individual event is linked to its becoming history and tradition; tradition however is understood only as a recomposition of events. Thus, a hermeneutic circle is established between the individual event and the tradition to which it belongs, which are comprehensible only if they are connected to each other. From a sociological point of view, the circularity of understanding appears most clearly in the modern world, in which the link between tradition and pre-judgement is revealed thanks to an increasingly autonomous subjective reflexivity. In the modern world, the close link between pre-judgement and understanding becomes increasingly evident. If there is history, there is pre-judgement: the autonomy of the subject cannot reflexively erase the whole tradition to which it belongs and the set of pre-judgements that – through tradition – makes understanding possible.

Habermas' critique stems from this point. Where does the critical intention of hermeneutics go if we surrender to the inevitability of prejudice? Hermeneutic interpretation can be truly critical if it can reflexively recognize prejudice and question it. Otherwise, behind the authority of prejudice reappears that of tradition, and little is needed at that point to legitimize authority tout court: "Gadamer transforms the recognition of prejudice as a structure of understanding into a rehabilitation of prejudice as such" (Habermas 1979, p. 63, translation mine). What prevails within the tension between prejudice and reflexivity? While for Gadamer the inevitability of the former seems to prevail, for Habermas it is necessary to unfold the full potential of the latter. For what would become of a critique of ideology that stopped at the inevitability of prejudice? By overcoming hermeneutic fear, which retracts from what it discovers, the moment of reflection, which hermeneutics contains and restrains, must be unleashed in all its critical potential.

Habermas goes a step further. For him, it is necessary to set up an external normative point of view from which to support the critique. This is a different theory of language. Unlike Gadamer, dialogical understanding excludes something, and if it does not recognize this exclusion, it condemns itself to blindness. Indeed,

> The objective nexus by which alone social actions can be understood is constituted together by *language*, *labor* and *power*. In the systems of labor and power the event of tradition is relativized (…). Sociology *cannot therefore be reduced to interpretative sociology*. It requires a system of reference (…) that does not submit to an idealism of linguisticity and sublimates social processes entirely into cultural tradition.
>
> (ivi, p. 69, italics mine, translation mine)

The 'idealism of linguisticity' brings with it the rehabilitation of prejudice. Against a merely dialogical conception of social relations, against a sociology that is only interpretative, the structural realities of society, labour, and power must reappear.[20]

However, it seems to me that Habermas misses an important point in Gadamer's position. In Dilthey, historical consciousness replaces Hegel's Spirit. Mannheim's concept of dynamic synthesis is also an attempt to take up the theme of unity, of totality. Gadamer seems to substitute language for Spirit in its being simultaneously absolute and historical. But hermeneutics, against prejudice, allows a dimension of openness against the systemic spirit. As Gadamer writes, there is

> A certain legitimate ambiguity in the concept of historically effected consciousness (*wirkungsgeschichtliches Bewußtsein*), as I have employed it. This ambiguity is that it is used to mean at once the consciousness effected in the course of history and determined by history, and *the very consciousness of being thus effected and determined.*

Moreover, "historically effected consciousness is so radically finite that our whole being, effected in the totality of our destiny, inevitably transcends its knowledge of itself" (Gadamer 2006, pp. XXX, XXXI). Put simply, we are always more than what we know, about ourselves and the world. As Adorno says, "people are even now better than their culture" (Adorno 2005, p. 46). The contribution of Gadamer's hermeneutics is to deliver to the critical endeavour a possibility not locked within the narrow confines of a critique of ideology, with the determinism they bring with them. I believe there are great affinities between this ongoing tension between openness and closure and the phenomenological tension between intentionality and reflexivity: both testify to the ineradicable character of human culture as both determinate and indeterminate.

Paradoxically, this debate is taking place in parallel with the conflict promoted by social movements, notably youth and feminism. Are the narratives of these movements new ideologies? Are they meta-narratives? Or do they have new characteristics? What type of subjectivity do they bring into play? Taking up again with Lyotard, in the new world emerging after 1989, and with the new processes of globalization, "each individual is referred to himself. And each of us knows that our *self* does not amount to much". This new post-ideological self is very little, but

> No self is an island; each exists in a fabric of relations that is now more complex and mobile than ever before. Young or old, man or woman, rich or poor, a person is always located at 'nodal points' of specific communication circuits, however tiny these may be.
>
> (Lyotard 1984, p. 15)

These are, to use the terminology used in previous chapters, identities characterized by a multiplicity of belongings, living in an increasingly differentiated society, full of narratives of a new and unpredictable nature. We are faced with a new world, which needs new critical perspectives, not anti-ideological but devoid of this outdated concept.

Enlightenment and Ideology

The end of ideologies does not imply the end of a theory of ideology. The concept of ideology is older than ideologies. I am referring to the school of *idéologues* and their conceptualization of ideology as a science of ideas. This is an important group of French intellectuals, working at the turn of the eighteenth and nineteenth centuries, as earlier stated. Their philosophy poses the question of the genesis of ideas through the study of man in society, a question embodied in the theme of the relationship between theory and praxis, between speculation and action. What is the relationship between political positions and their philosophical justifications? This is also an important question because, unlike the *philosophes* who preceded them (Hélvetius, Voltaire, Rousseau, Condillac, d'Alembert), they act in the civic and political life of France at the time, taking often hegemonic positions. They thus became undisputed protagonists in the not only intellectual affairs of their time but also giving rise to a second flourishing season of the French Enlightenment.

From this philosophical and political position, one can understand their interest in a scientific study of ideas, how they are produced in society, and how they are affirmed and translated into social and political practices. As the science of ideas, ideology constitutes the culmination of the empiricist and sensible method, based on observation, that goes back to Locke. Their thought takes up the English intellectual tradition that had already been the basis of the *Encyclopédie* authors, that of Bacon, Hobbes, and Locke. It enters into direct connection with the American one of the time, represented by Franklin,[21] Paine, Jefferson, and Adams. It circulates throughout Europe, contaminating in Scotland the epigones of the great tradition of Scottish moral philosophy, influencing the Italian cultural context, and its more liberal and progressive components, among them Romagnosi, Gioia, and the young Manzoni. Tracy's most important book, the *Élemens d'idéologie*, was promptly translated into Italian by Compagnoni as early as 1817. As Moravia writes, "these intellectuals contributed to the overthrow of the *ancient régime* (...); they helped dissolve its main moral and religious principles (...); they went about preaching a metaphysics without divine seals, a methodology without transcendent guarantees, a psychology without the soul, an anthropology without the spirit, a society without absolute power, an art without the holy impulses of the *Coeur*" (Moravia 1986, p. 25, translation mine), thus arousing, even before the wrath of Napoleon,[22] those of reactionaries, Catholics, and Romantics.

The idea behind their thinking is that the relationship between philosophy and politics can only be mediated and, therefore, requires a dedicated science. Behind it, a profoundly Enlightenment cultural background operates: the idea that it is possible to shed light on the mechanisms that regulate the relationship between ideas and praxis; the criticism without concession of the dogmas and obscurities that tend to mystify reality; the belief in the educability of humankind; and the possibility of a moral and political regeneration of society. The *idéologues* are perhaps the first modern intellectuals, inspired by a genuine and real civic vocation, firmly convinced in the public function of knowledge, in its usability in the face of the most current problems. Another important aspect was their cosmopolitanism, the aspiration to speak to humanity, with the aim of giving it an awareness of its own reality, not only moral but also civil and political, based on the universality of human values. There is still in them intact hope and conviction in the harmonizing function of reason, but without its becoming a court without appeal to which praxis must submit. That philosophy becomes praxis has a function, if one may say so, of mutual domestication: thought puts itself at the service of reality, not dominating it from without. Learning processes go in both directions: especially under the influence of American thought, of Jefferson and of Franklin, philosophy and praxis converse without either having the last word or shouting the loudest. The tradition of the *philosophes* becomes contaminated with the concrete and realistic enlightenment from overseas, producing a more cautious and forward-looking, though no less convinced, thought.

Of the early Enlightenment, the strong charge of social critique remains: "the civil maturation of the *idéologues* takes place (...) through becoming aware of the profound political, social and economic injustices present in the world of the *ancient régime*", in the light of a "humanitarianism that (...) derives from Voltaire, from Voltaire the defender of the oppressed, the patron of the innocent persecuted or unjustly condemned" (ivi, p. 87, translation mine). There remains the idea of the relationship between intellectuals and politics, which proposes

> To perform, according to a purely Condillacian methodology, a work of collecting *faits*, and then a series of *analyses*, of *comparaisons*, of *calculs*,

> in order to arrive finally at determining that framework, or *plan de travail*, which will implicitly contain the solution of the proposed problem. It is the *philosophie* that offers to *éclairer* with its *lumières* the political power.
> (ivi, p. 93, translation mine)

The areas of direct intervention are many: slavery, the subject of a *pamphlet* by Condorcet and then at the centre of the discussions and proposals of all the *idéologues*; health care, which Cabanis deals with above all; education; poverty and mendicity; the situation of prisons and asylums;[23] etc. In all these areas, the most problematic issues are addressed by interweaving scientific and socio-political aspects, in a combination within which the former is functional to the latter and vice versa. For example, the issue of health involves technical-scientific domains but also, and perhaps above all, the ability to cope with the social and economic distortions and inequalities that produce a humanly unsustainable situation.

The importance and novelty of the method adopted should be stated: from wherever one starts, from abstract scientific research or from a live situation in a hospital, it is a matter of constantly relating real problems, more general social aspects, and suitable systematic skills. One moves, in a profitably circular way, from the abstract to the concrete, from the particular to the general, in search of non-pre-packaged solutions, which should emerge from a work of mutual and continuous interaction between knowledge and reality. Always supported by a pressing and demanding call for moral and civic commitment made complementary to an awareness of the power that a scientifically and rationally inspired method can have. As Cabanis says, "charity is not an instinct but a technique" (quoted in ivi, p. 104, translation mine). This is a conception that today we can call progressive, to which the *idéologues* probably lay the groundwork: "not paternalistic assistance, but the offer to the destitute of a job is the instrument with which the problem of unemployment and poverty must be addressed" (ivi, p. 105, translation mine). In essence, what the *idèologues* are working on could be defined today as a grand and complex plan of social reform, underpinned by a genuine democratic and anti-despotic spirit. Without democracy, no reform is possible: it is a conception based on the universal right to citizenship; the need for constitutional and representative government; and the public role of philosophy.

This is a democratic-liberal political vision, which is nourished by a profound awareness of the importance of popular participation that goes well beyond the ballot paper. The main reference theorists for the *idéologues* are Sieyés and Condorcet. While the former sketches a model of democracy capable of managing conflicts through the parliamentary instrument, supported by an idea of a nation in which all social components are recognized, Condorcet promotes the idea of a genuine diffuse popular self-government, proposing the constitution of decentralized assemblies, with the purpose of connecting people and institutions. Foreign to this attitude is the conservative realist view, typical of Montesquieu and later Tocqueville, whereby the wisdom of politics lies in adapting institutions to the characteristics of the body politic, of society as a whole. In this way, one inevitably ends up superimposing the real order with the just order. The thought of the *idéologues* is, on the contrary, animated by a deep critical and innovative drive, committed to subverting unjust institutions.

Hence comes the accusation of abstractness that Napoleon will address to them.[24] Also from here comes that continually open tension between theory and reality, between abstract and concrete that characterizes their reflection. To maintain this tension is to avoid a twofold risk: that of subjecting reality to theory, the concrete to the abstract, as many theorists of the Revolution do, but also the opposite risk of adapting to a reality without alternatives. On the one hand, there are no general laws defined by thought to which reality can/should subject itself; on the other hand, reality itself is not the only yardstick. It is, in a word, an anti-dogmatic thought, capable of proposing itself as a political program.[25]

Within this framework we can place the theory of ideology proposed by Destutt de Tracy. For Tracy, 'ideology' is "a necessary neologism (…) because metaphysics was too discredited and psychology implied a knowledge of the soul, knowledge which no one could any longer claim to have" (Kennedy 1979, p. 354). The intent is to replace metaphysics and psychology with a scientific approach analogous to the natural sciences, capable of shedding light on the processes of construction of ideas, all ideas, whether they have to do with the subject, society, or nature. *Eléments d'idéologie* was to constitute, in its author's plan, after an introduction on the notion of ideology, a systematic study of grammar and logic (part one); economics, morals, and social organization (part two); physics, geometry, and calculus (part three). The systemic and rationalizing spirit typical of the Enlightenment appears evident here. Tracy takes up the materialist and sensible monism of de La Mettrie and d'Holbach, for whom all ideas are the product of sensible perception. This is a monism that opposes Cartesian dualism of mind and body, and takes up the English empiricist approach, especially Locke's: ideas are the result of perceptions, and the mind is nothing more than a percipient activity, to be studied with a physiology of perception approach.

Ideology, as the science of ideas, is the fundamental science because it investigates the formation of ideas through sensible experience, providing us with knowledge about the ways of knowing. From basic simple ideas, through complex mechanisms of composition and recomposition, complex ideas are composed. The method of analysis serves to deconstruct this complexity, showing how each element occupies a position within this ordered process, which goes from the simple to the complex. Empirical observation and analysis allow the social sciences to pursue the same results as the natural sciences: objectivity and clarity. Ideology, for Tracy, is "a system of truths closely tied together, all stemming from this first indubitable fact, that we know nothing except through our sensations, and that all our ideas are the product of the various combinations we make from these sensations" (quoted in Head 1985, pp. 36–37). This approach is an outright polemic against metaphysics and its empty categories. The study of the mind and the study of the body are part of one general and natural science: for ideology, everything perceptible – whether subjective, social, or natural elements – can be similarly transformed into ideas. Head points out that "whereas the *content* of ideas was largely determined by experience, education and environment, the *structure* of the mind itself was stable and predictable owing to its physiological foundation" (ivi, p. 38).

Thus a nexus of continuous interaction is constructed between ideas and perceptions: the former are knowledge of the world also because they are a direct product of the world itself. In this sense, ideology "was particularly suited to the task of clarifying ideas, making concepts more precise, and thereby promoting scientific understanding of phenomena in every field" (ivi, p. 40), freeing the human mind from all the empty abstraction of metaphysics and religion, not anchored in any empirical fact. The ideological approach, which allows all reality to be subjected to analysis, would like to have an effect of collective clarification and liberation, also through the instruments of training and education. A radical and seemingly dogmatic monism thus ends up translating into a liberal and anti-dogmatic socio-political approach, contrary to the fanaticism of the revolutionaries, but also to the authoritarian anti-democratic Napoleon. As Head writes, Tracy's work "constitutes one of the most comprehensive and interesting attempts at the beginning of the nineteenth century to elaborate a liberal theory of individual, society, education and politics" (ivi, p. 4)[26] Tracy is not against morality: he seeks to counter the influence of religion in the name of a scientific morality that takes human interests and desires into account. His liberalism – since it wants to be ideologically grounded, that is, scientific – approaches utilitarianism.

To conclude, for the *idéologues*, "practical activity (…) was a direct embodiment of their philosophical activity" (Moravia 1986, p. 8, translation mine), which produced "the cosmopolitan ideals, the all-secular and worldly morality, the aversion to all forms of metaphysics and transcendence, the defense of positive sciences, *observation* and rational *analyse* in every field" (ivi, p. 607, translation mine).

No intention is here to reintroduce a theory of ideology in keeping with Tracy's. Many of its elements sound dated today, partly because they are an expression of a historical and cultural context far removed from our own and lack that capacity, typical of the ideas of great thinkers, to remain ever relevant. What remains extremely interesting, beyond a use of the term ideology completely out of tune with what we are accustomed to, is the attempt at a rational enquiry into the relationship between ideas and action, holding together both instrumental and normative aspects. The sense in which ideology can be thought of again as a science of ideas, particularly as a reflection on the relationship between theory and praxis within a finalistic conception of social action, will be the subject of the next section.

Theory of Ideology

The heart of the discussion revolves around the relationship between theory and praxis. The key question can be formulated as follows: is the former capable of providing normative principles to direct just praxis? Capable of unmasking unjust praxis, sometimes deceptive in appearance? Its task would be to show the injustice present in reality and that contained in the ways of thinking that mask it. As we have seen, the concept of ideology carries with it that of critique of ideology, because, by definition, ideology is false and distorted thinking. It differs however from simple error or lies: those immersed in an ideology not only live inside a false reality but are systematically unable to see it as such. This is that twofold aspect highlighted above: the critique of ideology, according to Marx, must be able to show the falsity of the world and that of the interpretation that conceals that falsity.

This dual aspect has recently been emphasized by Jaeggi (2009). Her analysis springs from the paradox shown by Adorno that ideology is both true and false. Jaeggi uses, as an example, the Marxian critique of the bourgeois ideals of freedom and equality. They are true because, in fact, capitalist and worker relate to each other within the labor market as abstractly free and equal subjects. They are false not only because, again de facto, workers have no alternative, but more importantly because it is precisely those ideals that help produce the conditions that lead workers to offer their labour. In Jaeggi's words, "according to Marx, the ideology of freedom and equality itself is a factor in the production of the coercion and the inequality" (ivi, p. 67). In short, there is a real reality – that of the inherently unequal and shackled labour market – that is ideologically presented as immune to the distortions it contain, as if it were the realm of freedom and equality. But even the truth of reality contains its moment of falsity.

The circularity highlighted above emerges, whereby one does not understand what is true and what is false. Ideology is a necessary false consciousness, that is, it is "necessarily false" (ivi, p. 68). But if consciousness is false as a true reflection of a false reality, what is true and what is false? How does one have a true consciousness? And how does one decide that a reality is false? In the Italian edition of the essay, Jaeggi cites a passage from Habermas that is emblematic in this regard: "consciousness itself becomes false because of the – sometimes exact – mirroring of a false reality" (quoted in Jaeggi 2016, p. 70, translation mine). It's mind-boggling.[27] How is it possible to criticize "both the false understanding of a situation or state of affairs (in a society) and the properties and conditions of this situation itself" (Jaeggi 2009, p. 69)? What is the nature of the consciousness that can operate this double unmasking? To whom does it belong and who can enjoy it? The critique of ideology, from this perspective, should criticize false representations of a true reality because it is real, but false because it is distorted.

Added to this not-insignificant problem is another. According to Jaeggi, the critique of ideology today can no longer refer to a conception of human essence, as Marx could. In a sense, it is without foundation.[28] Where then does it derive its normative character? The first possibility might be to refer to external normative standards, which come from normative theory in a strong sense. This is a division of labour that Jaeggi rejects. The critique of ideology must be able to be directly *critical analysis*: noun and adjective must form a unicum. Analysis must not be mere description, and criticism cannot be a mere external claim; it must enter into the living body of the existing. We are at the opposite pole of Weberian avalutativity: description and evaluation, within an approach of critique of ideology, are the same thing, not even distinguished from each other. How then to acquire "a non-normative critique that is normatively significant" (ivi, p. 69)?

The critique of ideology must show that our understanding is wrong and that the reality we understand is false. It must do so immanently, that is, without reference to external criteria. Nor can it simply rely on the gap between what is promised and what is done, between ideas and reality. Jaeggi criticizes Walzer, according to whom criticism shows the gap between the self-representation a community makes and the factual reality within which that community lives. For Jaeggi, it is not enough to say that American democracy promises freedom and equality as its fundamental principles and then show how and why it is unable to deliver on these promises. The major flaw in this critique, according to Jaeggi, lies in the fact that the criterion of the critique refers to the norms present in the self-representation of the community, it remains particularistic.[29] The critique of ideology, on the contrary,

> Criticizes particular social practices *as deficient*; but it does this following a pattern of determinate negation (or of a 'dialectic process of development'), or, in other words, according to a principle that is crucial for the Hegelian variant of immanent critique: the right follows from a 'sublating' overcoming of the wrong.
>
> (ivi, p. 73, italics mine)

She aims for a process that is non-particularistic because it is universal and potentially applied to every particularity.

The problem lies in recognizing social practices 'as deficient': who can do that? Moreover, deficient with respect to what? Adorno, for example, proposes his own different solution to the question: for him – where it is no longer possible to identify the truth, in the light of a dialectic that can only be negative – the only possible criterion becomes suffering. It is a given: where there is suffering, there unequivocally is deficit. In *Minima moralia*, Adorno writes, "the splinter in your eye is the best magnifying-glass" (Adorno 2005, p. 50). This is perhaps too empirical a criterion, but in itself it is unequivocal. Jaeggi, on the other hand, entrusts this task to the normative character of analysis. A proper analysis contains a critique of the reality that it describes: in her words, "the descriptive turns normative, and the normative descriptive" (Jaeggi 2009, p. 74). Analysis is at one with the description and is part of a process – arguably an endless one – of *problem solving*, understood as a continuous process of development and learning. There is no longer any external normative correctness: it is a matter of initiating processes of critical self-understanding capable of activating as many processes of transformation of reality. The critique of ideology "is the ferment of a *practical process of transformation* that pertains to both (social) reality and its interpretation" (ivi, p. 69). Beautiful expression, but without foundation.

This process, for Jaeggi, has three characteristics: (1) the contradictions are not logical, but practical, that is, internal to human praxis; (2) the critique is necessarily constructive, because it takes place in the Hegelian manner of determinate negation; and (3) the process is experiential, meaning it concerns the lives of each of us, and it is progressive, because it brings with it a transformation towards the better. Jaeggi herself identifies other, and not simple, problems that her idea and such characteristics entail. For example, it is impossible to be sure that there is an actual improvement if it is no longer possible to envisage an ultimate end towards which the whole process moves, in the light of which to evaluate actual steps forward. Moreover, the problematic nature of the existing, highlighted by subjective analysis, is the result of interpretation and is therefore inevitably arbitrary. Finally, it is impossible to guarantee that the position of the subject experiencing an ideology coincides with that of the subject of criticism and equally difficult for the latter to offer universal criteria to the former.[30]

This complex issue is taken up in another and larger text, devoted to alienation (Jaeggi 2014). Jaeggi tries to reuse this concept for the critique of social relations, and she does so, in a refined and interesting way, starting from the analysis (understood in the way briefly described above) of some everyday life situations. In all these cases, alienation is a situation that is deficient with respect to individual or collective self-realization.[31] Alienation is an "impeded appropriation of world and self" (ivi, p. 151). It is the impairment of our ability to be ourselves, within social relationships that do not allow for self-actualization. In short, "alienation is a relation *of relationlessness*" (ivi, p. 1). It is a relation, but a deficient one. The subject overcomes his alienation by recognizing, through critical analysis, the ways in which distorted paths of self-actualization manifest themselves in his daily life: overcoming alienation "is an active and collective appropriation of the world" (Jaeggi 2017, p. 333, translation mine). Here, too, the problems highlighted above appear: how to recognize such impairments only immanently?

These are problems that lead to a definitive overcoming of the concept of ideology and ideological critique. Since the substance of argumentation lies in the analysis of the relationship between ideas and reality, between structure and superstructure as Marx would say, I would like to propose a theory of ideology that, in the direction proposed by the *idéologues*, takes up this theme without the argumentative structure underlying the unmasking technique. My proposal is much less ambitious than that of the *idéologues*: it does not set itself the task of an actual science of ideas, as it was in their formulation, as much as the far more modest one of reasoning about the ways to read the relationship between theory and praxis in a post-metaphysical or, rather, post-ideological era. Always keep in mind that the end point is the proposal of a new articulation, also post-ideological, of the relationship between society and politics. For simplicity, I will set out my proposal in points.

1. The starting point can be formulated as follows: *there is always mediation between theory and praxis*. In this sense, critique is not immanent critique. According to Jaeggi, "immanent critique, then, does not confront, as Marx put it, reality with a prefabricated ideal, and it does not just extricate such an ideal from it but instead develops it from the contradictory dynamic of reality itself" (Jaeggi 2009, p. 81). This is, in short, a refined re-presentation of Marx's *Eleventh Thesis* on Feuerbach. To abandon this thesis is to abandon the Hegelian-inspired Marxian vocabulary. The concepts of contradiction, alienation, dialectic, determinate negation, etc., can be set aside, with all the problems they bring with them. Reality is dynamic, but it does not contain internal contradictions that thought can only recognize.
2. Since the relationship between theory and praxis is always mediated, a *factual and autonomous intervention of reason* is possible within it. Its task is to mediate – in the literal sense of constructing a relationship of mutual mediation – between thought and reality, whereby thought means not only scientific theory but also, and perhaps above all, narratives. Human action is rational because it is finalistic. As is well-known, in Weber action is rational in two ways: instrumentally and with respect to value. In both ways, to be rational means to syndicate a relationship, that is, to mediate. To act means to believe in the pursuit of a given end and to prepare modes of operation that make it reasonably pursuable.[32] This is the sense in which Weber assigns a central role to the ideal types of rational acting over the affective and traditional ideal types. It certainly does not mean forgetting the importance of the latter: we can consider, to take just one example, the role that the concept of charisma – strongly affectively connoted – plays in his theory. The point is that to give oneself autonomously and consciously an end – to act in a way endowed with meaning – implies the inevitable involvement of rational activity: without the latter, there is no acting in the proper sense.
3. The concept of action is inherently *normative because it is finalistic*. To act means to choose rationally – although affect and tradition, I insist, are of paramount importance – between alternatives, that is, to hold that one end is more important to us than others. Reason, at least in the Weberian conception, does not tell us which choice is normatively right. Action is meaningful insofar as it involves a process of decision-making, a choice that is an expression of a valuing process. Regardless of whether our decision and the meaning we give to the action are in themselves, a priori or

a posteriori, right. In this perspective, our action is not instinctive but is deeply human. This is an important point, to which I will return later.

4. Schütz develops the Weberian approach by introducing the idea that intended meaning refers to a pool of common sense available to subjects, who act intentionally, but seldom reflexively. In this direction, the finalistic conception of acting fits into a fully inter-subjective framework since it refers to an inter-subjective dimension of meaning. Moments of reflexivity are rare, and their rarity is directly proportional to their importance. They are the moments when the meaning of what we are doing becomes apparent to us, that is, the end, or ends, for which we are striving. Since pursuing an end, any end, implies a relatively coherent set of interrelated actions, Schütz introduces the concept of the *project of action*. What I am now doing I am doing without necessarily having to reflect on the fact that several months ago I made the decision – among alternatives I had – to write this book. A project that I was very much involved in, but which, I confess, sometimes, thinking back, in the face of the difficulties I have encountered, made me rethink at times of the alternatives I dropped. But as Caesar once said, "alea iacta est". Caesar's expression testifies to the autonomous strength of the project of action, that is, the strength of the decision made that became a daily commitment. For this very reason, I think we can usefully distinguish between established, habitual projects of action and unconsolidated, more open-ended, and less defined projects of action. On this important point, too, I will elaborate below. In the last chapter, I will present the notion of utopia as a particularly far-reaching project of action.
5. The distinction between intentionality and reflexivity carries with it a conception of *critique* that does not refer to the Hegelian vocabulary of alienation. This is because recognizing – in the rare moments when, regardless of or prompted by circumstances, we reflexively work on our projects of action – the non-natural character of our actions, and of the valourization processes that have brought them about, can enable a change of course. Reflexivity, bringing to light the meaning that has become implicit and hidden in our projects, may call into question what we took for granted. For my part, I confirm, now that I am thinking about it, that the writing of this text continues to fascinate me. Perhaps the only way to make sense of our identities is precisely this drive to maintain internal coherence and consistency in our projects of action. Three aspects are worth noting. The first: reflexivity can apply to any project of action, whether right or wrong.[33] The second: reflexivity that denaturalizes common sense is not dialectical, it does not bring to light a particular made universal. Put differently, the naturalization typical of common sense does not coincide with the universalization of a particular, with the masking of an interest. The reality of the world is far more complex and diverse than this mechanism. The third: reflexivity does not imply change. It makes it possible, but not compulsory.[34] Now that my plan of action towards this book is

back under the scrutiny of my conscious reflexivity, I decide not to leave it; on the contrary, I renew my intentions with greater conviction and determination. All three of these aspects are related to the fact that there is mutual mediation between thought and praxis.

6. The last statements lead to the recognition, at the same time, of the *autonomy of praxis* and its *limitations*. The two are closely interconnected: human praxis is autonomous, therefore it is limited, and vice versa. The concept of limit is all internal to the decision that propels the project of action: being a choice between alternatives, it accomplishes something by denying others. Knowing what one does, one is also aware of what one does not do.[35] Were it not so, praxis would not be autonomous, because the dimension of choice, of valuing one end over others, would be missing. Autonomy and limitations of praxis are a consequence of its normative nature, in the sense discussed above.
7. Similarly, *thought is also autonomous and limited*. There is no possibility that our ideas are capable of grasping the essence of reality; they can be fully attuned to it; they can consequently make it conform to themselves. The point merely echoes the critique of totalizing ideology as argued by Bell. A narrative, ideological or otherwise, that claims to transform society radically and totally is no longer conceivable. A differentiated and articulated reality such as ours makes it virtually impossible for any of the social subjects in it to have a comprehensive and privileged view of the whole. Thought must also recognize its own limitation: ideas, in short, are not weapons.[36] They are important up to the point where they do not become blind to the world.
8. To retain the use of the term unmasking, it may be used in the sense of unmasking the process of naturalization. Keeping in mind that all common sense is, albeit in varying degrees, naturalized sense. Unmasking is the result of reflexive activity on intentionality. It does not unmask a lie, or an ideology, in the light of a truth: it unmasks a naturalization, showing its not natural but socially constructed character.[37] As pointed out above, naturalization does not coincide with the universalization of a particular in order to disguise it and make it unrecognizable. This is a typical mechanism of common sense, without necessary bad faith. Unmasking can be directed at any social practice and the meaning embedded in it.
9. As complex as the topic is, a separation between description and evaluation is possible. This aspect is grasped by dwelling on the notion of reflexivity: in the first instance, it brings to light meaning in its objectivity, in the way meaning was realized within the project of action. In the second instance, it might reactivate the valourization process that led to the definition of those ends, even calling them into question. The two moments can be conceptually separated. First, in highlighting the meaning contained in the project, we aim to get a good understanding of what we are doing and why, and what are the ends we have set. Then

we can think about questioning them. How does Schütz's disinterested observer deal with this delicate issue? As we saw in the previous chapter, this observer is only partially interested in syndicating the valourization process that has identified some specific ends within the individual project of action. Theirs is not an evaluation of those ends: I do not expect a social scientist to tell me whether I was right to choose to become a sociologist. The finalist theory of action would like to identify some basic mechanisms capable of interpreting the ways through which the subject constructs, within the social world in which that subject lives, their own personal perspectives of action, but it does not set itself the direct task of evaluating them because, in principle, it is not driven by specific interests. Of course, such a theory might be wrong because it is inconsistent, full of errors, and internally contradictory, but not because it is interested. From Schütz's point of view, this seems to me to be the distinction between theory and narrative, between science and common sense.

10. To summarize, a *theory of ideology* sets itself the task of reflecting, within a finalistic theory of social action, on the ways in which thought and action interact reciprocally, maintaining their autonomy and, consequently, respecting their limits. It reflects rationally on the ways in which ideas become actions, and vice versa. The idea that there is always a mediation between theory and praxis is based on Adorno's position that there is always a gap between concept and thing. Critical thinking is a 'reflection on damaged life', a meditation that does not have a correct point of view. In a nutshell, the theory of ideology is a *reflexive technique of translating values into ends*, descended from the idea that values – understood as final ends – cannot, and must never, be realized.

In what sense does the finalistic character of acting carry with it a normative conception? The two aspects highlighted above – acting means giving oneself an end, valuing it among alternatives – in their complementarity are part of a single vision. Acting in a finalistic way is the way in which the subject aims at autonomously constructing his own identity, within the pre-constituted inter-subjectivity within which he moves. For the reasons advanced above, this identity constitutes a narrative, which is both the result and the condition of acting. Actions are just in the sense that they allow – or prevent – the unfolding of the autonomy of individuals, that is, they ensure that someone's autonomy is not obtained at the expense of others, through mechanisms of constraint.

Project of Action and the Process of Valourization

The project of action is a process: it makes possible continuous adjustments between what is thought and what is done. It implies a continuous mediation between thought and action. As it unfolds, within daily life, much of this process happens automatically, without thought lent to the project and the meaning it contains. Any adjustments mostly concern the daily steps of the project, not the structure of meaning on which it is based. Students who decide to enrol on the graduate program that I teach on then forget the reasons behind their choice and set out, diligently, to attend lectures, participate in the scientific life of the department and take exams. They will decide from time to time which courses to prioritize; which seminars to attend; which examinations to take and in what order; and, in the end, with which lecturer to graduate and on which topic. From a certain point of view, it is well that they do not return to the motives and causes behind their choice. It may mean that they are doing well, that it is satisfactory to them, and that everything is flowing as expected. If their path is a linear and rewarding one, the crucial questions around their future will come back to prompt their planning soonest after their graduation.

In the previous chapters, we looked at how we form the shared repositories of meaning from which we draw for our daily projects of action, and what their characteristics are. To continue the discussion, we need to take a closer look at the concept of projects of action. What are the motives behind a project of action? Can they be classified through a typology? Schütz distinguishes between *in-order-to-motives* and *because-motives*. Here again, the point of reference is Weber. According to Schütz, Weber's theory of action functions as a model of 'natural' action, of what the actor takes for granted. The distinction between causes and ends serves to problematize that model, introducing the problem of human freedom, of the subject's ability to make sense autonomously of his actions within a project of action. In Schütz, we have seen, it is as if two different planes of consciousness are given: the intentional one, understood as the indistinct flow of everyday experiences; the reflexive one, understood as the subjective capacity to momentarily suspend that flow in order to focus on separate moments endowed with meaning and to grasp the linkages that connect moment to moment. Consequently, meaning is internal to the stream of consciousness, but not to objects as such: the world acquires meaning through a particular grasp of consciousness on the part of the subject. Building on the Weberian idea that only a limited part of reality is meaningful to us, the world within which we operate our selection is, for Schütz as well, pre-given with respect to our experience and thought. In this way, "it is the meaning of our experience and not the ontological structure of the objects which constitutes reality" (Schütz 1962, p. 230). In sum, meaning is always an expression of a relation, between the subject and its experience, between the subject and the world, and between the subject and others. On all this, its character of uniqueness and unrepeatability depends.

The reflexive identification of meaning from the common sense repository can take place in a more or less active or passive form. This is not a cut and dry alternative, a dichotomy, but rather a continuum, ranging from a maximum to a minimum of freedom. It is difficult to think of a subject who entirely freely, without being impelled by any external factor, pauses reflexively on the content of his actions, driven only by an abstract need for reflexive awareness. Just as it is equally unlikely for a subject to be merely driven by circumstances and the changes they bring with them. Within this inevitable continuum, however, it is possible to identify motives that come from conditions, from their changeability, which can be seen as causes; and motives that, on the contrary, embody the normative nature of action, the freedom of the subject, understood as the subjective capacity to freely give oneself ends. In sum, for Schütz, the actor employs his or her reflexivity primarily when confronted with alternative courses of action, which appear to him or her – unless the actor encounters a Martian – within a background of meaning that is relatively familiar to him, and which significantly he has been constituting through previous choices and conditioning. To stay with the student example, this is the general conceptual framework within which students will, for example, reflect on whether to take the political economy or public law exam first. There is discretion, but not total freedom. Not least because the alternatives arise within projects of action that have the subject themself as the protagonist.

Subjective discretion, for Schütz, is organized within different systems of relevance. Correctly, Muzzetto points out that, for Schütz, "the processes involved in the problem of relevance have their basic reference point in the 'selective nature of the spirit'" (Muzzetto 2021a, p. 6).[38] In the Schützian model, there are three types of relevance: *thematic*, *interpretive*, and *motivational*. Let us look briefly at these. First, all three can be more or less active or passive. Thematic relevance concerns the themes that the subject identifies within a shared background. Certain experiences may be thematically relevant at some times and not at others, but also may never be thematically relevant. Even the varying relevance that experiences may have for us, this continual turning to them or retracting from them, constitutes a history of different and sometimes alternative discretions and produces a sedimentation of meaning that contributes to forming that context within which we then continually thematize. The fact that my students have thematized the choice between giving an exam or taking an internship, while ignoring the hypothesis of beginning to think about the thesis, constitutes a precedent that contributes to structuring a context of experience, even as they will again thematize these, or other, aspects of the background of experience they experience. In the process of thematization, the subject does not necessarily submit to reflexivity all the experiences that have settled within his or her context of experience. A clear and distinct knowledge of all those elements or factors that, more or less consciously, push us in one direction rather than another is not necessary. Possibly only later, reflecting on the past, may elements come to light that could have conditioned our thematizations, which remained unreflected over time.[39] To summarize, thematic relevance – which can be, let's recall, either voluntary or involuntary, triggered more or less actively or passively – acts against the background of a familiar sense, selecting certain experiences so as to bring them to the subject's attention: these experiences are thus thematized. They are no longer taken for granted but are problematized as they are subjected to the actor's reflexive attention.

At this point, interpretive relevances intervene. They operate within the various typical experiences that constitute the background of knowledge available to the subject. We find here the same problems characteristic of the hermeneutic circle: interpretation constructs the background of reference and, at the same time, is internal to it. To recall Schütz's well-known example of the rope, when I see an object at a relative distance, I interpret it from my background of knowledge: if I am a sailor, and that object appears to me on the deck of the ship, I will assume, even if I do not see it perfectly, that it is a rope. If I live in the country, and I see that object at the back of the room and with little light, I will think that it is perhaps a snake that came in through the window. Habit builds interpretation, but habit, as the word itself says, is the result of past interpretations. As a hermeneutic circle, we are always dealing with interpretive relevances, never with logical inferences, which instead belong to other reflexive processes. As Schütz writes, "Husserl has clearly shown that what we call *interpretation and interpretive relevances originate within the pre-predicative sphere* and are as such not inferential" (Schütz 1970, p. 43). All this supports the distinction already discussed between theory and narrative, between science and common sense.

Interpretive relevances also shed light on the relationship between in-order-to-motives and because-motives. The distinction between causes and ends depends on the different attitudes towards time that reflexivity brings. If the reflexive gaze is exercised from the initial moment of the action project, the motive appears as the goal of action, and I regard each moment of the project as an intermediate stage, motivated by the final end. In contrast, if the reflexive gaze dwells on the act performed, which is reconstructed ex post, causal motives appear, and the linguistic use of the concept of cause may suggest that one is really in the presence of a causal network. If my students reflect upon the moment they enrolled in the degree program, they each may see the actions they performed thereafter as a whole motivated by the ultimate goal they intend to achieve – to graduate. If, on the other hand, they reflect upon enrolment as a completed act, trying to reconstruct ex post the motives for it, they may see the advice of friends, parental influence, university location, etc. as causes of their choice. However, what appears as a cause to the retrospective gaze is always only a prior project of action: causes are ends in false guise, which are viewed retrospectively, so that the retrospective gaze makes them appear in a different light. What looks like a cause is always the expression of a motivating element, of the internal normative tension in action, which, as such, is always aiming at an end:

> 'causal relevance' (…) is nothing else but the objective corollary to what is subjectively experienced as 'motivationally' relevant. With respect to human action, in short, any statement of causal relevancy can easily be

> translated into terms of motivational relevance and the adherent systems of interpretational relevance.
>
> (ivi, pp. 49)[40]

The concept of cause appears, within the project of action, as an end achieved: the in-order-to-motives for which the action was designed appear now to the reflexive gaze as if they were because-motives. What really appears to the reflexivity are always and only the motives, that is, the system of relevance that – applied to the situation, within a background – constitutes the meaning of action, in its inseparable mixture of autonomy and conditioning. In this perspective, I believe phenomenological constructivism can be interpreted.[41]

What role do motivational relevances play in this framework? They emphasize the aspect of motivation behind the project of action. Above all, they emphasize the relationship between the means to be adopted versus the ends to be pursued. In a nutshell, to interpret means to diagnose, that is, to cogitate the means-ends relationship. To stay with Schütz's example, is it a rope or a snake? When in doubt, I will use a stick to see whether it moves or not. The importance of the correct interpretation

> Consists in the fact that not only the means to be chosen but even the ends to be attained will depend upon such a diagnosis. The satisfactorily plausible degree of interpretation opens a relatively high subjective chance of meeting the situation efficiently by appropriate countermeasures (…). We shall call this type of relevance the *motivational relevances*.
>
> (ivi, p. 46)

Here too the hermeneutic circularity appears: is it the correct interpretation, or presumed as such, that motivates action or is it the end that does? It is still a matter of thinking about the concept of cause, and the distinction between causes and ends. It is a matter of seeing how much force the background of meaning has toward my autonomy. Again, with the example of the rope, Schütz points out how a subject who has a great fear of snakes will be driven, even unreasonably, to move the object with a stick, because the person is motivated not so much by the end – for example, entering the room to open the window – but by the fear, which acts as a background of reference.

The discussion of relevance shows the complex articulation of autonomy and conditioning that characterizes human action, bringing to light the theme of freedom. Autonomy is also exercised vis-à-vis the self, that is, the background of meaning available to us, which is also the result of both active and passive processes. Discussing relevances also means addressing another aspect: "there are no such things as isolated relevances" (ivi, p. 43). In fact, relevances

> are all situationally conditioned. We have to *learn* what is interpretatively relevant; we must learn in the course of our actual experiences how to

> recognize interpretatively relevant moments or aspects of objects already experienced as typical. Furthermore, we have to learn how to "weigh" the outcome of our interpretations, how to determine the impact of circumstantial modifications inherent in the situation in which such interpreting occurs, how to complete and to coordinate the interpretatively relevant material, and so on.
>
> (ivi, pp. 43–44)

In sum, the action project is *made by doing*, it is a continuous learning process, because it is, at the same time, determined and open-ended. It possesses an end, but its enactment does not exclude continuous reflexive intervention. Such intervention is not only useful in adapting the various intermediate actions in view of the end but may perhaps question the end and come to modify it. I know many students who have painfully and problematically changed their course of study, moving from one degree program to another, sometimes very different from each other. The opening of the project of action has directly to do with the relationship between intentionality and reflexivity: being completely reflexive gets us nowhere, it locks our action into systematic doubt; living completely within the intentional flow of duration can get us somewhere, only to find out later that it was not where we wanted to be.

Therefore, it is a matter of reasoning about the meaning in the departure and the meaning contained in the arrival. First, there is no real departure and no real arrival either, except only biographically. Subjective reflexivity opens a passage within the motivational flow, trying to reconstruct its paths. But such reconstruction is always arbitrary and partial: where does it begin and where does it end? For example, where do I stop the retracing of aspects that explain my being a sociologist? Did I study sociology, in part, because my parents did not send me to piano school, as I would have liked as a child? Otherwise, would I have become a pianist and not a sociologist? With what results? For Schütz, an outside observer can never perfectly reconstruct subjectively intended meaning. If it cannot be done from the outside, it is perhaps equally difficult from the inside: no one is completely transparent to himself, and reflexivity does not allow us to achieve this. We are always reasoning about arbitrarily selected pieces of experience, based on systems of relevance, our courses of action. The social scientist can identify the characteristics and operation of this selection.

A first point to emphasize is that every project of action is dominated by an instrumental logic and a finalistic logic. This is the Weberian perspective: action moves in an instrumentally rational manner with respect to desired ends. Since the normative, that is the inherently human, character lies in the ability to give ends to action as autonomously as possible by coordinating our actions within relatively coherent projects, it becomes crucial to reflect on the nature of this normativity. What does it mean to choose between alternatives? It is raining, so I open my umbrella is not an action in the proper sense. In a sense, it is as if there is no alternative. From the Weberian perspective, we have seen, acting requires the presence of a clearly intended meaning. This idea is complemented by the concept of the project of action and the systems of relevance that characterize it. There is a normativity of acting connected to the simple possibility of freely making sense of our action, within projects of action. Choosing between going to the movies or having a beer at the pub is much less demanding, from a normative point of view, than choosing to consume organic products instead of mass distribution products. Or, to take an even more radical example, choosing to take up arms in the face of military aggression by a foreign country. Therefore, this issue needs to be addressed at multiple levels.

In the first instance, the finalistic conception of action involves normativity as it implies a choice between alternative ends. This is a dimension independent of the benevolence of ends. The presence of one or more ends is sufficient. If the taken for granted completely predominated, and our action moved only in pure unreflexive intentionality, we would not be able to exercise our freedom. To choose between alternatives means, in the first place, to step out of the taken for granted. It does not mean, of course, to disown it. We can see what we do and decide that we will continue to do it, knowing that we are doing it. And, after a while, return to the starting point, so that what had become visible becomes opaque again. In its essence, choosing among alternatives means valuing certain ends over others. As Weber says, our action is rational with respect to value insofar as it aims to bear witness to the value of reference. Such witnessing, as already discussed, becomes concrete as the value takes shape in a given end. How can we bear witness to the value to us of the nation to which we belong, our family, respect for the environment, etc.? Only by working towards ends that we believe are attuned to those values, within a spectrum of possible ends, which are not necessarily mutually exclusive. Around that choice, we build our projects for action.

Such projects imply the design of a series of mutually coordinated actions, each of which could at any time reactivate that system of the interconnected relevances described above, starting with thematic, then interpretative and, finally, motivational relevances. In general, once the project has been outlined in its design, it constitutes a kind of taken for granted with respect to the actions that will then be implemented within it. We hardly question the project every time we choose which single action is best to undertake, but each time the delicate question of how best to articulate our choices, giving greater weight to the instrumental dimension or to the testimonial dimension, might arise again. This is a delicate balance: motivation that is only instrumentally efficient would constitute a betrayal of the value of witnessing, but the opposite is also true: pure witnessing could be instrumentally ineffective. It is a matter of putting two logics at work, internal to Weber's two ideal types of rational action, reasoning their infinite possible interactions. All this, regardless of the worthiness of the end, of its intrinsic value: it depends on the choice, on the values we want to witness.

Thus, a second normative dimension appears: acting is normatively connoted because it involves a choice, but also because this choice involves a process of valourization. In making our choices, we value some aspects over others. This is a process that can be made opaque, but not erased. Choosing between ends means, in essence, valuing something rather than something else. Many elements may come into play, some passive and some active, and the different degrees of awareness one has of one and the other. In any case, the end we intend to achieve is something that has value for us. Normativity of action is therefore characterized not only by the fact that our action has an end, but also by the fact that that end is important to us, certainly to which we are not indifferent. Generally, we give little importance to those actions whose end is unimportant to us. Or, put even better, is undemanding of us. The process of valourization thus carries with it two dimensions: the breaking out of the taken for granted; a decision around the relevance of what is at stake.

We can thus better articulate the relationship – already partly analysed in the first chapter – between ends and values. A value may be the result of *hypostatization of an end*, which can be produced by the valuing process that leads us to select an end among alternative ends. Acting is normative because it involves identifying an end that has value for us and involves significance that engages us: an important project is one that aims to achieve an *important end*. What happens, however, is that importance outshines the end, the adjective overshadows the noun. We no longer see the end, but the value, which has become something independent of the end. This is a well-known process, already looked at in the second chapter about the formation of common sense. A content of meaning becomes objectified; it becomes independent of the process that produced it. At the same time, it withdraws from the reflexive gaze, becomes opaque. In this case, the process of valourization – through which we select among alternative ends the one that is most meaningful to us – first transforms an evaluation, that is, a judgement, into a content of meaning; then it renders that meaning opaque, removing it from reflexivity. The concrete end, through this hypostatization, thus becomes the ultimate end, the most worthy to be achieved, removed from any further evaluation and choice.

Thus, meanings are produced that are independent of the process of valourization: values are produced. The deeper this mechanism goes, the more values appear to us with an independent reality, which we take for granted, and which we think are the object of our action in the world. Realizing value is an empty expression, which can lead to considerable dangers. When value appears to us as the end of action, through a substitution produced by its hypostatization, much of the process of valourization is taken for granted, and the dimension of choice becomes opaquer. Ends seem already given, taken for granted, based on a value that has been removed from our reach, for the realization of which any means can become licit, any course of action justified. All this becomes possible because the process of valourization is anesthetized, taken away from its fundamental function: to identify achievable ends. We could say that this process is deactivated because of its own success. Success that brings with it a form of cognitive economy: instead of reflexively imposing on ourselves the commitment to decide on worthwhile ends, we eliminate the process by using acritically the product of that process. After all, this is the same mechanism that produces common sense: a meaning abstracts from reflexivity to become disposable meaning. In this way, it is not the end that justifies the means, but the value. Ends that have withdrawn from the reflexive gaze, which become final ends, that is to say, they have become values in themselves, justify anything. This is the mechanism that produces, among other things, the totalizing ideologies denounced by Aron and Bell.

The hypostatization of ends into values, that is, the construction of values as realities, becomes particularly significant in the modern world. In the pre-modern world, the ends of human actions have a foundation, whether metaphysical or religious, that is realized within identity-based communities. This is quite evident, to give just a few examples, in Aristotelian ethics, but also in medieval religious ethics. Therefore, the normativity of human action, and of the projects of action within which it takes shape, is predefined externally to action.[42] Any attempt to construct an immanent critique – from Hegel onwards – is a way of coping with the failure of fundamentals while maintaining the idea of a necessary critique.

The modern production of values is highlighted in a short text by Schmitt (2018). As is often the case, it is conservative thinkers – with a more or less pronounced reactionary connotation – who shrewdly point out the fundamental mechanisms of the modern world. Schmitt is adept at showing the quantitative and economic nature of the modern concept of value, an expression of the centrality that economics assumes in modernity. The ancient virtues are replaced by the cold calculation of interests, by the domination of the market. And, like all other commodities, values are put on the market. His analysis, paradoxically, resembles that of Marx and Engels, who in the *Manifesto* shows how the bourgeoisie succeeds in imposing a world in which human relations are dominated by interest, and human dignity becomes a value of mere exchange. To transform virtues into values is to make "the incommensurable commensurable" (ivi, p. 8). The most interesting aspect lies in the fact that, for Schmitt, "value *is* not, rather it *holds* (…). Value precisely lusts after actualization. It is not real, but directed toward realization and longs for enforcement and implementation" (ivi, p. 27, italics mine). This is because its nature "lies precisely therein, that instead of being it only has a holding. The setting is consequently nothing, if it is not put through; the validity must be constantly actualized, that means: *made* valid, if it is not to be dissolved in mere appearance" (ivi, p. 31, italics mine), so that "the compulsion to validity of value is irresistible, and the strike of those who value, de-value, raise in value, and valuize (*Verwerter*), is unavoidable" (ivi, p. 35). Value becomes the arbiter of ethics, imposing its practical realization, for which no price is too high. In a situation without foundation, the process of hypostatization advances irrepressibly, so as to create that situation, perfectly described by Weber, in which worlds struggle against worlds, with no possibility of mediation. The market is dominated by the logic of value; at the same time, a market of values develops, each of which yearns for its implementation. At this point, one can believe without faith. As Eagleton writes, "to place one's credence in the slogan as rhetorically valid is to perform a fictional act, whereas to take it literally is to fall victim to a myth" (Eagleton 1991, p. 191).

Against all this, it is important to keep alive the dimension of critique, presented here from a phenomenological perspective. Critique is exercised on every content of meaning, through the use of reflexivity but, to take up Jaeggi's argument, also on *certain* contents, fixing a doubly reflexive gaze upon them: should values suggest to humankind scenarios of perfect worlds, which present themselves to human action as truly actionable ends, that process of valourization must be reactivated. Values are not the end of action. They can be, in the Weberian manner, witnessed. When Walzer proposes an idea of an internal critique that is exercised on the gap between values and reality, one must forcefully argue that values do not have to be realized. Jaeggi's critique directed at Walzer, that the criterion of critique remains *internal* to a community and does not become universal, misses the decisive aspect of the matter: a community that fulfils its ideals would be hell.

To highlight the centrality of the valourization process is to dispense with any metaphysics of values. In the modern post-ideological world, the real finalistic, and therefore open-ended, nature of human action can finally appear, no longer subservient, as it was in the pre-modern world, to a metaphysical or religious dimension external to it. Nor is it any longer subservient to modern totalizing ideologies.

To conclude, a finalistic theory of action carries with it a double connotation of normativity: it is normative because it imposes a choice, through the identification of ends; it is normative because, through a process of valourization, it endows its ends with value, which produces the risk of hypostatizing values as an independent reality. A new theory of ideology, in the wake of the Enlightenment project and aware of the risks of hypostatizing values, proposes itself as a critical reflection on the relationship between ends and values, theory and praxis, culture and structure, putting itself at the service of a project of democratic implementation of democracy.

Politicizing Society

One final task now remains, announced at the beginning of the chapter. Once ideologies have lost their ability to bridge, how do we rebuild meaningful connections between society and politics?[43]

A first response is populism. The idea is that of a return to the people, to their centrality and authenticity.[44] Populist movements, whether right-wing or left-wing,[45] start from the realization that the functioning of democracies today is at risk because of a fracture between institutions and parties on one side and society on the other. The reason for this separation lies in the fact that institutions and parties have increasingly become the place where self-referential élites clash, unable to represent anything beyond their own narrow sphere. Political conflict no longer expresses the plurality of collective positions and interests present in society, but only the interests of an 'elected few'. All this produces disinterest in politics, poor election turnout, and distrust in the system as a whole. The solution is to give the people a voice again, in a trend against the system, or at least against this type of political representation. Certain characteristics are shared by all recent populisms: an anti-system attitude although, at least formally, not always anti-democratic; criticism of the processes of globalization, which distort and erase identities; opposition to political and economic élites, unable to promote the collective interest, especially in times of global crisis; aversion to political professionalism; and a call to the people, their identity and unity.

The rise of populism goes hand in hand with the de-politicization typical of neo-liberal policies. It is reductive to see neo-liberalism only as an economic system, one that has been emerging since the last decades of the last century. On the contrary, neo-liberalism constitutes a complementary and original combination of elements involving capitalism, the market, and democracy. It is a new form of social organization, endowed with its own perspective capable of becoming shared common sense. It was born and established as a reaction to the stagflation crises of the 1970s, as an evolution and overcoming of Fordist capitalism, and as an alternative to social democratic welfare policies. Beginning with the ideas of von Mises, von Hayek, and Friedman, economic freedom and the principle of competition are to be placed at the foundation of society. The latter is conceived as the best means of coordinating human efforts and interests because, as an abstract and impersonal mechanism, it is the only method by which we can adjust our activities without arbitrary and coercive intervention by authority. Political freedom has its basis in economic freedom, and in the impersonal mechanism that regulates the latter, namely the market. Neo-liberalism brings with it a specific idea of the individual, based on the centrality of economic interest and the idea that anyone who wants to can realize themself, the supremacy of market logic, the centrality of economic enterprise and, more generally, of the economy.

Paradoxically, neo-liberal de-politicization and populist re-politicization are closely related, not only in the sense that the latter can be seen as a reaction to the former but also as a form of apparent rebalancing of the tensions and inequalities produced by the new global capitalism. Populism and neo-liberalism are only seemingly in opposition. In both directions, we have a contraction of the autonomy of democratic politics: neo-liberalism would like to reduce it to technical matters; populism would like to make it the direct expression of an identity, that of the people, with which to attune. These are two different forms of de-politicization and naturalization: the former is technical; the latter is identity based. While, on the one hand, the abstract individual is placed at the centre, an equally abstract idea of the people is set against it. The full freedom of the former is just as false as the equally full freedom of the latter. Just to give a clear example, the slogan 'less tax', an expression of criticism of welfare policies, would like to meet the interests of the people, but basically also those of international markets.

Democracy thrives on participation, within an institutional framework that guarantees and sustains freedoms, rights, and pluralism. The latter is fundamental, but if it remains on the merely formal level of procedures, it is not sufficient to guarantee the democratic quality of the system as a whole. There may in fact be illiberal democracies, that is, regimes that only formally guarantee a whole range of democratic procedures – elections, party system, presence of elective chambers, etc. – but which, in fact, employ these elements as empty shells, serving new autocracies. The substantial difference is made by the quantity and quality of participation. Therefore, it is necessary to reflect on the political disintermediation enacted by neo-liberalism and the apparent response constituted by contemporary populisms. As we have already seen, in a complex and differentiated society, within which subjectivities have become increasingly disjointed and the system of social stratification can no longer be read with the categories of the past, participation cannot coincide only with electoral participation. The fact is that the system of interests and identities cannot be traced back to simple aggregative nuclei – classes, generations, and territories, to give a few examples – which the party system should then directly represent. The variety, fragmentation, and intersection of interests and identities require new models of transforming social demand into political supply.

Populism, through the idea of the people, remains anchored to the idea of representing an identity subjectivity in its unity. It remains anchored to the idea of a Subject. It thus aims at a re-politicization of society that downplays, or even erases, its internal plural articulation, especially in the ways in which pluralism seems to be taking shape today. At least three errors are attributable to populism: (1) trying to recompose pluralism into an abstract idea of the people; (2) substituting for the conflict between left and right – which is horizontal, if it remains within the democratic institutional framework – the conflict between high and low status, between the people and élites – which is vertical and as a result, can develop anti-system positions; and (3) thinking that civil society can become directly political, without mediation, erasing the autonomy of politics. Overcoming disintermediation thus leads to the rejection of all mediation.

Neo-liberalism and populism therefore converge on another point: the idea of a conflict-free society. In the first case, because the abstract individual – what Bauman calls the de jure individual – produces conflicts that cannot be aggregated, the individual being alone against all; in the second, because the idea of the people nullifies within the homogeneity of a real subjectivity the possibility of conflict. In sum, neo-liberalist de-politicization and populist re-politicization are two different forms of political disintermediation. The question to be addressed is that of an *anti-populist democratic re-politicization,* which is nurtured by mediation between the two spheres, that of society and that of politics, each recognized in its autonomy.

In this perspective, it is appropriate to reflect on a further feature of the project of action. Within the project of action, as we have seen above, both instrumental and value-related rationality operate. However, it is possible to trace a third idea of rationality, which interacts with the first two. The project of action, produced by the activation of a whole system of relevance, requires a certain amount of *coherence*. First of all, in order for it to be identified as such, and to prevent the multiple and heterogeneous set of actions that compose it from being lost in the great murky sea of happenings. A project has its own relative identity, for the actor, for the others with whom it enters into relationship, for the eventual disinterested observer. Anyone, upon reflection, can recognize that the meaning of an individual action comes from the more general meaning of the project in which it is embedded, even if they are not at that moment reflexively aware of the implications this may entail. Second, instrumentality and witnessing both require some temporal scope and, consequently, that multiple actions be connected to each other so that the whole becomes meaningful. This connection must rely on a shared meaning that serves as a background of reference but is also capable of creating meaningful relationships among the parts of the project. In short, connections are as important as the things that are interconnected. They too are based on meaning and produce meaning.

There is a certain amount of coherency even within common sense. Without it, our daily life could become unlivable, and each moment might stand as an absolute, detached from the rest. All the more so, coherence becomes important when, within the everyday, we identify projects of action as an expression of our autonomy. Coherence is the result of a systematic and reflexive exercise: from these two characteristics, its rationality derives. Indeed, we say we are inconsistent when there is no connection of meaning between one action and another. Just as with the system of relevance, here too we are not dealing with logical inferences, but only with interpretive ones, which are therefore also subject to the hermeneutic process mentioned above. What is coherent for ego may not be coherent for alter, although ego may argue with alter with respect to the sense in which coherency is given for him. The coherence of an entire project of action is thus subject to a process of interpretation, because at its origin is the activation of interpretive relevance.

Coherence rationality has an impact on the other two rationality models, possibly affecting the actor's decisions. For example, one may choose to act in a way that is not entirely rational with respect to purpose in the name of greater coherence, or vice versa. The three dimensions of rationality – instrumental effectiveness, reference to value, and coherence – interact with each other, going on to formulate, on the basis of choices made using the relevances, projects of action that are also relatively recognizable by others. Such recognizability is made possible by the common reference background, within which actors carve out, through selection, their own personal projects.

To stay with the example of the university students, in my eyes not only is each student's project recognizable but also those of their peers enrolled in other degree programs.

That said, I believe that the link between society and politics can be constituted by a process of *politicization of the social*. This process lies opposite to political socialization typical of the world of ideologies. Within that past world, ideologies created from above were made available to social subjects through socialization processes, enacted by parties, institutions, mass media, families, etc. In our world, on the contrary, the problem is no longer to bring politics inside society, but rather society inside politics. This is a process that must be carried out, again, by politics vis-à-vis society, in the opposite direction of that of the past. Now the contents present in the living body of society must become politics and policies. The autonomy of politics is manifested in a new way because, above all, society has become more autonomous. The basic premise is a dual recognition: society and politics have different and complementary roles, which must be made critically complementary, embracing the autonomy of both.

Society is characterized by a complex system of identities and memberships, which must be maintained, valued, and enriched. However, it is difficult to identify relatively coherent social subjectivities from which, using their worldviews, to build political projects. Gender issues, environmental issues, those related to a new model of development, the assertion of rights, and the maintenance and strengthening of peace are all issues promoted by social subjects such as women, ecologists, and pacifists, and by the collective imaginaries that these subjects promote and develop, but the fundamental political question is to link all these aspects within relatively coherent and identifiable political projects. I insist on the point: in an ideological world, social classes were bearers of ideologies, that is, of overall visions of reality that, starting from the world of labour, thought they could embrace all aspects of collective life. Today, this is no longer possible: there is no longer the Subject protagonist of history.

In the world of ideologies, civil society was hetero-directed: grand narratives gave social subjects a relatively coherent and reliable vision of their place in the world, sustaining their collective identity, including through forms of political and union representation, from a perspective that tended to defend interests and identities. *Political* ideologies used to be able to provide *social* identities. Today the question must be upended: *social* imaginaries must be translated into *political* identities.

In this context, it is counterproductive to regret the socializing function of the mass parties of the past. While it becomes extremely important for a new political sensibility to develop, one capable of giving voice to issues that civil society, in its rich and complex articulations taking shape within the new social imaginaries, poses with insistence and continuity. Civil society today is all too full of issues, narratives, and imaginaries. There is an ongoing ebullience that demands consideration and representation, and transformation into policies. These are issues that, in different and disjointed ways, are sometimes confused and contradictory, but always with a clear and strong voice, civil society raises: the expansion of rights; the reduction of inequalities; a model of sustainable development; the promotion of a circular economy, capable of replanting roots in the social; the adherence to new models of consumption; policies of inclusion towards weak subjects; a new vision of the relationship with nature; the need for sociality; the critique of an alienating globalization; a new management of human relations, time and space; and so forth.

The task of politics, and of a renewed party system, is to bring these demands, and many others I have forgotten, from the social to the political plane. This is not, of course, a process of 'colonization' that politics does vis-à-vis society: the latter continues to maintain its autonomy, its own modes of organization and socialization. It can continue, indeed in Putnam's critical perspective it *must* continue, to give voice to these needs, finding concrete and operational ways to realize new and shared experiences. Politics, for its part, must organize them into a relatively coherent system of pursuable ends, into a political project recognizable by citizens.

The task of politics is no longer to provide *identity values*, but rather to construct *identity projects*, capable of speaking to significant, and potentially majority sections of civil society.[46] The political system has before it a twofold task: to secure, protect, and implement those democratic values and procedures that constitute the ineradicable framework of our advanced societies; and to provide alternative projects through which to articulate political conflict, within that institutional framework. The *values*, and the imaginaries behind them, are, and will increasingly be, a product of civil society, which elaborates them by constructing that dense puzzle of intersecting identities typical of our societies; the *ends* – a relatively coherent system of ends, which takes the form of a political project – are the political contribution to the smooth functioning of democracy.

I offer an example. Defense of labour and defense of the environment do not always go together. The processes of valourization, which can lead to the hypostatization of labour and environment as independent values, must be relocated, in their concrete operation, within projects of action that identify – on the basis of rationality from coherence, with respect to value and instrumental (coherence rationality, value-rationality, and goal-rationality) reasonably pursuable ends. There will always be a gap between these ends and the abstract values of imaginaries.

New narratives are always being produced in society. Society thus remains the source of thinkability of the impossible, where imagination can continue to maintain that degree of freedom from necessity that alone can guarantee freedom from the present. In this way, a criticism emerges that thinks the unthinkable: *social criticism* can afford to be free from the necessity of coherence, reasonableness, realism. It can even afford to be an irresponsible critique because it is the critique of imagination. Values can offer themselves in their guise of absoluteness, as hypostatizations of a desire that wants to be satisfied. *Political critique*, on the contrary, is the critique that is exercised on the adequacy that exists between the individual project and its reference imaginary, and between political projects that are different and antagonistic to each other. In essence, between ends and means. If the social imaginary is the world of the possible, politics is that of the feasible. It translates values into actionable ends: this translation is the opposite process of the hypostatization of values. The latter lose their character of objectivity: praxis imposes the choice between alternative ends, so that from values we return to the process of valourization.

The pluralism of values characteristic of our societies is nothing more than an expression of the loss of the ultimate foundation. Paradoxically, our present one is not a world without values, but with many, and perhaps too many, values. In the absence of an ultimate foundation, everything requires justification and many arguments. The process of valourization, which is becoming freer and more open, with an increasing number of different social actors as protagonists, continually hypostatizes new values. Who would have thought of the importance of animalism imaginary only a few years ago?

To summarize: society produces narratives, and by hypostatizing ends consistent with those narratives it always puts forth new values. The latter, in their irreconcilability, hardly constitute relatively coherent and organic worldviews. All this has repercussions for identities, which are increasingly resembling Harlequin's costume. Politics has a task of synthesis. Through their own systems of relevance, parties develop political projects[47] understood as a system of ends that are relatively coherent with each other, that is, reasonably pursuable not individually, but as a whole. This process involves the translation of values into ends, that is, narratives into political practice. At this point, the voter, but more importantly the citizen, identifies with a project even if it does not fully realize his or her reference values, his or her imaginaries, because the latter are in fact unrealizable. A living and mature democracy can only value and promote the proliferation of social pluralism (multiplicity of imaginaries) and political pluralism (multiplicity of identity projects), starting from the recognition of the limits of human praxis.[48]

Notes

1 Present especially in the *Economic and Philosophic Manuscripts* of 1844 (Marx 2007). The central idea is that the objectification of human essence takes place through free activity, capable of producing, through labour, objects in which to recognize oneself. The appropriation of self thus occurs through a becoming other than self, through a process of alienation into objects that are not only ends in themselves but also instruments of subjective self-awareness. Since work is always social work, there is a need to pursue those forms of sociality that enable a free activity capable of realizing the subjectivity of each and all. Human history is thus a process of progressive liberation of human activity through the gradual development of production techniques and the social relations these bring.

2 Note that Marx and Engels, using the metaphor of the camera, conceive of the human mind as a mechanism that passively records external data, in line with the strictest empiricism. But if so, how is it possible to introduce an alteration from empirical evidence? How can the human mind lie, conceal, distort, in a word produce ideology?

3 The cultural basis of bourgeois ideology is not only idealist: there is an important materialist, mechanistic, and positivist culture that nourishes bourgeois and capitalist culture, without which the bourgeois revolution would not have been possible.

4 For example, is feminism an ideology? Are women 'compelled' to universalize their interests by presenting them as being common to all? Does feminism carry with it false consciousness? Does it imply a misperception of reality to be unmasked? And if so, who can do it? These are questions that it would perhaps be senseless to answer, probably because they make sense only within a conception of history that views social classes as the sole protagonists. In historical materialism, there is no autonomous space for other subjectivities, nations, communities, generations, etc. Unless the term ideology is used as a simple representation of the world, in which there is nothing to unmask. At this point, one can simply be mistaken, or be in bad faith, without necessarily having a false consciousness.

5 Later, the example, taken up by Jaeggi, of Marx's critique of bourgeois freedom and equality, seen as an expression of class domination, will be discussed. For Mannheim, the fact that

> the calculating attitude is to be sociologically imputed to the aspiring bourgeoisie does not amount at all to a notion of reality (which would be incorrect as such) according to which every individual bourgeois always maintains this attitude toward his environment, but it amounts simply to the claim that a systematically consistent and fundamentally novel inclination toward quantifying everything in the world was brought into the realm of possibility out of the will brought to the world by this new stratum, which had borne the rise of capitalism.
>
> (Mannheim 1997e, p. 157)

The calculating attitude, in Mannheim's example, is not in itself false because it is bourgeois; it can become a possibility available to all; the bourgeois is not always and only calculating. This does not mean that the attitude is right: it only means that it is not false because it is bourgeois.

6 I remember a high school literature teacher of mine contrasting the revolutionary poetry of Majakovsky with the bourgeois poetry of Leopardi.

7 From this perspective, human subjects can only express a reality that is imposed in its objectivity on their consciences. Eagleton reports in this regard an anecdote concerning Wittgenstein.

> The philosopher Wittgenstein is said to have enquired of a colleague why people considered it more natural to hold that the sun moved round the earth rather than vice versa. On being told that it simply looked that way, he enquired what it would look like if the earth moved round the sun. The point, of course, is that one does not here simply derive an error from the nature of the appearances, for the appearances are in both cases the same.
>
> (Eagleton 1991, p. 88)

8 For Marx, the fact that religion is the opium of the people is not entirely negative. He does not mean that, like opium, religion distorts reality, altering it to others' ends. Rather, he is referring to the medicinal, soothing property of opium: this is a merciful, and rather unnecessary, concern for suffering. It will be mainly later Marxism that will emphasize the distortion aspect.

9 Capitalism, according to Marx, is true, as real; it is false, as alienated reality. Existential truth and moral truth are intertwined in an attempt to make both objects of scientific analysis. But the concept of true as an expression of an existence is one thing: capitalism is true insofar as it exists in the same way that anything out there exists. It is quite another thing, however, to make a moral judgement of a social reality. Marx's effort is aimed at showing that capitalist alienation cannot be assessed only from a moral point of view, but is real, that is, independent of the moral judgement that can be made of it. The critique of capitalism must be scientific, not moral, and its heart of reality is expressed in the theory of exploitation. Hence the Marxian effort, contained primarily in his theory of value, to demonstrate that exploitation is real, a concrete theft and not an expression of moral judgement. As is well known, this demonstration – related to the problem of the transformation of values into prices – is largely problematic and, after the work of Sraffa (1975), was abandoned. It is another thing to see in Marx not a scientist of capitalism – as he perhaps preferred to consider himself – but a moral thinker, making his critique of capitalism not a scientific critique but an ethical one. The debate on the point is open and the related literature enormous. According to Mannheim, "the primacy of volition over cognition is an implicit cornerstone of Hegel's system and a conscious axiom of Marx" (Mannheim 1997d, p. 42). In recent times, an interesting ethical reinterpretation of Marx has developed that repudiates the Hegelian-inspired dialectical method (Cohen 2000; 2001).

10 The intertwining of these issues can be well illustrated by the following passage from Engels: "Ideology is a process carried out by the so-called thinker consciously, in truth, *but with a false consciousness*. The real motives that impel him remain unknown to him, otherwise it would not be an ideological process at all. So he imagines false or apparent motives" (Engels' letter to Mehring, July 14, 1893, italics mine). Now it is the bourgeois thinker who has a false consciousness: he masks nothing, he can only produce ideology. It follows that he is entirely blameless. How could he who has a false consciousness think correctly?

11 As an example, the first interpretation is espoused by Ricœur (1986) and the second by Althusser (1993). Unlike Marx, for Ricœur – once he sets aside "the concept of ideology as opposed to science" in favour of what "may be the most primitive concept of ideology, that opposed to praxis" – what is "most basic to the ideology-praxis contrast is not opposition; what is most fundamental is not the distortion or dissimulation of praxis by ideology. Rather, most basic is an inner *connection* between the two terms" (Ricœur 1986, pp. 9, 10). This is a way of overcoming Marxian determinism.

12 According to Eagleton, "what Lukács has in effect done is to replace Hegel's Absolute Idea – itself the identical subject-object of history – with the proletariat" (Eagleton 1991, p. 98).

13 In his second thesis on Feuerbach, Marx writes: "the question whether objective truth can be attributed to human thinking is not a question of theory but is a *practical question*" (Marx 1974, p. 121). Ricœur – about the famous eleventh thesis, according to which "the philosophers have only *interpreted* the world, in

various ways; the point is to *change* it" (ivi, p. 123) – rhetorically wonders if "we can change without interpreting" (Ricœur 1986, p. 70).

14 Mannheim himself has firsthand experience of these processes in his native Hungary.

15 At least two texts should be mentioned: Aron (2001); Meynaud (1961). Aron makes a scathing criticism of those leftist intellectuals *engagés* (Sartre, Camus, and Merleau-Ponty) who, out of loyalty to Marxist ideology, fail to grasp the dramas produced by Soviet communism. For Meynaud, there is an actual decline of ideologies, which manifests itself in poor participation, although this does not mean a weakening of political confrontation. In particular, he does not believe that a technocratic approach, in fact complementary to a generalized apathy, can really replace an idea of politics understood as opposition between different sides. In sum, a pragmatic approach – embodied by American society – can never eliminate the need for a broader perspective, a need that inevitably ends up unfolding in a plurality of different positions.

16 Bell, in the *Afterword* to the new 1988 edition of his book, recalls that it was Camus who first spoke of the end of ideologies as early as 1946: the hope was that with the end of the war the 'absolute' utopias, as Camus calls them, would also end.

17 "What is not considered an ideology today? Ideas, ideals, beliefs, creeds, passions, values, *Weltanschauungen*, religions, political philosophies, moral systems, linguistic discourses – all have been pressed into service" (Bell 1988, pp. 433–434).

18 The debate between Habermas and Gadamer – in which von Borman, Bubner, and Giegel also participate – consists of a series of essays published between 1967 and 1970 (Apel, Gadamer, Habermas 1979). See also Ricœur (1981). On the relationship between Ricœur and Habermas, see Thompson (1981); on that between Ricœur and Schütz, see Sacchetti (2012).

19 In Aristotle, *phronesis* is practical knowledge, as opposed to abstract knowledge, capable of directing the choice behind action in view of the ultimate goal, which coincides with happiness.

20 As is well known, the aspects here will be developed by Habermas in his theory of communicative action (Habermas 1984), which contains a different theory of language than that of Gadamer. In a nutshell, after the dispute with Gadamer, Habermas clarifies his position in light of the theory of validity claims, going beyond the consideration of work and power. The validity claims internal to language are the presupposition of hermeneutic understanding. B can understand A because he understands the validity claims of A's linguistic expression. Hermeneutic capacity results from the inter-subjective nature of linguistic communication. This has as a further corollary that there can be no pre-linguistic self-awareness. An adult, an infant, or a dog can have the same pre-linguistic consciousness that results from having a bellyache. But our own self-awareness presupposes linguistic communication.

21 Franklin appears to them as "the standard bearer of a free and democratic society" (Moravia 1986, p. 78, translation mine).

22 After an initial phase characterized by mutual sympathy and cooperation, culminating in the coup d'état of 18–19 Brumaire (November 9–10, 1799), "the *idéologues* will constitute for Napoleon a kind of recurrent obsession. Few other things disconcerted and irritated him more than these intellectuals, weak as a political party, unable to sober public opinion (…), yet almost all of them stubbornly non-aligned, refractory to any integration into the system" (ivi, pp. 461–462, translation

mine). For Napoleon, "they were guilty of having theorized and propagated the theories of democracy, equality, the right of self-determination and in some cases of insurrection of the people, and then of having elaborated and propagated a secular and earthly conception of laws and of political and civil power, putting the creative capacity of the assemblies, the expression of the popular will, before any right of religious origin in this field" (ivi, p. 601, translation mine).

23 For Cabanis, a madman must preserve human and civil rights. Moreover, he argues that the reasons for crimes are to be found more in society than in individuals.

24 After all, these are Marx's own criticisms, first found in The *Holy Family*, then in *The Capital* (Marx 2010; 1992).

25 Their political program would be defeated in the fiercest moments of the revolution, when "they would be overtaken on the left by a party not only more resolute, but also and above all more sensitive to the politico-social anxieties present in the French people" (Moravia 1986, p. 183, translation mine). At those moments, they had manifested their ideal, "the ideal of an interclass and inter-party conciliation, inspired by goodwill and *raison*, and extraneous to the sterile and nefarious mixes of political life. A purely *philosophique* ideal, which few times as then revealed its historical inconsistency" (ivi, p. 189, translation mine). All this will lead them to denounce the fanatical, dogmatic, and pseudo-religious character that the Revolution was taking on under Robespierre. With dramatic personal consequences, since most of them were directly persecuted through execution or incarceration.

26 According to Tracy, "the idea of *liberty* arises from the faculty of willing; for, with Locke, I understand by liberty the power to execute one's will, to act according to one's desire (…). Thus there would be no liberty if there were no will; and liberty cannot exist before the birth of the will" (quoted in Head 1985, p. 75). More generally, "*idéologie* became a philosophy of perfectibility, defining progress in terms of diffusion of knowledge and its embodiment in rational institutions". For Tracy, "the obstacle to a free society (…) was the institutionalization of ignorance and prejudice which made possible the survival of oppression" (ivi, pp. 207, 208).

27 For Jaeggi, as socially induced, ideologies "are not merely an error or a cognitive mistake; in a certain sense, they are mistakes with better reasons, because they are grounded in the properties and conditions of reality" (Jaeggi 2009, p. 68). They are mistakes because capitalist reality is itself distorted and the bourgeoisie makes this distortion its own.

28 Jaeggi, emphasizing the importance of the issue, writes:

> the critique of alienation would always presuppose an (objectively grounded) shape of purpose of true human existence from which one has become distanced in the alienated condition. Saying that something is alienated or that one becomes alienated from something suggests that there is something essentially 'one's own' from which one has become alienated.
>
> (Jaeggi 2014, p. 27)

29 Jaeggi seems to make her own that which she critiques when she writes that "the critique of alienation can then be conceived immanently and negativistically as a contradiction between the promise of modern self-determination and its non-fulfillment" (Jaeggi 2017, p. 342, translation mine). It is true that modernity is not a community, but it is also true that the mechanism is the same: it is a matter of evaluating the gaps between what is ideally promised and what is not actually kept.

30 This point reproduces the old socialist issue that the working class, once it becomes aware of its social existence, must follow the theory, and not what it wants.

31 Jaeggi describes four situations in which loss of control towards one's own existence can be emphasized; total absence of critical awareness of one's social roles; splitting between reality and basic needs; and loss of interest in any projectuality within one's own life (Jaeggi 2014, pp. 51–154). What the four cases have in common is being alienated, that is, the presence of a systematic "impairment of willing that results from a disappearance of the possibility of appropriating – of making one's own – one's self or the world" (Honneth 2014, p. IX).

32 Jaeggi also picks up this point. For her, "'working' means not just running smoothly, but always also 'doing a good job' in both a functional and an ethical sense" (Jaeggi 2009, p. 78). For her, however, unlike the perspective I am trying to develop, something that does not work well is always an expression of a "practical contradiction" (Ibidem). An expression that, as we have seen, carries with it a good many unresolved problems.

33 Indeed, this is a point that Jaeggi radically criticizes. For her,

> "every way of understanding the world is (…) perspectival, 'constructed', and establishing norms (…). To show this, however, is in itself not yet to criticize it (…). The critique of ideology would remain negative in the sense that it could criticize the social practices and institutional arrangements only for restricting the field of possibilities in general. This, however, would mean criticizing *every single particular* social practice or institution for being what they are, rather than criticizing *certain* social practices as wrong.
>
> (ivi, p. 72)

I emphasize that, even to criticize *certain* social practices, it is necessary to recognize them reflexively. The exploited worker, the alienated housewife, the frustrated homosexual must become reflexively aware of the inner meaning of their projects of action, perhaps even helped by someone in this reflexive process of theirs. But without this stage, an active and conscious involvement of the worker, the housewife, and the homosexual is not possible. Otherwise, there will be someone acting for them and giving them a pre-packaged answer. Moreover, how does one, within the infinite social practices, recognize those specific, certain practices that are false in themselves? Who decides that, and how? Are there internal contradictions within reality that must be brought to light, and that mark the fate of the subjects working within them? Here again, Adorno's position seems consistent to me: when the dialectic can only be negative, and we become aware that "the whole is the false" (Adorno 2005, p. 50), then "true thoughts are those alone which do not understand themselves" (ivi, p. 192). From the perspective of criticism

> perspectives must be fashioned that displace and estrange the world, reveal it to be, with its rifts and crevices, as indigent and distorted as it will appear one day in the messianic light. To gain such perspectives *without velleity or violence, entirely from felt contact with its objects* – this alone is the task of thought.
>
> (ivi, p. 247, italics mine)

A dialectic that becomes negative eliminates not only the end point of the process but also the internal logic that leads to that goal. What remains is the negative moment which, taken reflexively, becomes the ability to recognize suffering. Certainly, not all suffering can be placed on the same level, and not all is equally deserving of the same recognition. But even the suffering of the incarcerated murderer is a symptom of a lack, of a gap between the real and the possible. The Adornian idea, for simplicity's sake, is that all our plans for action are ultimately wrong, because it is impossible not to wrong ourselves and others: it is not possible to avoid halitosis. It is a matter, for those with courage and willingness to reflexively recognize the limitations of the concept and those of the praxis that follows, of questioning themselves, pointing out 'rifts and crevices'. Criticism is, at least in the first instance, 'negative'. It emerges from the unblind contact of the concept with reality, where by reality is meant primarily our relationship with others. And it needs reflexivity.

34 As we have already seen within the discussion around common sense, there can also be unreflexive change. It is the consequence of each individual reactivation of common sense: reproduction is never totally so. This kind of change generally takes a long time and is not visible, precisely because it is not reflexive.

35 For Schütz, this aspect is a consequence of the way we make sense of the world. Indeed,

> to be familiar with an object of our experience means not only to know sufficiently for the purpose at hand what this object is, but also what it is not. It is also to know that certain objects do not exist, that certain means are not available or suitable, that certain actions cannot be carried out in terms of our knowledge (…). In this sense we may say that we are familiar as well with the negative, we not only know that "*S* is *P*" but also that it is "non-Q". *Our belief in the world as it is involves our disbelief in what it is not.*
>
> (Schütz 1970, pp. 153–154)

The continuous oscillation between believing and not believing creates the situation of doubt, of uncertainty. Without this oscillation, one would probably not give thought as such.

36 According to Bell, "ideology is the conversion of ideas into social levers. Without irony, Max Lerner once entitled a book *Ideas Are Weapons*. This is the language of ideology" (Bell 1988, p. 400).

37 Searle highlights these aspects effectively. As he writes, "there are portions of the real world, objective facts in the world, that are only facts by human agreement. In a sense there are things that exist only because we believe them to exist (…) the complex structure of social reality is, so to speak, weightless and invisible". It seems as natural to us "as stones and water and trees". It always remains true, however, that "a social constructed reality presupposes a non socially constructed reality": the mountain I observe exists independently of my observation (Searle 1995, pp. 1, 4, 191).

38 On this topic, I point out the monographic issue in the journal *Sociologia e ricerca sociale*, with texts by Muzzetto, Nasu, Belvedere, Takakusa, Lopez, Venturini, Dreher, Santos and Susin, Meyer, and Oberzaucher (Muzzetto 2021b).

39 For Schütz, there is also a non-conscious dimension, which is not, however, entirely passive. It does not concern elements that are by definition excluded from the possibility of becoming reflexive, but only aspects that compose sedimentations of meaning that have remained contingently outside the 'cone of light' of reflexivity, from the application of thematic relevance. Schütz's use of Freud implies a concept

of the unconscious understood as a potentially active reservoir of meaning. On this point and, more generally, for the whole discussion on the subject of relevance, see Schütz (1970).

40 Schütz takes up here the Weberian theme of the transformation of causes into ends. For Weber, as is well known, the reconstruction of a historical event does not allow the identification of real causes, in the sense in which the concept is used in the natural sciences, but only allows the identification of more or less adequate means to motivate that event. The Sarajevo bombing – in which Bosnian Serb patriot Gavrilo Princip kills Franz Ferdinand, heir to the throne of the Habsburg Empire, and his wife Sofia – causes the outbreak of World War I only in the sense in which an accurate reconstruction shows that without that murder the war would not have broken out. It shows that that murder is more or less adequate means to an end, comparatively with other relevant events. The question to be asked is: without that murder, would the war have broken out equally? In the Weberian setting, this means two basic things: that that murder is not the sole cause of the outbreak of conflict and that the cause-effect relationship must be read as a means-end relationship. On this issue, see von Wright (1971); Psillos (2011).

41 To be constructivist is not to claim that all reality is just interpretation: the mountain in front of me is real, and it is not a mental construct of mine. Instead, the way I act towards it (do I return home or start the climb?) is the dense, and in some ways inextricable, result of my own autonomous reflexion, from more or less established plans of action. If I am an experienced climber, I will know how to correctly assess the danger of the thickening clouds ahead of me, since its interpretation is a process with which I am familiar: I interpret it from a background of knowledge within which the phenomenon I see becomes legible, on the basis of the past projects of action that have constituted that background. Only in this direction can past final motives appear to me, apparently, as causal motives.

42 On this point, I refer, for example, to MacIntyre's analysis of virtues (1981).

43 I do not set myself the task here to develop a normative theory of democracy, but only to show the possibility of a democratic and critical articulation of the relationship between civil society and the political sphere.

44 According to Laclau, "'the people' is not something of the nature of an ideological expression, but a real relation between social agents. It is, in other terms, one way of constituting the unity of the group" (Laclau 2005, p. 73). How is such a way constructed?

> We will call a demand which, satisfied or not, remains isolated a *democratic demand*. A plurality of demands which, through their *equivalential articulation*, constitute a broader social subjectivity we will call *popular demands* – they start, at a very incipient level, to constitute the 'people' as a potential historical actor. Here we have, in embryo, a populist configuration.
>
> (ivi, p. 74, the second italics are mine)

The two requirements of populism are: "1. the formation of an internal antagonistic frontier separating the 'people' from power; and 2. an equivalential articulation of demands making the emergence of the 'people' possible" (Ibidem). The people is a concrete relation that appears very abstract, however, because it is based on equivalential demands. As Laclau himself admits,

> there is a third precondition which does not really arise until the political mobilization has reached a higher level: the unification of these various demands – whose equivalence, up to that point, had not gone beyond a feeling of vague solidarity – into a stable system of signification.
>
> (Ibidem)

Everything seems a bit vague. The recognition of equivalential questions presupposes the existence of the people, the subject with respect to whom those questions, and not others, appear to be so. Moreover, antagonism towards power is opposed to what exactly? And with what level of radicality? What happens, finally, to the pluralism of questions if, if anything, 'a stable system of signification' were to be realized?

45 On leftist populism, see Damiani (2020). According to Damiani, populist parties of the radical left can be seen "as a political category intent on transforming the existing political equilibrium while excluding anti-systemic revolutionary action", within a situation "characterized by the fracture of the 'people' versus the 'élite'" so as to accelerate political disintermediation, "by facilitating direct appeals to the people against the governing élites responsible for, in this view, the conditions of widespread economic and social hardship experienced by a large part of the European population" (ivi, pp. 2, 4, 6).

46 Taking up a well-known Weberian category, the political leader no longer has the task of proposing values and constructing identities, but the equally challenging task of coherently articulating within a coordinated system of ends, values, and narratives that are not immediately complementary. One could thus speak of the *charisma of ends*.

47 I mean *political projects* and not *political programs*. A project is something broader than a program. The latter is the concretization of the project at, for example, election campaigns. A project can sustain the identity of a party and its constituents for a relatively large period, materializing over time in different political programs. The identity character lies in the project and not in the program. For example, one may share the former and not the latter. The reverse is unlikely to be true.

48 The Adornian conception of suffering resurfaces. One of the great problems of history is that we have always tried to realize values without thinking about the human costs. The first essential constraint on action must therefore become the conscious elimination of potential human costs from our projects of action.

5 Utopia

A Brief History of Utopia

We do not live in the everyday alone. Sometimes, a fresh wind blows through our lives. It comes from afar and sweeps us farther forward. Utopia is an expression of this wind. A present compressed into the everyday is an empty, meaningless space. Our actions would be mere praxis in their repetition. According to Adorno, "since Utopia was set aside and the unity of theory and practice demanded, we have become all too practical" (Adorno 2005, p. 44). To pose the question of utopia today is to oppose that unity, in search of a meaning that does not coexist with everyday practice, aware that a world dominated by production and consumption flattens us inside a series of disconnected moments. Gratification, recognition, and self-realization need time because they involve the investment of meaning. This is an ancient and profound truth, one that is pressing upon us with dramatic urgency today.

Within its complex history, "the word utopia stands in common usage for the ultimate in human folly or human hope" (Mumford 1962, p. 1). The nexus of madness and hope is found in the complex interplay between the two meanings of utopia: that of *eutopia*, or good place; and that of *outopia*, or non-place. Folly lies in thinking that hope can be fully realized. It lies in thinking that the good place can be a real place. The distinction between the two meanings and the risk of its erasure are already present in Bacon. The underlying mechanism is quite simple: every human community carries with it the ideal image of how it could be and in fact is not; consequently, it is inclined to think that the gap between real and ideal can be overcome.

This mechanism produces the conflict between conservation and change. Realized utopia is the attempt to eliminate this conflict, to think of a world in which no more change is possible because ideal and real coincide. Folly is thus a world with no more hope and no more conflict, desired by those who want to realize an ideal world, but also by those who oppose all change. The perfect future world and the irreducible defence of the present are two different ways of erasing hope, of thinking that the best has been achieved. Utopia itself can become an instrument of conservation, since hope can foster "inequality between the positions of élites, more or less aware of the

DOI: 10.4324/9781003229339-6

illusory nature of the proposed goals, and those of the masses that are all the more easily manipulated the more driven they are by uncontrolled needs for" (Crespi 1997, p. XI, translation mine).

The hyper-realist reactionary and the visionary dreamer basically make the same mistake: thinking that the best has already been achieved, or that it is ahead of us, attainable at any cost. The concept of utopia, in its meaning of a good place, needs the gap between ideal and real to be maintained: utopia, to survive, must remain a non-place. A history of utopias is therefore the history of how human communities have given themselves their own ideal image and how they have related to it. In most cases, they have remained abstract, unattainable, and unachieved models that have functioned as an ideal frame of reference. They are interesting, from a historical point of view, to reason upon how those who came before us would have liked to be and never managed to become.

The main classical utopias are an attempt to depict in detail an abstract world. Fantasy and substantivity form a strange and fascinating mixture. Utopia is the finishing point, the realization of eutopia, rather than the process by which humans react to their unhappy condition. The model par excellence is Plato's *Republic* (1981). This is a small community, perfectly integrated into its territory, in which balance and justice reign. Here justice is an expression of balance: the community functions because the divisions within it are organically organized, in equilibrium. Everyone performs their assigned task, and everyone has a task suited to their aptitudes. The division into classes is governed by the possession of virtues typical to each class: the ruler is the person who possesses wisdom and knowledge, not the child of rulers. The same is the case with warriors, who must possess the valour and courage necessary to defend the community. Temperance is the virtue of workers. The three virtues and the three classes are in harmony within the framework of a general spirit of citizen fellowship.[1] In this way, happiness is being oneself inside the community, because the community is able to recognize each citizen's aptitude and provide the citizen with the way to realize it. In modern terms, we might say that Plato's is not a political or even a commercial unit, but a civil union, based on the social relations among its individuals.

What really matters are the relationships between the functions exercised by different social classes, the balance between them, and the harmony between social function and subjective gratification. In a sense, it is a natural community, reproducing within itself the balance of nature, not least because it maintains a balanced relationship with the nature surrounding it. The key lies in the management of desires: happiness lies not in the explosion of desire and its satisfaction, but rather in the practice of those virtues that enable individual and collective equilibrium to be maintained. The community is happy because it is orderly. Education and training serve to create the conditions for this harmony to be maintained and not to be broken. The common good does not lie in increased consumption, nor in the conquest of foreign lands. It is not in the expression of trade or war. It lies in the maintenance of order, that is, the observance of justice and the achievement of happiness. Plato's Republic is historically impossible: it is the non-place that makes historical places possible. It can have no place except as the marker of a shortcoming.

After Plato, one has to wait for More for another secular utopia. Meanwhile, the otherworldly Christian utopia emerges, for which happiness is not for this world. It is the most typical example of what Mumford calls *utopias of escape*. Hope is projected into a reality that is not the result of human action, but the latter, in the name of that perfection, certainly does not refrain from demonstrating its folly. Interestingly, the Platonic idea of a balance based on rules and virtues is not entirely forgotten. An important example is the medieval monastic orders, which try to reproduce the maximum possible earthly perfection within functionally regulated communities. Consider, for example, the Benedictines or the Franciscans.

More's Utopia is the island that is not there, but it is perfectly and meticulously described (More 1965). It has 54 cities and one capital, Amaurota. The basic activity is agriculture, which everyone knows and can practice. Everyone works, so the workday is rather short, generally not exceeding six hours. Each family can freely meet their needs by taking from large public warehouses, as production is able to provide everyone with the necessities. The most menial and strenuous work is carried out by slaves, comprising the people who have committed crimes. Magistrates are entrusted with the task of giving those who have produced less, for reasons independent of their own will and effort, the surplus created by others. The whole island is thus one big family. Meals are eaten in communities, inside large buildings. Public kindergartens exist so that women can devote themselves to food preparation. There are also large hospitals, and the sick are given the best food.

Social organization – as well as economic and political organization – has at its base the family. Every year, 30 families choose their magistrate; for every ten magistrates, an arch-magistrate is chosen; all magistrates choose a prince – who remains in office for life – from a list of four people nominated by the inhabitants. All political organization is aimed at regulating and controlling economic activity. War is something of a residual activity: it is justified for the defence of the territory and is entrusted to the worst subjects, so that the best are preserved. As for the family, spouses can separate for good reason. Lastly, on the island, all religions are tolerated, as long as they do not cause violence.

The governing virtues are inspired by agreement with nature. This agreement has a rational basis, because nature and reason are in harmony with each other. To live in society is to live in accord with nature and reason: personal advantage cannot and should not result in any disadvantage to others. Even the pleasures people pursue are natural and dictated by reason: inordinate wealth 'without reason', for example, is not a pleasure. It is therefore necessary to recognize what fulfils the inhabitants as such – on the island, for example, education, reading and study, the art of music, etc., are encouraged – from whatever may distract them in futile and dangerous ways, such as power, wealth, and vainglory. Life in common, as in Plato's Republic, helps each person to be oneself, based, of course, on a definite idea of what it means to be.

The City of the Sun described by Campanella is a fantastical and far-fetched place suspended between dream and reality, a blend of astrology and mechanical invention (2018). It is a wonder that appears before the navigator who has become lost at sea. It has seven circles, four gates, and a huge temple dominating it. It is inhabited by an ideal community in which there is no private property, equality of the sexes reigns, and wives are communal. There is no slavery, because labour is worthy of respect. The inventions of technology reduce the workday to a few hours. The needs of the community prevail over those of individuals, creating a climate of thrifty and frugal communal living. Bacon's New Atlantis can be considered a variation on the theme (2008). The centre of this community is the scientific and technical activity that takes place in the House of Solomon, a kind of vast laboratory where a wide variety of experiments concerning mechanics, medicine, physics, agriculture, etc. take place. The basic idea is that science is the only tool that can really change the human condition: from a utopia based on collective virtues, we move, with Bacon, to a modern utopia, which believes in observation, science, and technology.

The later utopias, related to the development of the industrial revolution, follow the course indicated by Bacon. Equilibrium and justice are no longer the expression of a natural order, capable of bringing the parts and the whole into harmony, in an idealized world whether it is set close to home or beyond the oceans. Rather, they are the result of the feverish and human construction of social institutions capable of controlling and directing human passions: just as technology and industry transform the natural world, similarly they can provide the knowledge for a new world of harmony. Philosophy and the philosopher are replaced by technique and the social engineer, justice by science, temperance by organization.

The phalanstery of Fourier is the most striking example (1971). It is a small ideal community, within which the search for balance between public and private is no longer made in the name of philosophical or natural ideals but through the division and organization of labour, large-scale production, and the development of technologies. Material, social, and intellectual activities all respond to a common rational logic, so, inspired by it, institutions and concrete structures such as the factory, refectories, and libraries develop. Greatness and perfection are no longer the result of parsimony and frugality, but of production and its organization. Balance is no longer the consequence of the pursuit of the minimum but is achieved through the attainment of the maximum. Although the phalanstery[2] continues to be based on agriculture, its dominating spirit is that of the new industrial bourgeoisie, which Fourier seeks to bring out to its best.

The chaos produced by the uncontrolled liberation of productive capacities must be brought back within an order capable of making the most of those potentials, correcting the imbalances, injustices, and traumas that industrialization brings with it. All this is possible through the construction of small communities: in the face of the explosion of large urban aggregations, the management of numbers remains central. However, quality is pitted against quantity: the explosive power of large numbers must be subjected to mechanisms that can work only within circumscribed and replicable communities. The need for the rational organization of these communities makes the analysis of details all the more central: a feature that, in earlier utopias, takes the guise of fantastic and imaginative description – think of the City of the Sun – now takes the form of minute disquisitions on how it is most efficient to organize communal meals, access to libraries, division of labour, etc. The freedom of imagination is replaced by the rigour of early forms of planning.[3]

Henceforth, the utopias "become vast reticulations of steel and redtape". Mumford emphasizes "how little human significance remains in the post-eighteenth century utopia (...). These utopias are all machinery: the means has become the end, and the genuine problem of ends has been forgotten" (Mumford 1962, p. 147). These are *utopias of reconstruction*, in Mumford's words, comparing them to those of escape. The latter return in two important works: that of Morris (1970) and that of Wells (2006). Wells in particular, in *Modern Utopia*, depicts a world yearning to return to the classic models, aware of the problems that industrial modernity has produced. The society he envisions is the result of a great common project, taking shape in a world state and a single civilization. It is a kind of enlightened, multiracial, and tolerant technocracy governed – like Plato's Republic – by a caste of intellectuals, the Samurai, who live a simple and disciplined life. The utopia of the project lies in bringing to synthesis technique and humanity, autonomy and social order, individual and collective welfare, politics and the market. Work is embedded in a cooperative framework, within which everyone is expected to make his or her own contribution without the exploitation characteristic of capitalist enterprise. The world is interconnected and organized as a whole through a dense and functional network of transportation, a common energy system, and the development of modern communication technologies. Science and morality are complementary: the Samurai, who are entrusted with decisions on the most important economic and social initiatives, ensure such harmony on the basis of their superior learning.

All these utopias have much in common. In the classical ones, the element of communism, the idea of a satisfying life and frugal happiness, the pursuit of perfect harmony between part and whole, the management and compression of desire, the absence of money, the containment or cancellation of war, and the presence of an intellectually superior caste are elements that outline a natural perfection opposed to the corruption and degradation of the real world. In general, nature and reason find their own syntony by re-establishing a balance that can be broken in many ways but is eventually recomposed in the reconciliation of man and environment, whether social or natural.

After the upheavals wrought by the Industrial Revolution, the role of technology becomes central even in the world of utopias. Order and balance seem achievable through organization and planning, social control, and scientific development, even to the point of raising again the question of a balanced management of the relationship between science and humanism.

In general, I have always found all these utopian models claustrophobic. The prevailing sensation they provoke in me is the lack of ways out. Everything is meant to be precise and perfect, but with no exits. Within them, it seems to me that we live a repetitive and boring everyday life, rather than a serene and natural one. As Mumford encapsulates perfectly,

> The classic utopian writers, in attempting to extract the ideal element from the matrix of contemporary society, often by that very effort to achieve a purer form of community left out many necessary components which, like the baser elements in an alloy, fortify the precious metal and make it more serviceable.
>
> (Mumford 1962, p. 2)

The rational and systemic spirit, the idea that a perfect, working model can be constructed, make us forget that mud is just as useful as gold and is sometimes more fun. And, above all, they make us forget that reality is made of copious amounts of one and rare amounts of the other.

The End of Utopias?

Mannheim was among the first to sound the alarm. The end of ideologies and the world in which they prospered must not lead to the end of utopias. In *Ideology and Utopia*, Mannheim matches the three major ideologies – conservatism, liberalism, and socialism – with three forms of utopian mindsets: the *conservative ideal*, the *liberal-humanitarian ideal*, and the *socialist-communist utopia*. This correspondence is explained, according to Mannheim, through the complex relationship between conservation and change: social classes capable of carrying with them an entire worldview produce ideologies and utopias depending on whether their underlying predisposition is better aimed at conserving or at changing the world. For Mannheim, not every transcendent model is a utopia. Utopia is a set of ideas that not only transcends reality but also aims to transform it. Therefore, it is not easy to distinguish ideology and utopia. The same model can be both: "what in a given case appears as utopian, and what as ideological, is dependent, essentially, on the stage and degree of reality to which one applies this standard" (Mannheim 1997a, p. 176). In the modern world, gone is the idea that utopia is something unattainable in principle; utopia means something "which seems to be unrealizable only from the point of view of a given social order which is already in existence" (ivi, p. 177).

It is important to stress the change undergone. In classical utopias, utopia is the ideal model of a real, fundamentally united community. The community finds its core values realized to the fullest in utopia. The detailed description of life within the ideal community is intended to demonstrate the gap between perfection and imperfection, the latter identified in its various guises: think, for example, of the various forms of degeneration of the Republic described by Plato. In the modern world, by contrast, the community is internally divided, and utopias are expressions of the conflict running through it. Thus, what is ideology for some is utopia for others, and vice versa. Utopia acquires a relative character because it is an expression of the dynamic and conflicting character of modern society, expressed by the social classes and their different and opposing worldviews. In this way, the relationship between the two meanings of the term also changes profoundly: what is eutopia for some may not be so for others, and, at the same time, what may seem utopian today may be ideology tomorrow. In Mannheim's words,

> Whenever an idea is labelled utopian it is usually by a representative of an epoch that has already passed. On the other hand, the exposure of ideologies as illusory ideas, adapted to the present order, is the work generally of representatives of an order of existence which is still in process of emergence.
>
> (ivi, p. 183)

All this profoundly changes the relationship between theory and praxis. Utopias are projects for the transformation of the world, sustained by social subjects who do not recognize themselves in the existing order. This is why utopia is no longer the lost island beyond the oceans. The distinction between ideology and utopia expresses the mutual indictment between conflicting subjects: those who want to change accuse those who want to preserve, of ideology; the latter, in turn, will say that the former's world is a vain dream, a utopia. For both, for ideology and utopia, there is a need for the formation of a collective consciousness capable of producing political history, through social conflict. It is necessary, for example, for class consciousness to develop, to use the Marxian term. Moreover, there is a need for a model of utopia that is entirely different from the Platonic model, which is abstract and absolute, static and outside of history. Instead, the ideas that make up a utopia are rationally conceived ends that, projected into an abstract future, become regulatory models of everyday action: "the utopian view sees the world moving in the direction of a realization of its aims" (ivi, p. 202).

History is set in motion by the social conflict between subjects of various contrasting worldviews. While

> the deepest driving forces of the liberal ideas of the Enlightenment lay in the fact that it appealed to the free will and kept alive the feeling of being indeterminate and unconditioned (...) conservative mentality as such has

> no predisposition toward theorizing. This is in accord with the fact that human beings do not theorize about the actual situations in which they live as long as they are well adjusted to them.
>
> (ivi, p. 206)

What the Enlightened projects into the future, the conservative finds already realized in the present.[4] Liberal abstraction contrasts with conservative concreteness.[5] Finally, the socialist utopia, for Mannheim, on one hand, takes up the liberal conception of an idea that is projected into the future; on the other hand, it "places this future at a much more specifically determined point in time, namely the period of the breakdown of capitalist culture" (ivi, p. 216). The liberal realm of future freedom becomes a clearly identifiable and tangibly achievable goal from the concrete historical dynamic.[6]

Utopia is now an expression of the modern way of reading the relationship between theory and praxis and of considering the historical force of ideas:

> A veritable Copernican revolution occurred when man began to regard not merely himself, not merely man, but also the existence, the validity, and the influence of these ideas as conditioned factors and the development of ideas as bound up with existence, as integral to the historical-social process.
>
> (ivi, p. 220)

From utopia understood as an abstract model of perfection, we turn to the idea of the possibility of realizing that perfection concretely: eutopia can become a place since ideas act in history. It is a possibility contained in the present and only needs to be realized. The idea becomes the internal leaven of a historical process, of a more or less ineluctable tendency, which pushes towards its realization. Praxis is now capable of realizing the idea. Incidentally, while classical utopias were very detailed non-places, communism, for example, is an indeterminate place, the exact details of which are not well known. The latter, if one trusts the idea, will be the result of the historical process, of that fundamental historical tendency that only needs to be indulged and to which, of course, someone holds the keys. The strength of the idea, together with the indeterminacy of the result, thus ends up justifying virtually everything.

The end of ideologies, namely the end of a society divided into recognizable social classes, marks the end of this possibility. The mutual unmasking, the general use of the total conception of ideology, ultimately proves that the good world is good for some, and not for all, because it is someone's world and not everyone's. Along with ideology, according to Mannheim, utopia is thus in danger of disappearing too. While the end of the former indicates only the overcoming of a specific way of articulating the relationship between culture and structure, in essence of a certain form of social stratification, the end of the latter may imply the end of the possibility of thinking of a future. Can our existence be enclosed within a relentless present? According to Mannheim,

> It would require a callousness which our generation could probably no longer acquire or the unsuspecting naïveté of a generation newly born into the world to be able to live in absolute congruence with the realities of the world, utterly without any transcendent element, either in the form of a utopia or of an ideology.
>
> (ivi, p. 230)

Mannheim, making himself the speaker of a generation that is still sensitive to the world in which it lives, thinks it is necessary and incumbent to construct new narratives projected into the future. His sociology of knowledge seeks to be an original reading of the relationship between being and thought, between structure and superstructure, capable of being, at the same time, an analysis and diagnosis of reality.

The answer, of course, does not lie in the new totalitarian narratives. They are, for Mannheim, no longer ideologies but new modern mythologies, which merge substantive irrationality – the reference to irrational myths, such as nation or race – with instrumental rationality – the unscrupulous use of technology and planning as instruments of social control. Not surprisingly – unlike conservative, liberal, and socialist ideologies – fascism, according to Mannheim – is incapable of producing its own utopia. Just as realized communism, in its becoming totalitarian madness, is incapable of keeping alive the hope of change. Are totalitarianisms realized utopias? That they think they have built the place within which only adaptation is possible, and all sensibility must be silenced? As we have seen, totalitarianism, if the category can have a scientific and not merely polemical sense, is a social reality that imposes itself as something with no alternative. Mannheim is effective in showing that the end of the active dimension is achieved both in a perspective of preservation – fascism – and in that of change – realized communism. A perfect world erases the protagonism of social actors. Within it, collective consciousness is a mere reproduction of the ruling narrative.

All this takes place within the time of humankind, and not in a transcendent dimension external to history. As Taylor writes, in the modern world

> We are dealing with a story in purely secular time. The sense that the present, post-founding order is right has to be expressed in terms that consort with this understanding of time. We can no longer describe it as the emergence of a self-realizing order lodged in higher time.
>
> (Taylor 2004, p. 175)

A praxis that has lost the reference to an external abstract model – whether metaphysical or religious – yields a credible realization of the impossible within history:

> People become capable of making a decisive break with age-old forms and structures that impede or distort the moral order. Suddenly it becomes possible to carry out the demands of this order as never before. There is a heady sense that everything is possible.
>
> (ivi, p. 176)

The totalitarian myth and the myth of the revolution – whether of class or race – are the expressions of this liberation, of the very real possibility of disproportion, of the lack of limit.

How to deal with this question today? Is utopia still possible? Reflecting on the end of ideology, Bell writes that

> There is now, more than ever, some need for utopia, in the sense that men need – as they have always needed – some vision of their potential, some manner of fusing passion with intelligence. Yet the ladder to the City of Heaven can no longer be a "faith ladder", but an empirical one: a utopia has to specify *where* one wants to go, *how* to get there, the costs of the enterprise, and some realization of, and justification for the determination of *who* is to pay.
>
> (Bell 1988, p. 405)

Attention must turn to the process, with in mind, of course, an idea of the point of arrival. But this point must not justify everything.

The utopias briefly described so far are characterized by emphasizing the characteristics of the ultimate point of arrival, of the *model* to be built, forgetting the nature and strength of the *process* by which we get there. The theoretical aspect, the ability to draw the model in the abstract, takes over from the practical, the actions that will actually lead to the realization of the model. As we have seen above, if praxis needs narrative frames of reference to set itself in motion, at the same time theory is always concretely realized, and this embracing of the rigidity of the abstract model can penalize the creative and dynamic role of practical human actions and the possibilities they can always unlock. Utopias thus run the risk of designing an abstract perfect world, which becomes hideous the moment someone believes they can actually realize it.

Bell is right: utopia must no longer be a ladder of faith because the stronger the faith, the greater the damage. But nor can it be empirical: if it were as Bell describes it, it would be a common project of action, highly detailed, but not a utopia. Utopia need be neither 'utopian' nor 'realistic'. It is about identifying that point of no return where hope becomes folly. It is about controlling the disproportion of thought that justifies all praxis. The endeavour, then, is to give voice to hope that is a little crazy, but not insane.

Real Utopias

In the literature of recent years, this theme is very much present. Emerging is the need to rethink utopia, to restore meaning to human experience, and this includes through narratives that can provide an image of the future. In a period of accelerating time (Rosa 2010), in which the past disappears as soon as it has been experienced and the future is so mysterious that it eludes all prediction, there is a need to construct far-reaching horizons, without which both individual and collective identity dissolve.

In this context, a new conception of utopia must include the potential for building projects of experience of a certain scope within the relationship between theory and praxis, valorizing both. As Weber would say, a balance must be pursued in the relationship between values and means, conviction and responsibility, action and beliefs. This becomes crucial in a world that appears increasingly dominated by technology and a technology-centred narrative that wants to be neutral but is not neutral. The autonomy of the medium, as Weber makes clear, is always and only apparent: it is always in the service of an end, which can be concealed, but not obliterated. The critique of rationalization consists precisely of this: the neutrality and objectivity of technology are only presumptions; they construct a world, not the world. It is therefore a matter of recognizing the nature of that world that is being built around us without apparently anyone wanting it, to collectively regain responsibility for choice. In this sense, democracy and utopia can be closely intertwined with each other today.

Utopia therefore appears in the form of the process, rather than that of the result. Of a directed process, but one that possesses its own autonomy as the story of a progressive unfolding that tends to pursue a goal, never perfectly attainable. In this perspective, two recent proposals seem to me to proceed: the *real utopias* of Wright (2010) and the *everyday utopias* of Cooper (2014). The character of reality and that of the everyday come to meet the need expressed above: that of having *concrete utopias* available, which have the character of both projection into the future and action in the present.

Wright's book fits into a Marxist frame of reference. It is a wholly particular Marxism, which, without making use of the Hegelian dialectic – and which therefore dispenses with the notions of alienation, contradiction, immanent critique, ideology, reification, etc.[7] – seeks to reinterpret the concepts of self-realization and emancipation within a model of radical democracy. To be sure, other central elements of classical Marxism are missing. For example, Wright notes that a theory of transformation somewhat akin to Marxian historical materialism is completely unworkable today: "I do not believe that this classical theory or the immanent tendencies of social change is satisfactory, but neither do I believe that any compelling alternative has yet been developed" (Wright 2010, p. 28). Acknowledging this situation, which signals an unbridgeable gap between the knowledge available and the long-term horizons of social change, defines a decisive feature of the concept of real utopia: on one hand, the substantive requires a courageous gaze that looks far ahead; on the other hand, the adjective requires a precise definition of tangibly achievable goals on the basis of the knowledge currently available. Moreover, Wright rejects statist solutions, such as that of real communism: the role of capitalism and the market, which are mutually detachable, must be evaluated on the basis of the concrete needs of democratic institutions and not condemned a priori: "capitalism is not the root of all evils in the world today" (ivi, p. 38). Finally, Wright criticizes the Marxian theory of the implosion of capitalism, which he says can be identified in four aspects: intensification of crises, theory of progressive proletarianization, theory of the development of class consciousness, and theory of revolution. In essence, according to Wright, the internal determinism of this position should be criticized: capitalism can be transformed, not necessarily wiped out.

The aspect of Wright's proposal mostly in keeping with the perspective of a finalist theory of action lies in its focus on the motivations of actors. According to Wright, "our real task is to try to think of institutions which themselves are capable of dynamic change, of responding to the needs of the people and evolving accordingly, rather than institutions which are so perfect that they need no further change" (ivi, pp. IX–X). Real utopia is embodied in institutions that know how to change to meet people: therefore, it is not a point of arrival, and it does not match perfect institutions. On the contrary, utopia lies in the provision of institutions capable of continuous evolution, which therefore recognize their inherent imperfection. It lies somewhere between the design of abstract perfect models and the achievement of small reforms potentially achievable in the immediate term: in short, it is a forward-looking and radical reformism, able "to provide empirical and theoretical grounding for radical democratic egalitarian visions of an alternative social world" (ivi, p. 1).

Emphasis is placed on the political sphere as the dimension that enables the unfolding of social power. The model of radical democracy designed in its broad outlines by Wright is the instrument that, through the reabsorption of the economy under democratic control, aims to develop social participation and power of subjects as much as possible. A social science of emancipation, according to Wright, has the task of making a critical diagnosis of society, imagining alternatives to reality, and designing paths of transformation. These three tasks must put at their centre the analysis and transformation of institutions: the criterion by which to evaluate their efficiency and performance lies in their ability to realize individual potentialities. The egalitarian principle tends to eliminate as much as possible not only, and perhaps not primarily, class inequalities but also those related to race, gender, education, and disabilities so that potentially everyone has free access to the material and immaterial tools necessary for individual self-realization. In keeping with Fraser (2008; Fraser, Honneth 2004), the politics of recognition must be complementary to the politics of material distribution of goods. The idea of self-realization coincides for Wright with that of real individual freedom: "people should have as much control as possible over those decisions which affect their lives".[8] This possibility can be guaranteed, as stated above, through a model of radical democracy: " 'democracy' is the power to participate in the effective control of collective choices that affect one's life as a member of the wider society" (Wright 2010, p. 18).

While capitalism is not the root of all evils, it does produce many. In a nutshell, for Wright, the current economic system perpetuates eradicable forms of suffering; prevents the universalization of opportunities for human prosperity; reproduces eliminable deficits of personal freedom and autonomy; violates egalitarian principles of social justice; produces inefficiency; induces an ineradicable tendency towards consumerism; is destructive of the environment; threatens established communitarian values; fuels militarism and imperialism; and tends to limit democracy (ivi, pp. 33–85). There is enough to look for alternatives. Wright's proposal lies in democratic development: that is, there is a need to develop a "democratic egalitarian organization of economy and society" (ivi, p. 89), of a profoundly socialist inspiration. Leaving all forms of determinism behind, according to Wright,

> The best we can do is to think of the project of emancipatory social change as a voyage of exploration. We leave the well-known world with a *compass* that shows us the direction we want to go, and an *odometer* which tells us how far from our point of departure we have travelled, but without a map which lays out the entire route from the point of departure to the final destination.
>
> (ivi, p. 108, italics mine)

Consequently, the greater part of the author's proposal is to define what a socialist compass can consist of today, having abandoned the Marxist presuppositions mentioned above. It is the harmony between democracy and socialism: "if 'democracy' is the label for the subordination of state power to social power, 'socialism' is the term for the subordination of economic power to social power" (ivi, p. 121). Wright's socialism proposes itself as a real and viable alternative to capitalism and statism and, by leveraging the development of social power as opposed to state and economic power, aims at strengthening a model of democracy whose beating heart is civil society, capable of independently managing market and state.

If this is the compass, Wright points to a number of possible steps that can gradually increase social empowerment. Particularly interesting among these are the development of the social economy, through which civil society, instead of acting as a curb on economic power, directly organizes various aspects of economic activity; the various forms of direct democracy, such as participatory municipal budgeting or random-selected citizens' assemblies; the development of associations and associational democracy; an unconditional basic income, which should enable every person to have a decent life; the development of the cooperative market economy; etc. These are steps in the right direction, even if the end result is not perfectly defined or even guaranteed. Since the heart of Wright's socialism lies in the development of social empowerment, it will be precisely civil society, exercising its power, that will define case by case how to adapt to the circumstances the aims indicated by the socialist compass.[9] In short, "the idea of 'real utopias' embraces this tension between dreams and practice" (ivi, p. 6).

Everyday Utopias

We find the same productive tension between dreams and practice in Cooper's work. Her attempt is to transport utopia to inside everyday life: real utopias are for her *everyday utopias*. The underlying idea is that invention within the everyday may have a conceptual reach beyond its situational boundaries. Through the description of six real cases – the realm of touch and feel within equality governance, public nudism, the ethics of care in a public Turkish bath for women and transgendered people in Toronto, the role of non-monetary economic transactions in the development of integrated communities in the West Midlands, the idea of property as belonging developed in Summerhill School, and the market play unfolding at Speaker's Corner in Hyde Park in London – Cooper seeks to show how the practice of everyday invention can have an unexpected reach and can become a harbinger of broader innovations. What is striking about the six cases is precisely the mixture of practical aspects, which impact the everyday lives of individuals, and the general scope of the issues they raise and potentially bring to public attention. Everything stems from the belief that change can have its basis in the micro-social dimension, in the ordinary and only seemingly mundane gestures of everyday life, capable of becoming the basis of new narratives. There is no theory that shows the way from the outside: rather, it is innovative social practices that point to possible broader strategies, bringing general issues to the table, even unintentionally.

Subjects become protagonists in their everyday lives and, in doing so, show paths of hope. The possible and the alternative are not thematized, but rather practiced within experiences that remain niche. As Cooper writes,

> Everyday utopias don't focus on campaigning or advocacy. They don't place their energy on pressuring mainstream institutions to change, on winning votes, or on taking over dominant social structures. Rather they work by creating the change they wish to encounter, building and forging new ways of experiencing social and political life.
>
> (Cooper 2014, p. 24)

The possible becomes immediately doable because it loses its cognitive dominance: it is innovation which becomes a reality that impacts the world of possibilities, opening up its perspectives. In this way, practices become the engine of deliberation, since they are not the implementation of an abstract model, but the direct concretization of an innovative idea within the everyday. The process that is activated, even through its failures, needs continuous adaptation and change, thus stimulating reflexion.

Let us see, in summary, the main characteristics of these experiences. Everyday utopias do not need an abstract model to refer to; they are not realized in imaginary worlds, but close to home. Their presence does not form an extraordinary occasion but invades the everyday because these are available and accessible places that focus on being in proximity. The critique they embody is not abstract and ideal but concrete and operational because it is based on innovation that has made itself real. They do not cover the entire experience of the subjects involved, but they cut across it in significant ways. Theirs is not the intention to completely change people's lives, but only the more modest intention of offering alternative glimpses, places of self-realization, and experimentation. They do not, by any means, constitute perfect places. They are expressions of social pluralism, in the same vein in which I have tried to characterize it in the previous chapters: the subjects who populate these experiences are ordinary citizens and include women, the poor, immigrants, transgenders, and other minorities. The politics that inspire them are varied and multifaceted, as they concern social democracy, queer feminism, egalitarianism, communitarianism, localism, etc. Most importantly, in Cooper's intentions, they have the potential to revitalize a radical progressive perspective through the operationalization of concepts such as equality, property, market, labour, etc. in alternative ways to the dominant ones. In this way, they can also provide the impetus for a broader conceptualization of those concepts, potentially capable of offering a broader and more general impact.

All these aspects raise the question of the relationship between everyday utopias and social transformation. For Cooper, everyday utopias seem to be able to serve a dual function: to construct alternative real experiences; to offer the cue for a more general conceptualization, useful for broader processes of transformation. As the book's subtitle states, these inventive social *promising spaces* can have *conceptual life* beyond their size. They are small, everyday realities capable, however, of showing the way, raising questions, and issuing challenges that pure reflection would not be able to see, or at least would see in a more abstract, merely formulaic way. The issue, in my view, is at the heart of Cooper's book and underlies the concrete examples studied. It is thematized as the relationship between imagination to actualization: the former emphasizes the dimension of fantasy and abstraction; the latter that of concreteness, of real structures and praxis. Imagination that wants to become reality in the immediate, without building the perfect world of the future, must necessarily circumscribe its impetus: the future is here and now, inside this steam room, in this specific corner of Hyde Park, in this particular school. Cooper starts with the idea that "concepts are not abstract generalities floating above the 'real' world; they are not elements in some kind of autonomous mental film through which a material life 'below' becomes intelligible" (ivi, pp. 35–36).

This fact redefines the relationship between success and failure:

> If concepts are not representations of states of affairs, and if practices lend themselves to dissenting readings, the failure of practices is never

> really a failure. The non-coincidence between how the practice is imagined and how it is enacted offers continuous resources for re-contextualizing it.
> (Croce 2016, p. 17, translation mine)

Moreover, thinking, for example, about the potential of the concept of equality not only on the abstract normative level but within concrete practices – as in the example of nudism, or Summerhill School – can highlight other various concrete possibilities as yet unexplored. It is not only the imagination that moves practices, but the latter can stimulate the former, providing glimpses of new alternatives and prompting speculation.[10]

That said, what then can be the relationship between concept and reality, between theory and practice? Cooper's answer is in keeping with what has been argued in previous chapters: "since neither imagination not material practice can ever adequately capture or respond to the other, oscillation remains inevitable and ceaseless" (ivi, p. 37), so that "what is imagined and what is done reinforce each other" (ivi, p. 225). The point, for a theory of utopia that does not remain confined to the albeit significant everyday practices, is how to enhance the potential of both practices and concepts. Discussing oscillation and mutual reinforcement is important, but it cannot suffice. We need to find a theoretical and practically viable arrangement that articulates the relationship between imagination and actualization, between theory and praxis, more explicitly and coherently.

Freely Feasible Utopias

I call *freely feasible utopias* broad projects of action that can involve several generations.[11] How broad the scope of the utopias,[12] both in a temporal and spatial sense, depends on the project of action they incorporate. Of course, the more visionary and challenging the latter is, the more utopian the utopia it entails.

This has to do with distance from the everyday. Every project of action is in fact embedded in the everyday. If I am now tired of writing and plan to go out to get coffee at the coffee shop below my house, this project will consist of a series of actions – save the file, turn off the computer, leave the house, get to the coffee shop, etc. – mutually coherent and striving towards the end. The project incorporates causal motives – tiredness? – and final – taking a walk and enjoying a coffee. In all this, there is nothing utopian, and the project seems entirely feasible. It is firmly anchored within the everyday and depends almost solely upon myself and has nothing utopian about it. The intentional sense, once I have reflexively made the decision to go out, flows without predictable hiccups, unreflexively, because it is dominated by daily routines. Even my entire day, which while it may include several such unplanned projects of action, generally flows within the routines of common sense.

I can, however, always recognize by a reflexive act increasingly broader ends, which extend beyond the temporal bounds of the single day and break out of the everyday. I thus trigger a process of *progressive departure from the everyday*, depending on the temporal and spatial scope of the project that I reflexively bring to light. The closer I stay to the present, to the everyday, the opaquer my vision remains, trapped in routines. My now-and-thus remains opaque to myself as long as it remains so. The reflexive act that gives meaning to the present requires a projection of the gaze that extends to the temporal dimension, which articulates my now-and-thus within a past projected into the future. The writing of the book that is now engaging me is part of a project of action that goes beyond a single day, which has covered much of the last few months and will cover several more. Meaning appears only within the project, which becomes visible by lifting me out of the opacity of the present: it is the connection between actions that constitutes meaning in its narrative. Of course, this specific project could also be part of an even larger design, the broad outlines of which I may have defined, but the details of which I now, in the specific moment I am actually living, do not know. The farther I move away from the everyday, the more the plan of action becomes less precise and detailed, and less coherent, because, by engaging the reflexive and imaginative effort, it involves a distancing from routines. The meticulous planning of extensive projects, covering years or even decades of subjects' existences, not only appears in itself inhuman and a form of absurdity, but it obviously encounters obstacles and contingencies independent of subjective intentions, which belong to the external, social, and natural world to which the subjects belong.

The feasibility of utopias implies however the impossibility of defining them in detail. Unlike the classical and literary utopias, in which fantasy and desire to design a perfect ideal world prompt meticulous details, far-reaching projects of action do not allow the same precision. We have seen above that the project of action is done by doing: this is all the more true for utopian projects. Every choice corresponds to a crossroads, which excludes some possibilities while it opens up unknown ones. The relationship between intentionality and reflexivity – which allows one to question the taken for granted and to continually adapt the project to circumstances and imagination – cannot be defused. Change has no internal law that indicates its necessary point of arrival: change shifts internally all the time, especially if one constantly keeps open the potentially critical mechanism that underlies the production of meaning. Of course, it is possible to keep the rod straight towards a goal: but the more long term and demanding this goal is, the more one can only define its general and indispensable features, features that will undergo unforeseen variations over time. Let us now use our compass in a broad and undefined territory. In this sense, freely feasible utopias concern the future, but above all they engage the present: the character of doable concerns our concrete relationship with the everyday, the steps we take every day. The sense of possibility internal to feasible utopias is not a precisely delineated goal concerning an inaccessible, dreamed future: rather, it implies a close connection with everyday reality.[13]

The relationship between intentionality and reflexivity, that is, the fact that one can still reflect on the beliefs underlying our intentions at any time, guarantees a certain elasticity to one's project of action, an elasticity that reasonably increases as one moves away from the everyday. If I were to set myself the task of writing an encyclopaedia of the knowledge produced by the social sciences in the coming decades, I would have to reckon not only with the boundless utopian ambition of the project but also with a number of conditions that make it difficult to foresee, no matter how much I might plan for it, how the project might unfold. Moreover, any step in that direction can only be internal to my everyday life, since it is the only place that belongs to me, outside of which nothing else exists. Even the largest and craziest project imaginable can only be based on an ineradicable *rootedness in the everyday*. The most ambitious and far-reaching utopia, which pushes desire and imagination beyond all reason, can only move within the everydayness of human beings and its ineluctable predictability.

The inescapable connection between departure and rootedness in the everyday is directly related to the finalistic structure of action and the complex and unpredictable relationship between intentionality and reflexivity. In a sense, the everyday is everything, because subjective experience is concretized there; at the same time, it is nothing, because it always refers back to something else, to the ineradicable relationship between meaning and time, ignoring which we would be left with only the blind mechanism of routines. The intended meaning of which everyday life is full always refers back to that structure of time which, pushing behind us, projects us into a future, more or less uncertain and definite, that lies ahead. Be it even the coffee waiting for us at the café downstairs. In this vein, all utopias are everyday, in the sense that, although they are projects of action that most of all distance us from the day-to-day, they nevertheless remain rooted in it, subject to the logic that governs it.

Of course, not all the quotidian is utopian. The everyday utopias discussed by Cooper are utopias because they carry with them something that is beyond the ordinary, that is not yet realized in it, and that is not common sense. The politics of equality, nudist demonstrations, the questioning of property relations, the use of an unofficial currency, and a market that plays itself out express an unrealized desire, a capacity for imagination that has not yet materialized into taken-for-granted routines. They are concretions laden with potential, potentialities that may remain opaque to the protagonists, but that emerge powerfully at the topical moments of their activities, thus providing the cognitive fuel capable of sustaining the broad projects of action embedded therein. What matters, beyond the concrete specificity of the cases studied, is their utopian 'conceptual power', the ability to challenge significant pieces of common sense by realizing practical and alternative experiences.

For simplicity's sake, I have spoken of individual utopias – in my case, writing not only a book but even an encyclopaedia – but the underlying conceptual structure would not change if projects of action involving larger collectivities were set in motion. In this case, the progressive departure from the everyday also increases under the influence of this latter variable: the larger the reference group, and thus the more extensive and universal the project of action, the more necessary a far-reaching reflexive gaze becomes. To take one example, even communism – understood as the society where human nature finds its fullest realization, which realizes the complementarity of freedom and necessity – thus displays all its utopian nature, despite the fact that one may think, as a certain Marxism did, that one arrives at it guided by a positive science of society. In short, the freely feasible utopia is a *determinable indeterminacy*: every possible thematization always continues to contain something unthought of that reflexion can bring to light. It is, as it were, a journey with an end, but never-ending.

The available stock of knowledge makes it possible to predict the future in the form of anticipation, under the assumption of repeatability in their typical form of past-occurring events. To take a trivial example, I am not surprised if a traffic light turns red, and I know how to react, automatically. At the same time, that stock forms the fundamental sense base from which to define new projects of action, broadly defining their course. The new project of action connects with the original available stock of knowledge, interacting with it and in some ways modifying it. What is realized, the determinable doable, thus always brings with it new potentialities, opening up a new indeterminacy. It always remains that "the limit beyond which the subject's action stops is represented by the project" (Sacchetti 2013, p. 41, translation mine). The indeterminate is not entirely so, because it is grafted onto the dimension of the possible from what has been determined. The utopian project extends in time this unbreakable link, projecting the present into a far-reaching temporal space, a present oscillating perpetually between the poles of opacity and transparency, of intentionality and reflexivity.

As Schütz writes, "the assumption of a perfect knowledge of future events by a finite mind leads to unsoluble inconsistencies" (Schütz 1962, p. 281). The example of Tiresias clarifies. Unlike the seer, the ordinary individual interprets their placement in time from an available stock of knowledge; they are directly involved in what they anticipate and are never simply a disinterested observer; the subject is placed within a fully socialized situation, and their experience is not an expression of an entirely private world.[14] How is the anticipation of common sense distinguished from utopian anticipation? While the former remains mostly within routines – my project of having a coffee at the café – utopian anticipation expands the relationship between determinacy and indeterminacy, moving from the former to open up the world of the possible within a far-reaching project of action. The validity of the first type of anticipation "is founded on the assumption that some or all of my fellow-men will find in their stock of knowledge at hand typically similar elements" (ivi, p. 282). The validity of *utopian anticipation*, while necessarily also having to rely on the kind of predictability typical of the former, is more open-ended and unpredictable: reflexivity continually at work uncovers feasible possibilities that are not necessarily realizable. In a sense, "all anticipations in commonsense thinking of daily life are made *modo potentiali*, in term of chance" (ivi, p. 287). Ultimately, I cannot rule out that the café below is closed, or that on my way down the stairs I receive a phone call that compels me to postpone the coveted coffee. Instead, it makes a difference that my project of action will involve open horizons, open to a temporal extension that is difficult to control and predict, full of anticipations whose content will be fully evident to me only when the anticipated event happens.

There is, however, a profound difference between *projecting* and *fantasying*: "projecting is more than mere fantasying. Projecting is motivated fantasying" (ivi, p. 289), rooted within the system of relevance that structures the project. Here, too, the dimension of utopia introduces a specific element. While in abstract and literary utopias we have fantasy without a project, and in everyday life mostly projects without fantasy, the sphere of freely feasible utopias articulates this relationship in an original way, combining fantasy and project in an endless dynamic. The utopian project cannot be closed to fantasy, not only in the moment of design but also within its realization: it always, again, requires both project and fantasy. The feasibility of the utopian possibly implies a continuous exercise of projectual imagination because it requires the ability to handle events beyond subjective control and requires an ineradicable relationship with the unexpected: "my anticipations concerning events in the world beyond my control are codetermined by my hopes and fears" (Ibidem). Utopia continually tests our ability to manage hope and fear because it lives in the unstable and precarious balance between the certainty and reliability of everyday opacity and the unexpectedness of the possible. When we project "we know that what we anticipate carries along open horizons" (ivi, p. 293). Most of our horizons lie in the opaque repetition of routines, so that only the unexpected reminds us of that openness that the everyday conceals. The horizons we envision in utopian projects, on the contrary, always keep alive if they do not want to deny their nature, that dimension of openness, of a possibility that continually brings hopes and fears into play.

The freely feasible utopia constitutes an inextricable nexus of predictability and unpredictability, within which the latter is not only a consequence of external factors but also an indispensable ingredient of the utopian project, characterizing it in its essence. According to MacIntyre, four sources of *systematic unpredictability* are given in matters human. The first is related to radical innovation, which cannot be predicted. MacIntyre gives the example of the wheel: predicting the invention of the wheel is impossible, because while making my prediction I try to describe the object of invention and, by describing it, I, in fact, invent it. The second is related to the fact that the unpredictability of our future actions produces unpredictability at a social level. For example, if I have not yet decided whether to spend or save my recent pay rise, the unpredictability of my future action has – minimal – implications for the current unpredictability of markets. This unpredictability can be put another way: since "omniscience excludes the making of decisions" (MacIntyre 1981, p. 96), it is very difficult to eliminate unpredictability from the social world. The third recalls the difficulties in applying game theory in social life. Individual reflexivity implies the impossibility of effective prediction: for example, playing chess, in order to predict the move of alter, I must predict that alter predicts what I predict that alter predicts ... ad infinitum: at each stage of the game, "each of us will simultaneously be trying to render himself or herself unpredictable to the other" (ivi, p. 97). Each situation is always characterized by imperfect knowledge. Moreover, each situation brings into play multiple games that are played simultaneously at the level of both identity and interests, sometimes inexplicit.[15] Finally, unlike simulations performed ex post, actors in real life find themselves in a situation that is not as transparent to them as it is to those facing it head on, based on known conditions that do not change. The fourth source is simple contingency. MacIntyre gives the paradoxical example whereby Cleopatra's nose is the basis for the founding of the Roman Empire. Contingencies, beyond the paradox contained in the example, matter.

The four sources of unpredictability are systematic, which precludes the fact that in the future a genie – or a supercomputer – can make predictable what is not predictable today, avoiding the conditions of social unpredictability. Recalling Wittgenstein, according to MacIntyre the language used by that genius, as a mere private language will always and inherently prove to be completely unintelligible. The decisive point is that unpredictability and predictability are closely intertwined. Thus, there are at least as many sources of predictability of human actions. The first derives from the notion of project of action, or, to use MacIntyre directly, "from the necessity of scheduling and coordinating our social actions" (ivi, p. 102). The second is related to statistical regularities: more gifts are given at Christmas than at any other time of the year. The third is the presence of natural causal regularities; the fourth is social causal regularities. The latter are not simply statistical regularities, but real causal nexus: in 1950s Italy, for example, class placement determined the opportunity for education.

However, the close connection between unpredictability and predictability does not imply inexplicability. The fact that the future is only partially foreseeable, that is, it is a mixture of predictability and unpredictability, does not preclude one from having an idea of it, and investing in it. MacIntyre's position, which I am briefly summarizing here, is that social life is the result of the relationship between the predictable and the unpredictable, which are intertwined in explicable nexus. Without the predictability of institutions and common sense, life would be meaningless, a collection of ragged and unconnected episodes. At the same time, each of us is aware of the unpredictability that pervades it. To pull the threads of the argument together, we can conclude that

> it is necessary, if life is to be meaningful, for us to be able to engage in long-term projects, and this requires predictability; it is necessary, if life is

> to be meaningful, for us to be in possession of ourselves and not merely to be the creations of other people's projects, intentions and desires, and this requires unpredictability.
>
> (ivi, p. 104)

We find here, phrased differently, the tension between determinism and voluntarism internal to Marxism, that tension whereby the final outcome of the historical movement, the perfect society, is both the product of science and the realization of the ideal, is both science and utopia, a synthesis of predictability and unpredictability. A tension, however, that in MacIntyre rightly remains unresolved. Just as it remains unresolved in the idea of a freely feasible utopia: the adverb carries unpredictability; the adjective, predictability. There is no contradiction, only the articulation, once again, of opacity and transparency, intentionality and reflexivity, predictability and unpredictability. An articulation that, present in all projects of action, becomes even more decisive the more the project engages the future, opening up ever broader horizons of predictable unpredictability. If all projects of action are done by doing, this applies even more especially to feasible utopias.

In this sense, utopias are historical, and therefore concrete and real. Hence, we must reflect upon the relationship that exists between the imaginative design of a perfect, or at least better, society and its feasibility. Especially with regard to the past, utopias constitute useful models to show the gap between reality and ideal, as such, not concretely realizable. Imagination finds its limit only in front of the self-representation of how one's community could be at its best. Otherwise, it can go so far as to paint fantastic and wholly unreal worlds. Plato's Republic is above all a mental experiment, a place designed by reason and its laws. The pre-modern world is full of fantastic places and happy islands produced by theogonies, belonging to mythologies or tales of origins. There is a strong intermingling of utopia and literature: to give a few random examples, think of the Christian Eden or the Golden Age, the Platonic Atlantis described in *Critias*, or the plans of Hippodamus of Miletus described by Aristotle in *Politics*.

Only with modernity does utopia become something truly feasible, an expression of the autonomous reflexivity of subjects. In this sense, utopian thought, if seen as thinking connected to reality, is exclusively modern. According to Lerner, utopian thought even constitutes a specific type of modern political theory: "Machiavelli sought to distinguish the realm of what ought to be and the realm of what is. He rejected the first for the second. But there is a third realm: the realm of what can be" (Lerner 1950, p. XLVI). The distinction between *what is* and *what must be* also belongs to the ancient world. The modern world adds a third possibility: *what can be*, even if it is not yet, because it is an expression of subjective autonomy. What can be does not necessarily coincide with what must be, and this is a thoroughly modern challenge. If utopia identifies the ability to think of a feasible better future, does it also mean that this future can be, as well as better, perfect? How far can modern hybris go? Is the end to which it aspires conceivable as an ultimate end?

In modernity, utopia is an expression of a normative theory acting in the world in an attempt to adapt it to itself. Therefore, the fascination with the impossible acquires an entirely specific force, capable of moving collective action and history. Utopia is the most authentic expression of an entirely modern predisposition to change. Change sees as its protagonists, autonomous social subjects who are pitched against other equally autonomous social subjects. This dynamic, already evidenced, is an expression of a divided world, which no longer represents itself as unitary, beginning with the fundamental split between an increasingly autonomous individual and the society to which each one belongs. The triggered social dynamic has directly to do with the question of the subject's freedom and self-realization, which must be articulated in a social structure that makes it pursuable for all. These are all matters unknown to the perfect worlds of antiquity, within which, if at all, there reigns an original innocence, later lost. In sum, utopia is thus a *rational, potentially realizable project*, a bearer of *change* with a view to a *better future*, understood as an expression of a specific *worldview* of some *social subjects* as opposed to others.

The moment utopias, having become feasible, aim to express the normative ideal of human autonomy, they take the form of freely feasible utopias. Thus, we have three models of utopia: (1) *unfeasible utopias*, the expression of an ideal to which reality will never conform; (2) *necessarily feasible utopias*, characterized by a freedom that has become a necessity, in which eutopia becomes a place; and (3) *freely feasible utopias*, produced by an autonomous capacity, individual and collective, to imagine the future, preserving it from any possible perfection. The relationship between intentionality and reflexivity, the tension between project and imagination, a relationship between theory and praxis that avoids the predominance of one over the other, and the sense of possibility understood as a way of explicating the inextricable nexus of predictability and unpredictability are all contributions that lead to the possibility of thinking, within a modernity increasingly characterized by meaningless change, broad projects of action, which I call freely feasible utopias. They stand as a conscious alternative to an early modernity in which the emergence of individual autonomy was still caged by models of historical evolution dominated by the logic of necessity. Let us see what may be other elements that characterize them.

Freely feasible utopias, while rational in the sense that projects of action are, are also the result of imagination and desire. The former is propelled by the latter and constitutes its yet unrealized, only imagined actualization. As Bloch writes, "we start out empty. I move. From early on we are searching. All we do is crave, cry out. Do not have what we want" (Bloch 1995, I, p. 21). Everyday life, however domesticated, always brings with it the initial void, that of childhood, that for which "a child grasps at everything to find out what it means" (Ibidem). The ploy, the joining of society, lies in "we also learn to wait" (Ibidem), articulating desire and imagination within time. The original, childhood longing becomes *desire* when it is connected to *imagination* and then materializes into a *representation*. Desire needs time. Therefore, imagination, which tries through fantasy to satisfy it, projects desire beyond the everyday, "daily into the Blue" (Ibidem), designing representations of an uncertain future that one would like to make into an everyday occurrence: since "our own life still lies a long way ahead, all distance is made more beautiful. The wish not only impels us towards this distance, but now it propels itself into it without a hiding-place" (ivi, p. 28). Our desire is an expression of longing for something distant of greater beauty, a wish that has given longing over time, through the work of imagination, its ability to produce a representation.

Hope plays a key role in particular, as we have seen. Bloch distinguishes between *filled emotions* and *expectant emotions*. The dimension of emotions also carries with it a tensional relationship between the present and future. Filled emotions – envy, gluttony, veneration – are those in which the dimension of intentionality has little impact, and the object of desire is really quite ready and available – even if not immediately obtainable – in the real world. Quite another matter for the emotions of expectation. They are those

> whose drive-intention is long-term, whose drive-object does not yet lie ready, not just in respective individual attainability, but also in the already available world, and therefore still occurs in the doubt about exit or entrance. Thus, the expectant emotions are distinguished, both in their unwish and in their wish, from the filled emotions by the *incomparably greater anticipatory character* in their intention, their substance, and their object.
>
> (ivi, p. 74)

Among the expectant emotions (fear, doubt, faith) hope has a central role: "the most important expectant emotion, the most authentic emotion of longing and thus of self, always remains in all of this – hope" (ivi, p. 75).

The close relationship between imagination and desire typical of freely feasible utopias is thus evident: on one hand, imagination cannot be harnessed in the detailed design of a pre-packaged future, but neither can it be constrained by the inevitable present; on the other hand, desire projects its intentionality not on immediately available objects, but on a wager that engages present and future. Hope, in short, feeds on an imagination that is always active, because the desire that sustains it is constantly expectant. Hope, like utopia, is consistently exposed to risk, disappointment, and uncertainty, but also happiness. Only when it rarely enters into a fragile connection with happiness does it take the unusual form of filled emotion. Happiness after all always belongs to the past: we know that we have been happy; we know that our hope has been able to be fulfilled. In one of his magnificent aphorisms, Adorno writes:

> To happiness the same applies as to truth: one does not *have* it but *is* in it. Indeed, happiness is nothing other than being encompassed, an

> after-image of the original shelter within the mother. But for this reason, no-one who is happy can know that he is so. To see happiness, he would have to pass out of it (…). He who says he is happy lies, and in invoking happiness sins against it. He alone keeps faith who says: *I was happy*. The only relation of consciousness to happiness is gratitude: in which lies its incomparable dignity.
>
> (Adorno 2005, p. 112)

The utopias of the past, especially the literary ones, are happy islands. The freely feasible modern utopia is left with the dimension of hope, in the knowledge that happiness is 'filled emotion' in a past incapable of projecting us per se into the future: the mother's womb, natural society, primordial Eden. Hope, however, is no small thing. It helps to keep up the torch of imagination, to turn longing and desire into representation. Keeping hope means that the goal to be pursued, however embellished by desire and imagination, can never coincide with the summum bonum. Feasible utopia is never fully realized, and the possibility enclosed in it retains a dimension of impossibility. In this, it is utopia in the sense of non-place. As in any project of action, a process of valorization is operative in utopias. The hope typical of utopia concurs to keep this process open, based on the existing dynamic between opacity of the present and imagination of the future, between intentionality and reflexivity. If the representation of the final goal coincided with a perfect society, with the hypostatized and absolute value, with the abstract ideal that has become static, the very openness of the process would lose much of its significance, because, in the face of a value taken for granted, the object of discussion would be only the most appropriate means of achieving it.

This is the drama of modern utopias: to think that a non-place can be a real, completely pursuable goal. At that point, action becomes indifferent to the human cost, and any means is justified. Hope can turn into madness. Indeed, Wallerstein writes that "utopias can be used, have been used, as justifications for terrible wrongs. The last thing we really need is still more utopian visions" (Wallerstein 1998, p. 1). Except then to argue, correctly, that it is only these kinds of utopias that we need to dispense with. What we need today, learning above all from the most recent dramatic experiences, is not "the face of the perfect (and inevitable) future, but the face of an alternative, credibly better, and historically possible (but far from certain) future" (ivi, p. 2).

To further clarify the sense of possibility encapsulated in the concept of feasible utopia, it can be said that possibility does not guarantee realization, nor does it exclude it, providing this does not coincide with perfect reality. This is the case, I insist, only if the value is not hypostatized into a final ideal that is closed to change. Freely feasible utopias as concrete utopias are contrasted, using Bloch's vocabulary, with abstract utopias, in which theory produces ideals that are detached from historical processes. But they also contrast with Bloch's concrete utopias, for which the ideal, in keeping with Marx, is concrete because it is capable of becoming one with the praxis of the subjects of transformation.[16] In short, the goal is attainable, but not in its abstract perfection. Notwithstanding the fact that it is unattainable, such perfection engages us in everyday processes, forcing us, from time to time, to evaluate what is most attuned to the imagination anticipated in the project of action. The freely feasible utopia may also already be partially present, as are Cooper's everyday utopias: in what has been accomplished, however, there is still something to be accomplished, which will probably never be accomplished. In this, freely feasible utopias are utopias: "something is missing".

A few last brief thoughts on the category of possibility. First, the possible is not boundless: "just as man is mainly a creature who enters into the Possible and has it in front of him, he also knows that this does not coincide with vagueness, that precisely his open character is definitely nothing arbitrary" (Bloch 1995, p. 224). *Longing* becomes *desire*, and desire through *imagination* becomes *representation*. The individual, it was said above, learns to wait. Not being boundless, the possible has limits, which are also social limits. Wright rightly points out that the "social limits of possibility are not independent of beliefs about those limits" (Wright 2010, p. 23). The possible is thus a social product: it depends on the imaginative potentials that society offers us and, to adopt the language used here, on the force of opacity that the everyday has towards our reflective imagination. Many authors have pointed out how, after the crisis of the great ideologies with their utopian promises, since the end of the last century the image of a future, unpredictable and threatening, without enchantment and leaving no room for imagination and hope, seems to dominate. The processes of time acceleration seem to force our existences into an increasingly narrow and opaque, windowless present that prevents us from looking back and forward. Increasingly, ours seems to be a world without possibilities, within which this category is monopolized by technology: the unpredictability of the future is dictated by technological development, by strategies that are fundamentally foreign to us all and that we cannot control.

The first step therefore lies in a new conviction with respect to the opening up of future possibilities, in the awareness that the category of possibility has immediate repercussions on our perception of the present. Freeing the imagination means gaining that distance from the everyday that enables us to operate consciously in it. It is about that autonomy of thought that nourishes the autonomy of praxis, triggering virtuous circles between the former and the latter. A realized possibility shows how much that is still feasible is contained in what has been done and requires realization. According to Bloch, "mankind and the world carry enough good future; no plan is itself good without this *fundamental belief* within it" (Bloch 1995, p. 447). It must be stated that this *fundamental belief* is an 'expectant emotion': as long as it is not blind and does not stifle hope.

Lastly, it is necessary to understand who can be the bearer of a utopian project, not least because "without the strength of an I and we behind it, even hoping becomes insipid" (ivi, p. 147). Every imaginary is a narrative. Since every short-term intention can acquire meaning only when embedded within a longer-term intention, the connections thus created are causal, producing identifiable contexts and temporal sequences. A meaning underlies contexts and sequences that has emancipated itself from everyday immediacy, a meaning that has become narrative: the intelligibility of meaning is therefore closely linked to the narrative, or narratives, to which it belongs. Each of us is both the actor and co-author of narratives: common sense (Schütz) and social representations (Moscovici) are narratives to which we have become so accustomed that we have naturalized them. But narrative is never closed and concluded: it is always interpreted and developed. Action and narrative are connected within the predictability/unpredictability nexus described above. The question is to understand the characteristics of utopian narratives, of *utopian social imaginaries*.

One of their main characteristics, we have seen above, is that the lengthy time frame on which they project themselves brings a radicalization of the tension between what is predictable and what is not, a tension that, on one hand, implies a distancing from the everyday, the opaque and the present; on the other hand, a return to the everyday, which takes on the task of realizing the impossible. Another significant characteristic is related to the structure of social stratification typical of our times. Simply put, it is impossible for utopian mentalities such as those described by Mannheim – marked by a stratification containing easily identifiable social subjects, like the social classes – to arise today. Freely feasible utopias are rooted in social imaginaries produced by a set of social subjects that do not coincide with a class, nor do they coincide with other well-defined types of social subjectivity. Thus, there is not the close correlation that was given, for example, between the liberal-humanitarian ideal and the bourgeoisie: imaginaries are not direct expressions of identities and interests that can be traced back to a clearly identifiable subject. Social imaginaries, as we have seen, are transversal and, rather than being an expression of identity, provide it to subjects from time to time who can identify with these.

Of course, not all social imaginaries are utopian. To give examples, we can think today of the existence of a pacifist utopian imaginary, of a pro-European one, and an ecological one.[17] None of these can be traced back to a precise social subject: they are vast repositories of meaning, full of narratives and representations, which have been built up over time through the desire and imagination of sometimes very different subjects. The contents we can find within them may also be relatively unstructured and loosely coherent, but they retain an air of familiarity, which makes possible common aggregations and actions among heterogeneous subjects. The utopian dimension they contain projects them into an uncertain and unpredictable future, but one worthy of pursuing.

The relationship that freely feasible utopias, and their corresponding utopian imaginaries, entertain with time can be so well synthesized by Bloch: "tomorrow in today lives, always wondering about it". And it is made alive by a hope capable of showing "*reality itself as the reality of the horizon*"

(Bloch 1995, III, pp. 1375, 1376). In conclusion, we can say that "it is a question of learning hope" (ivi, I, p. 3): because the future is neither in the care of a supercomputer nor of a philosophy of history. The only possibility is to roll up our sleeves with conviction.

The European Utopia

Europe is the freely feasible utopia of Europeans. As such, it is predictable unpredictability. There is no science capable of telling us exactly what, when, where, why, and who is capable of promoting its realization. It is realized within the process of its construction, which, by the way, we cannot even take for granted. The pro-Europeans' social subject is extremely heterogeneous and transversal: it is not given in the way of social classes, but neither in the way of generations, gender identities, or so on. Nor does it exist in the way territorial identities are given, because European identity is itself part of the process at hand. The project at its foundation, however, is not vague and generic; it is not built on the clouds of mere wishful thinking.

The idea behind Europe is the overcoming of the universalism typical of the nation-state in pursuit of peace. Europe and peace are therefore closely interconnected utopias. This is a connection clearly present in the *Ventotene Manifesto* (Spinelli 2006). This text is the best expression of the unprecedented force of a hope that becomes imagination. Europe is a true political miracle, first thought up by a few young anti-fascist intellectuals, confined to a remote island in the Mediterranean when the victory of Nazism seemed certain. The deep meaning of the term utopia is made clear here: a broad project of action, to be built collectively, step by step. With at its core, the idea of peace. Europe is the project of a new universalism that can ensure peace. Central to the *Manifesto* is the highlighting of the close relationship between the nation-state and modern warfare, so strong that it suggests that policy is nothing more than 'the continuation of war with other means', as von Clausewitz's well-known aphorism claims. European nation-states are historically guilty of producing a quantity of wars unmatched in human history, bringing internal conflicts to a global scale, making them planetary wars. These are processes that significantly connect with the export of the nation-state model across the globe. After decades of European peace – apart from the conflicts caused by the dissolution of the former Yugoslavia – the recent war in Ukraine has forcefully put this central issue back at the centre of pro-European attention.

Peace is not the absence of war, but a way of building social relations that must be placed at the centre of the daily *social* and *political* agenda. It is not an event that happens, only to then slip off our horizons: rather, it is a condition that must be maintained and implemented through continuous attention. It demands continuous and forward-looking care, covering both international and domestic relations. Peace is not stagnation and immobility, or even synonymous with death: in his *Preface* in *Perpetual Peace: a Philosophical Sketch*, Kant refers polemically to the fact that the inscription

'To perpetual peace' accompanied the depiction of a cemetery on the sign of a Dutch tavern (Kant 1991). The peace to be built requires continuous activity, because the conditions that make it possible are changing all the time. For example, it would be useful to set up a European Ministry for Peace to deal with all those policies capable of developing the conditions for it to flourish. At the moment, another important goal is the construction of a European army, capable of legitimizing an increasingly autonomous and decisive peacemaking role for the EU on the international stage. A political and social pacifism – which does not, of course, equate with anthropological, philosophical or religious pacifism, although it feeds on these latter – must be able to articulate reasonable ends to produce conditions through which wars, the arms race, and international power and neo-colonialist policies can be curtailed. The goals mentioned here – two among many possible ones – show well the sense in which utopia is made by doing: for example, to make or not to make a European army is an alternative that can shape profoundly present and future EU policies, and trigger markedly different processes of developing European cooperation. What the Europe of the future will be depends on choices like this, and others like it.

The idea of peace is closely linked to that of a mature democracy. Even the idea of democracy cannot be based on a definite and final set of conditions: it too requires continuous adaptation and development. Especially now, after the end of the foolish illusion that the fall of the Berlin Wall could mean the end of history, we are faced with a radical clash between democracy and autocracy, running through the West, but also affecting every other corner of the world. On this level, too, Europe can play a decisive role. In addition to promoting peace, Europe has the task of developing democracy and social justice, proposing an alternative to the economic and social disintegration produced by neo-liberal globalization. Habermas strongly emphasized these aspects. Within the democratic culture of the West, Europe constitutes a democratic model with its own specificities, all to be valued: a high level of secularization; a deep scepticism towards the presumption of neutrality of technology and processes of rationalization; the defence of the priority of the public over the private and of solidarity over efficiency; an awareness of the paradoxes of progress; the repudiation of the right of the strongest; and, finally, as a synthesis of all these aspects, precisely pacifism, a product of the historical experiences of the past, starting with Nazism (Habermas 2006). Moreover, central to European democratic development becomes the process of institutional reform, which must be able to create European institutions increasingly autonomous from national ones and increasingly an expression of direct popular participation.

Today Europe is in crisis. However, it should not be forgotten that it has been since it has existed, and probably always will be. In this crisis, economic aspects are important. However, they must be framed in a broader perspective. The question of identity, which is almost never asserted in political and cultural debate, is decisive: if not included in a process aimed at building a

European society, based on the awareness of sharing a common destiny, economic policies will remain instruments without an end. While not entering into the details, I believe that the social issue is the crucial one, not least because it is too often forgotten under the impellent nature of economic and legal issues. Europe must not assume the guise of a European nation. European universalism must not make all uniform, and must not build identities that erase distinctiveness, territorial and cultural, as nation-states have done. On the contrary, it must allow to shine the thousand identities deadened by the states. The Basque Country or Catalonia is not just at issue alone: at issue is the infinite articulation of diversities that have always constituted the complex European puzzle. The idea of a *welcoming universalism* must be developed.

This is a typically European issue. Europe has always had a universalist vocation and a localized reality, fragmented into a thousand identities. Its history can be read as a continuous tension between these two dimensions, which complement each other: the European spirit that thinks the universal is linked to local fragmentation, primarily geographical. Europe has no natural boundaries: it can be what it wants to be. The idea of Europe is closely related to that of a recomposition: a borderless jigsaw; composed of the warmth of the Mediterranean and the cold of the north; jaggedly fragmented into endless inlets, gulfs, valleys, regions, all with their own specificity; traversed and inhabited by a thousand peoples, each of whom has made adaptation its fundamental resource, thus going on to compose infinite cultural micro-climates, Europe, in its millennial history, has been forced to imagine itself as something unique and general, setting itself the task of being a unity. In a nutshell, it is something that must be wanted, otherwise it does not exist: it is a project, not a reality. For centuries, Europe's political and institutional history has caged, defined, confined: above all, nation-states have arisen by sequestering the living body of territories, uniting what was separate and dividing what was united. Consequently, if it is to be truly itself, Europe has before it the task of producing a *genuinely political universalism*, capable of direction, and a *genuinely social localism*, feeding on diversity, participation, and democratic vitality. It needs, especially today, a new social pact, policies capable of reviving social cohesion, so as to make possible policies for the environment, development, social justice, integration, and the implementation of rights.

For Bauman, Europe is "an adventure" (2004); for Rifkin, "a dream" (2005). I envision a freely feasible utopia, quite aware, just as Bloch writes, that "where nothing more can be done or is possible, life stands still" (Bloch 1995, p. 224).

Notes

1 The three virtues correspond to the three aspects of the human soul – rational, irascible, and concupiscible souls – thus emphasizing the harmony between public and private dimensions: each of the virtues is practiced with reference both to the individual and to the relationships between individuals.

2 The Phalanstery is a small, replicable agricultural-industrial community. All dwellings are gathered in a single building, described by Fourier in detail, a sort of large hotel within which everyone can find ways to satisfy their own inclinations. It is characterized by communal property, equality between men and women, and sexual freedom. The minimum of vital necessities is guaranteed to all. Family is abolished and the whole community takes care of children. Work is only a means of satisfying one's inclinations: hence it is neither a duty nor a right. It makes sense to work because one finds pleasure in what one does. The state is abolished and every decision is submitted directly to the entire Phalanstery.

3 This is planning that goes into outlining the minutest details. The Phalanstery is divided into Series, characterized by a common activity. To give a simple example of Fourier's organizational minutiae, there is a Series of pear growers, divided into 32 groups of about 10 people each, organized into 7 groupings according to the type of pears. Fourier outlines in detail as many as 132 Series of production activities. Another example of this systematic and organizational spirit, whereby almost every moment of each individual's daily life is regulated and predefined in the name of his or her interest and happiness, is nicely represented by Cabet's Icaria (2003). Very similar, however, is also the world of 2000 as Bellamy imagines it in 1888 in *Looking Backword* (1986).

4 In this vein, "in the case of conservatives, what corresponds to the *idea* is in substance, something quite different from the liberal ideas. It was Hegel's great achievement to set up against the liberal idea a conservative counterpart, not in the sense of artificially concocting an attitude and a mode of behaviour, but rather by raising an already present mode of experience to an intellectual level and by emphasizing the distinctive characteristic that mark it off from the liberal attitude toward the world (…). Meaning and reality, norm and existence, are not separate here, because the utopian, the 'concretized idea', is in a vital sense present in this world" (Mannheim 1997a, pp. 208–209).

5 I believe that the distinction between left and right arises within, and is an expression of, this dynamic. Both are different and opposite conceptions of the individual: the left thinks that the individual is what he or she can become; the right what he or she is, conforming to a reality that must be recognized (Santambrogio 1998; 2022).

6 On this point, Mannheim considers the polemical clash between Marx and Bakunin to be crucial, a clash that puts an end to the chiliastic utopia.

7 Here I find the collaboration between Wright and the authors of the so-called analytic Marxism interesting (Cohen, Roemer, Van Parijs, Przeworski, Steiner, Josh Cohen, Bowles, and others). Although Wright cannot be considered a full-fledged analytical Marxist, he shares with them a reading of Marx that eschews Hegel. On analytic Marxism see Cimmino, Santambrogio (1998).

8 On this point, Wright is in keeping with the positions of Van Parijs (1998).

9 One of the internal problems of the proposal lies in the presence of what Wright calls "nasty associations, based on exclusion, narrow interests, and the preservation of privilege" (Wright 2010, p. 146). That is, it is not necessarily the case that civil society associations are all democratic: even the Ku-Klux Klan, to take one example, is a civil society association.

10 For example, Cooper, concerning Summerhill, writes: "the conceptual lines community such as Summerhill facilitate, oriented to belonging rather than to control, gesture toward other ways of approaching property, ways that may hold value in other contexts" (Cooper 2014, p. 184).

11 This approach fits into the perspective offered by Bloch with his concept of *concrete utopia*, trying to develop it in a more sociological direction. For Bloch, utopia is concrete because it is able to valorize "the Not-Yet-Conscious", making it an element that can express "the Not-Yet-Being" in historical processes. This is a dynamic that Bloch summarizes in the concept of *anticipatory consciousness* (Bloch 1995, I, part two). For Bloch, "the Not-Yet-Conscious itself must become conscious in its act, known in its content" (ivi, p. 144). In this way,

> the thus determined imagination of the utopian function is distinguished from mere fantasizing precisely by the fact that only the former has in its favour a Not-Yet-Being of an expectable kind, i.e. does not play around and get lost in an Empty-Possible, but *psychologically anticipates a Real-Possible*.
>
> (Ibidem, italics mine)

The concept of meaning, in its articulation of intentionality and reflexivity, I believe can sociologically express this relationship between what nothing is yet known about and the process of social change. The utopian project of action is not an "empty possibility", not least because, in Bloch's words, "thinking means venturing beyond" (ivi, p. 4).

12 From here on, in speaking of utopia, I always mean my notion of freely feasible utopia.

13 The sense of possibility that is trapped in unrealized futures is addressed by Jedlowski (2015; 2017). For Jedlowski, the future before us also depends on the futures we have imagined in the past and the sense of possibility embedded in them.

14 Tiresias lives outside utopia because no project of action is possible for him: he

> lives an "out-of-time", solitary, unsharable existence. Blind to the present and to the environment in which he finds himself living, far from the needs, interests, concerns and doubts that characterize the way of life in everyday life, he places himself in a dimension of quasi-transcendence insofar as he possesses a clear, certain, immediate, original, incontrovertible knowledge of what is to come. A knowledge, however, that is not a tool for action since Tiresias is denied any power to intervene in the only reality that turns out to be within the reach of his "seeing".
>
> (Sacchetti 2013, pp. 42–43, translation mine)

Tiresias' foreknowledge renders the project, any project, useless, and action loses its value: his estrangement from the everyday is utmost.

15 We can recall MacIntyre's example. In trade union negotiations involving union leaders, government and business representatives, the former, if close to the end of their appointed term, might be interested in obtaining employment from the employers or the government, so as not to become just employees again; the business representatives might have interests with the government that go beyond the specific object of the negotiations; and finally, a government representative might want to run for office in a district where the workers' vote is crucial. These are just examples of other possible games being played – or 'hidden agendas' – behind the specific negotiations in hand (MacIntyre 1993, pp. 122–123).

16 Marxist Bloch argues that the

> ideal can by no means be instructed and corrected by mere facts (...). The ideal (...) has contact with the process of the world, of which so-called facts are reified-fixed abstractions. It has in its anticipations, if they are concrete, a correlate in the objective hope contents of the tendency-latency (...). Thus when Marx says the working-class has no ideals to realize, this anathema certainly does not apply to the realization of tendentially concrete goals, but only to that of abstractly introduced goals, of ideals which have no contact with history and process.
>
> (Bloch 1995, pp. 173, 174)

As we know, Marx criticizes the abstract utopias of utopian socialists. Feasible utopias are concrete differently from how Bloch intends, since rejecting the idea of the unity of theory and praxis, they are the result of a different way of understanding the same idea of hope.

17 The cosmopolitan utopia could also fit into this list. Arguably, a true cosmopolitan imaginary has not yet developed: in spite of considerable theoretical production, one thinks only of Kant, there is still no social embedding of these ideals and no actors who have become its interpreters. A key contribution to cosmopolitan ideals is the recent work of Rawls concerning the law of peoples, understood as an ethico-political theory of international relations (2001). I emphasize the fact that Rawls, by peoples' law, means a particular idea of just and justice applicable to the principles and norms of international law, going on to develop what he calls a realist utopia. As Maffettone writes, "Rawls' entire argument has a utopian flavor. However, it presupposes a factual realizability" (Maffettone 2001, p. XXVII). An interesting attempt to 'embed cosmopolitanism' within concrete social practices, with particular reference to Europe, has been made by Pendenza (2017). The point is that there is probably still no real cosmopolitan social imaginary.

Conclusions

A *finalistic theory of social action*, rooted in a phenomenological reading of Weber, highlights the autonomy of subjects, individual and collective. To act means to give meaning intentionally to one's actions, within generally extensive projects. There are no set tracks, predefined goals, or models to be followed, whether provided by religions or metaphysics. Nor is it possible that external, immanent, or internal criticism can provide a system of signposts, directions, warnings, or whatever else that can advise, direct, suggest, or promote. It is time to abandon the language of ideology, the last example of a system that claimed to distinguish – with a more or less clear line of separation – what is unworthy from what is meritorious, over the heads of subjects and their autonomy.

Our starting point is the *normative character* of social action: to act implies, first, identifying an end among alternatives and, second, giving that end a value that makes it worth pursuing. All this involves the definition of projects of action, variously structured and complex, within which the relationship between *meaning and time* takes shape in a relatively coherent way. The identity of the subject connects with significance to the meaning produced while maintaining the internal coherence of the projects: this is how we express our autonomy and recognize ourselves as the same subjects over time. What we are is the meaning we have given to our actions, to the common thread that binds them into recognizable nexus, for ourselves and for others. *Identity constitutes a narrative*, which is both the result and the condition of our action.

Within this process, active and passive elements operate. The passive character is constituted by the presence of external elements, difficult to change, natural, and social. Society constitutes a structured set of meaning contents that we take for granted – the reality that Schütz calls common sense and Gadamer tradition – that acts on us, intentionally prompting us to act unreflexively. This taken for granted is the result of an enormous collective work, operating behind us, in a historical and ontological sense. Being, in fact, the result of actions, it implies an active dimension of acting, which is rooted in the possibility of reflection on the intended meaning. Intentionality and reflexivity are thus the direct expression of the *intersubjective* character of the

DOI: 10.4324/9781003229339-7

construction of meaning: subjects are the product of the original intersubjectivity and contribute to its production. Actors, whether individual or collective, can articulate their understanding of themselves and the world whenever they reactivate the available reflexive dimension. Through these reflexive moments, meaning content emerges independent of practices, which can point them in one direction rather than another. Our identity is inherently social because it is tightly woven within the intersubjective context within which it emerges. Actions are right in the sense that they allow – or prevent – the unfolding of the autonomy of individuals; in other words, they ensure that one person's autonomy is not obtained at the expense of others, through mechanisms of constraint. There is no utopia, no island of human perfection, conceivable otherwise than through a progressive unfolding of each person's possibility of being oneself, that is, of being able to realize one's autonomy to the fullest. The perfect world, and one that for that very reason will never exist, is one that makes possible the affirmation of autonomy, that is, of self-actualization, of each and all.

To all of this, the destiny of democracy is closely bound. As far as we can know today, democracy is the only possibility, practical and therefore imperfect, through which to try to cultivate the autonomy of the subjects who inhabit it. Among the many alternatives that modernity offers us, democracy is only one of the options. It is not a given, and arguably it is also the most challenging and problematic. However, the structure of social stratification – as it has been shaped in the characteristics I have succinctly condensed into the concept of *society by differentiation* – does not exclude this option. Individuals engaged in the management of their identity – through the almost daily encounter with a multiplicity of affiliations, not necessarily attuned to one another – have before them the alternative between more reassuring responses, namely reducing complexity and settling for simple, linear identities; and others that are more demanding and challenging, involving the acceptance of complexity, and the risk of a wealth of alternatives and possibilities.

This book, reflecting on the concept of *political culture*, highlights the importance of a civic culture resulting from trust in democratic institutions, its procedures and values but, in particular, it highlights the increasingly evident importance of an effective and constant participation, not merely electoral, of citizens and their associations in collective life. Through the concept of *social imaginary*, it has been possible to reflect on the new configurations that collective narratives assume after the end of political ideologies, highlighting the problem that democracies today have in connecting social aspirations with political decisions. Social participation struggles to find adequate channels of political representation. A new *theory of ideology* could serve precisely to bridge this relationship, between an increasingly pluralistic and differentiated society and the political and institutional system. Finally, the concept of *freely feasible utopia* serves to show that it is also possible today to form social imaginaries with vast temporal and spatial reaches, capable of projecting the everyday into a broad project that engages the collective future. Political culture, social imaginary, theory of ideology, and utopia are concepts that variously articulate the relationship between meaning and time, a central aspect of the finalist theory of social action.

A *successful and radical democracy*, which places at its centre the conception that autonomous individuals can together realize themselves, is the greatest and most important of utopias. It is a great project of action that would not be starting from zero today; it can rely on deposits of shared meaning, arguably quite well established too, that have been sedimenting over the so-called modern centuries. A good example may be the modern imaginary as described by Taylor. At the same time, it is always vulnerable to the threat of desertion of freedom. Just as Mannheim, after the end of World War I, reflecting on the alternative between democratic and totalitarian planning, made it his own task to delineate, through a diagnosis of the times, a new model of democracy worthy of those times; we too have the same task today, albeit in an entirely different context. This is a commitment that must be taken up by everyone, by ordinary citizens, civil society associations, the most responsible political classes, and, of course, by intellectuals.

Bibliography

Abric, J. C. 1984, A Theoretical and Experimental Approach to the Study of Social Representations in a Situation of Interaction, in R. M. Farr, S. Moscovici (eds.), *Social Representations,* Cambridge University Press, Cambridge, pp. 169–183.

Adams, S. 2017, *Ricœur and Castoriadis in Discussion: On Human Creation, Historical Novelty, and the Social Imaginary*, Rowman and Littlefield, London.

Adams, S., Blokker, P., Doyle, N. J., Krummel, J. W. M., Smith, J. C. A. 2015, Social Imaginary in Debate, *Social Imaginaries*, v. 1, no. 1, pp. 15–52.

Adorno, Th. W. 2005, *Minima moralia. Reflection on a Damaged Life*, Verso, London and New York (1951).

Alma, H., Vanheeswijck, G. (eds.) 2018, *Social Imaginaries in a Globalizing World*, De Gruyter, Berlin and Boston.

Almond, G. A., Verba, S. (eds.). 1980, *The Civic Culture Revisited*, Sage Publications, Newbury Park, CA.

Almond, G. A., Verba, S. 1963, *The Civic Culture. Political Attitudes and Democracy in Five Nations*, Princeton University Press, Princeton.

Almond, G. A., Verba, S. 1980, The Intellectual History of the Civic Culture Concept, in G. A. Almond, S. Verba (eds.), *The Civic Culture Revisited*, Little Brown, Boston, pp. 1–36.

Althusser, L. 1993, Ideology and Ideological State Apparatuses, in Id., *Essays on Ideology*, Verso, London and New York, pp. 1–60 (1970).

Anitori, R. 2012, *Vite insieme. Dalle comuni agli eco villaggi*, DeriveApprodi, Roma.

Apel, K. O., Gadamer, H.-G., Habermas, J. 1979, *Ermeneutica e critica dell'ideologia*, Queriniana, Brescia (1971).

Appadurai, A. 2011, *Le aspirazioni nutrono la democrazia*, et al, Milano.

Appadurai, A. 2013, *The Future as Cultural Fact. Essays on the Global Condition*, Verso, London and New York.

Aron, R. 2001, *The Opium of the Intellectuals*, Routledge & Kegan Paul, London and New York (1955).

Aron, R. 2019, *Main Currents in Sociological Thought. Volume One: Montesquieu, Comte, Marx, De Tocqueville: The Sociologists and the Revolution of 1848*, Routledge & Kegan Paul, London and New York (1967).

Bacon, F. 2008, *The New Atlantis*, Floating Press, London (1627).

Banfield, E. C. 1970, *The Moral Basis of a Backword Society*, Free Press, Simon & Schuster, New York (1958).

Barry, B. M. 1970, *Sociologists, Economists and Democracy*, Collier-MacMillan, London.

Bauman, Z. 2000, *Liquid Modernity*, Polity Press, Cambridge.

Bauman, Z. 2001, *The Individualized Society*, Polity Press, Cambridge.

Bauman, Z. 2004, *Europe. An Unfinished Adventure*, Polity Press, Cambridge.

Beck, U. 1992, *Risk Society: Towards a New Modernity*, Sage, London (1986).

Bell, D. 1988, *The End of Ideology. On the Exhaustion of Political Ideas in the Fifties*, with a new *Afterword*, Harvard University Press, Cambridge and London (1960).

Bellamy, E. 1986, *Looking Backword*, Penguin Books, London (1888).

Berman, M. 2010, *All That Is Solid Melts into Air: The Experience of Modernity*, Verso, London and New York (1982).

Bloch, E. 1995, *The Principle of Hope*, III volumes, The MIT Press, Cambridge, Massachusetts (1959).

Bloor, D. 1991, *Knowledge and Social Imagery*, University of Chicago Press, Chicago (1976).

Bottici, C. 2014, *Imaginal Politics: Images beyond Imagination and the Imaginary*, Columbia University Press, New York.

Bottici, C. 2019, Imagination, Imaginary, Imaginal: Toward a New Social Ontology? *Social Epistemology*, v. 33, no. 5, pp. 433–441.

Brint, M. 1991, *A Genealogy of Political Culture*, Westview Press, Boulder, San Francisco, Oxford.

Brubaker, R. 2006, *The Limits of Rationality. An Essay on the Social and Moral Thought of Max Weber*, Routledge & Kegan Paul, London and New York (1984).

Bruni, L. 2021, *Solidarietà critica. Patologie neo-liberali e nuove forme di socialità*, Meltemi, Roma.

Cabet, E. 2003, *Travels in Icaria*, Syracuse University Press, New York (1845).

Campanella, T. 2018, *The City of the Sun*, Hardpress Publishing, Los Angeles (1637).

Castoriadis, C. 1987, *The Imaginary Institution of Society*, Polity Press, Cambridge (1975).

Castoriadis, C. 1993, The Greek and the Modern Political Imaginary, *Salmagundi*, no. 100, pp. 102–129.

Cimmino, L., Santambrogio, A. 1998, *Il marxismo analitico*, Studi perugini, a. III, no. 1, pp. 290.

Cohen, G. A. 2000, *Karl Marx's Theory of History*, Princeton University Press, Princeton, NJ.

Cohen, G. A. 2001, *If You're an Egalitarian, How Come You're so Rich?* Harvard University Press, Cambridge, MA.

Cooper, D. 2014, *Everyday Utopias. The Conceptual Life of Promising Spaces*, Duke University Press, Durham and London.

Costa, P. 2005, Introduzione. La modernità immaginata, in Ch. Taylor (ed), *Gli immaginari sociali moderni*, Meltemi, Roma, pp. 7–15.

Crespi, F. 1997, Crisi e rinascita dell'utopia, in L. Mumford (ed.), *Storia dell'utopia*, Donzelli, Roma, pp. VII–XII.

Croce, M. 2016, Premessa all'edizione italiana, in D. Cooper (ed.), *Utopie quotidiane. Il potere concettuale degli spazi sociali inventivi*, Edizione ETS, Pisa, pp. 9–18.

Damiani, M. 2020, *Populist Radical Left Parties in Western Europe*, Routledge & Kegan Paul, London and New York.

Destutt de Tracy, A. L. C. 1970, *Éléments d'idéologie*, Librairie philosophique J. Vrin, Paris (1817).

Diehl, P. 2019, Temporality and the Political Imaginary in the Dynamics of Political Representation, *Social Epistemology*, v. 33, no. 5, pp. 410–421.

Dittmer, L. 1977, Political Culture and Political Symbolism: Toward a Theoretical Synthesis, *World Politics*, v. 29, no. 4, pp. 552–583.

Durkheim, É. 1984, *The Division of Labor in Society*, Palgrave MacMillan, London (1893; 1902).

Durkheim, É. 1995, *The Elementary Forms of Religious Life*, Free Press, New York and London (1912).

Eagleton, T. 1991, *Ideology. An Introduction*, Verso, London and New York.

Edelman, M. 1976, *The Symbolic Uses of Politics*, University of Illinois Press, Chicago.

Edelman, M. 2007, *From Art to Politics: How Artistic Creations Shape Political Conceptions*, University of Chicago Press, Chicago and London.

Elkins, D. J., Simeon, R. E. B. 1979, A Cause in Search of Its Effect, or What Does Political Culture Explain? *Comparative Politics*, v. 11, no. 2, pp. 127–145.

Elster, J. 2000, Rationality, Economy, and Society, in S. Turner (ed.), *The Cambridge Companion to Weber*, Cambridge University Press, Cambridge, pp. 21–41.

Federici, M. C., Conti, U. (eds.) 2020, *Vivere i territori mediani. Identità territoriali, emergenze sociali e rigenerazione dei tessuti urbani*, Meltemi, Roma.

Ferrara, A. 1995, Presentazione, in M. Weber (ed.), *Considerazioni intermedie. Il destino dell'Occidente*, Armando Editore, Roma, pp. 7–40.

Festinger, L. 1957, *A Theory of Cognitive Dissonance*, Stanford University Press, Stanford.

Foucault, M. 1981, *The Order of Discourse*, in Id., *Untying the Text. A Post-Structuralist Reader*, Routledge & Kegan Paul, Boston and London, pp. 51–78 (1970).

Foucault, M. 1989, *Archaeology of Knowledge*, Routledge & Kegan Paul, London and New York (1969).

Foucault, M. 2020, *Power. The Essential Works of Michel Foucault 1954–1984*, Penguin Classics, London.

Fourier, Ch. 1971, *Design for Utopia: Selected Writings*, Schocken, New York.

Fraser, N. 2008, Riconoscimento e distribuzione delle risorse, *Quaderni di Teoria Sociale*, no. 8, pp. 97–112.

Fraser, N, Honneth, A. 2004, *Redistribution or Recognition? A Political-Philosophical Exchange*, Verso, London and New York.

Gadamer, H. G. 1979, Replica, in K. O. Apel, H. G. Gadamer, J. Habermas (eds.), *Ermeneutica e critica dell'ideologia*, Queriniana, Brescia, pp. 284–315 (1971).

Gadamer, H. G. 2006, *Truth and Method*, Continuum, London and New York (1960).

Gauchet, M. 2016, Tocqueville, America, and Us: on the Genesis of Democratic Societies, *The Tocqueville Review/Le Revue Tocqueville*, v. XXXVII, no. 2, pp. 163–231 (1980).

Geuss, R. 1981, *The Idea of a Critical Theory. Habermas & the Frankfurt School*, Cambridge University Press, Cambridge.

Gibbins, J. R. 1989, *Contemporary Political Culture. Politics in a Postmodern Age*, Sage, London.

Giddens, A. 1990, *The Consequences of Modernity*, Polity Press, Cambridge.

Gili, G., Ferrucci, F., Pece, E. 2017, *Il sociale nel social housing*, Rubbettino, Soveria Mannelli.

Goffman, E. 1959, *The Presentation of Self in Everyday Life*, Doubleday, Garden City, New York.

Goldman, H.1988, *Max Weber and Thomas Mann. Calling and the Shaping of the Self*, University of California Press, Berkeley, Los Angeles, London.

Graziano, P. R. 2010, Nuove forme di partecipazione. I gruppi di acquisto solidale, *Aggiornamenti sociali*, v. 61, no. 3, pp. 181–189.

Guidotti, F. 2013, *Eco villlaggi e Co-housing: dove sono, chi li anima, come farne parte o realizzarne nuovi*, Terra Nuova Edizioni, Firenze.

Habermas, J. 1979, *Su* Verità e metodo *di Gadamer*, in K. O. Apel, H. G. Gadamer, J. Habermas (eds.), *Ermeneutica e critica dell'ideologia*, Queriniana, Brescia, pp. 60–70 (1971).

Habermas, J. 1984, *The Theory of Communicative Action*, vol. I–II, Beacon Press, Boston (1981).

Habermas, J. 1992, *The Structural Transformation of the Public Sphere: An Inquiry into a Category of Bourgeois Society*, Polity Press, Cambridge (1962; 1990).

Habermas, J. 2006, *The Divide West*, Polity Press, Cambridge (2004).

Head, B. W. 1985, *Ideology and Social Science. Destutt de Tracy and French Liberalism*, Martinus Nijhoff Publishers, Dordrecht, Boston, Lancaster.

Hochschild, A. 1983, *The Managed Heart: Commercialization of Human Feeling*, University of California Press, Berkeley.

Honneth, A. 2014, Foreword, in R. Jaeggi (ed.), *Alienation*, Columbia University Press, New York, pp. VII–X.

Inglehart, R. 1988, The Renaissance of Political Culture, *American Political Science Review*, v. 82, no. 4, pp. 1203–1230.

Jaeggi, R. 2009, Rethinking Ideology, in B. de Bruin, Ch. F. Zurn (eds.), *New Waves in Political Philosophy*, Palgrave Macmillan, New York, pp. 63–86.

Jaeggi, R. 2014, *Alienation*, Columbia University Press, New York.

Jaeggi, R. 2016, Che cos'è la critica dell'ideologia? In Id., *Forme di vita e capitalismo*, Rosemberg & Sellier, Torino, pp. 61–89 (2009).

Jaeggi, R. 2017, Postfazione alla seconda edizione, in Id., *Alienazione. Attualità di un problema filosofico e sociale*, Castelvecchi, Roma, pp. 319–345.

James, P. 2019, The Social Imaginary in Theory and in Practice, in Ch. Hudson, E. K. Wilson (eds.), *Revisiting the Social Imaginary. Theories, Ideologies, Subjectivities*, Palgrave MacMillan, London, pp. 33–47.

Jedlowski, P. 2015, Futuri possibili. Immaginario, fantascienza, utopia, *Quaderni di Teoria Sociale*, v. XV, no. 2, pp. 11–32.

Jedlowski, P. 2017, *Memorie del futuro. Un percorso tra sociologia e studi culturali*, Carocci, Roma.

Kant, I. 1991, Perpetual Peace: A Philosophical Sketch, in *Political Writings*, Cambridge University Press, Cambridge (1795).

Kennedy, E. 1979, 'Ideology' from Destutt de Tracy, *Journal of the History of Ideas*, v. 40, no. 3, pp. 353–368.

Kim, Y. C. 1964, The Concept of Political Culture in Comparative Politics, *Journal of Politics*, v. XXVI, pp. 313–336.

Laclau, E. 2005, *On Populist Reason*, Verso, London and New York.

Lennon, K. 2017, *Imagination of the Imaginary*, Routledge & Kegan Paul, London and New York.

Lerner, M. 1950, Introduction, in N. Machiavelli (ed.), *The Prince and the Discourses*, The Modern Library, New York, pp. XXV–XLVI.

Levine, D. H. 1974, Issues in the Study of Culture and Politics: A View from Latin America, *Publius*, v. 4, no. 2, pp. 77–104.

Locke, J. 1988, Second Treatise, in Id., *Two Treatises of Government*, Cambridge University Press, Cambridge (1690).

Löwith, K. 2016, *Max Weber and Karl Marx*, Routledge & Kegan Paul, London and New York (1932).
Lukács, G. 1971, *History and Class Consciousness: Studies in Marxist Dialectics*, MIT Press, Cambridge MA (1923).
Lyotard, J.-F. 1984, *The Postmodern Condition: A Report on Knowledge*, University of Minnesota Press, Minneapolis (1979).
MacIntyre, A. 1981, *After Virtue. A Study in Moral Theory*, University of Notre Dame Press, Notre Dame.
Maffettone, S. 2001, Premessa, in J. Rawls (ed.), *Il diritto dei popoli*, Edizioni di Comunità, Torino, pp. VII–XXVIII.
Mannheim, K. 1997a, Ideology and Utopia,in Id., *Collected Works of Karl Mannheim*, volume one, Routledge & Kegan Paul, London and New York (1936).
Mannheim, K. 1997b, Man and Society in an Age of Reconstruction. Studies in Modern Social Structure, in Id., *Collected Works of Karl Mannheim*, volume two, Routledge & Kegan Paul, London and New York (1940).
Mannheim, K. 1997c, Essays on the Sociology of Knowledge, in Id., *Collected Works of Karl Mannheim*, volume five, Routledge & Kegan Paul, London and New York (1952; 1925; 1927).
Mannheim, K. 1997d, Essays on the Sociology of Culture, in Id., *Collected Works of Karl Mannheim*, volume seven, Routledge & Kegan Paul, London and New York (1956).
Mannheim, K. 1997e, Structures of Thinking, in Id., *Collected Works of Karl Mannheim*, volume ten, Routledge & Kegan Paul, London and New York (1982).
Mannheim, K. 1997f, Conservatism: A Contribution to the Sociology of Knowledge, in Id., *Collected Works of Karl Mannheim*, volume eleven, Routledge & Kegan Paul, London and New York (1986; 1927).
Marx, K. 1970, *Marx's Critique of Hegel's Philosophy of Right*, Cambridge University Press, Cambridge (1843).
Marx, K. 1974, Theses on Feuerbach, in K. Marx, F. Engels (eds.), *The German Ideology*, Lawrence & Wishart, London, pp. 121–123 (1845).
Marx, K. 1992, *Capital, v. 1, A Critique of Political Economy*, Penguin Classics, London (1867).
Marx, K. 2007, *Economic and Philosophic Manuscripts of 1844*, Dover, Mineola, New York (1844).
Marx, K. 2010, The Holy Family, or Critique of Critical Criticism. Against Bruno Bauer and Company, in Marx and Engels (eds.), *Collected Papers*, vol. 4, *Marx and Engels 1844–1845*, Lawrence & Wishart, Electric Book, pp. 5–211 (1845).
Marx, K., Engels, F. 1974, *The German Ideology*, Lawrence & Wishart, London (1845–1846).
Marx, K., Engels, F. 2014, *Manifesto of Communist*, Selected Works, International Publishers, New York (1848).
Meynaud, J. 1961, Destin des ideologies, *Etudes de Scienze politique*, n. 4, Lausanne.
Minkenberg, M., Inglehart, R. 1989, Neoconservatism and Value Change in USA: Tendencies in the Mass Public of a Post-industrial Society, in J. R. Gibbins (ed.), *Contemporary Political Culture. Politics in a Postmodern Age*, Sage, London, pp. 81–109.
Moravia, S. 1986, *Il tramonto dell'Illuminismo. Filosofia e politica nella società francese (1770–1810)*, Laterza, Roma-Bari.
More, Th. 1965, *Utopia*, Penguin Classics, London (1516).

Morris, W. 1970, *News from Nowhere*, Routledge & Kegan Paul, London and New York (1891).
Moscovici, S. 1961, *La pshycanalyse, son image et son public: Étude sur la representation sociale de la pshycanalyse*, Presses Universitaires de France, Paris.
Moscovici, S. 1984, The Phenomenon of Social Representations, in R. M. Farr, S. Moscovici (eds.), *Social Representations,* Cambridge University Press, Cambridge, pp. 3–69.
Mumford, L. 1962, *The Story of Utopias*, Viking Press, New York (1922).
Muzzetto, L. 2021a, Introduction to the Problem of Relevance, in L. Muzzetto (ed.), Alfred Schütz's Theory of Relevance, *Sociologia e ricerca sociale*, v. XLII, no. 124, pp. 5–15.
Muzzetto, L. (ed.) 2021b, Alfred Schütz's Theory of Relevance, *Sociologia e ricerca sociale*, v. XLII, no. 124, pp. 5–185.
Nasu, H. 2021, Alfred Schütz's Conception of Relevance and its Significances for the Social Sciences, *Sociologia e ricerca sociale*, v. XLII, no. 124, pp. 17–36.
Nussbaum, M. C. 2001, *Upheavals of Thought: The Intelligence of Emotions*, Cambridge University Press, Cambridge.
Parsons, T. 1968, *The Structure of Social Action*, Free Press, New York (1937).
Pasqualini, C. 2018, *Vicini e connessi Rapporto sulle Social Street a Milano*, Feltrinelli, Milano.
Pateman, C. 1971, Political Culture, Political Structure and Political Change, *British Journal of Political Science*, v. 1, no. 3, pp. 291–305.
Pateman, C. 1980, The Civic Culture: A Philosophic Critique, in G. A. Almond, S. Verba (eds.), *The Civic Culture Revisited*, Sage, Newbury Park, CA, pp. 57–102.
Pekonen, K. 1989, Symbols and Politics as Culture in the Modern Situation: the Problem and the Prospects of the 'New', in J. R. Gibbins (ed.), *Contemporary Political Culture. Politics in a Postmodern Age*, Sage, London, pp. 127–143.
Pendenza, M. 2017, *Radicare il cosmopolitismo. La sociologia cosmopolita di fronte alle sfide del futuro*, Mimesis, Milano.
Plato, 1981, *The Republic*, Penguin Classics, London (395–368 BC).
Psillos, S. 2011, *Causation and Explanation*, Routledge & Kegan Paul, London and New York.
Putnam, R. D. 1993, *Making Democracy Work. Civic Traditions in Modern Italy*, Princeton University Press, Princeton.
Putnam, R. D. 1997, Prefazione in Id., *La tradizione civica nelle Regioni italiane*, Mondadori, Milano, pp. VII–XII.
Putnam, R. D. 2000, *Bowling Alone. The Collapse and Revival of American Community*, Touchstone, Free Press, Simon & Schuster, New York.
Putnam, R. D. 2020, *The Upswing: How America Came Together a Century Ago and How We Can Do It Again*, Free Press, Simon & Schuster, New York.
Pye, L. W. 1972, Culture and Political Science: Problems in the Evaluating of the Concept of Political Culture, *Social Science Quarterly*, v. 53, no. 2, pp. 285–296.
Rawls, J. 2001, *The Law of People with "The Idea of Public Reason Revisited"*, Harvard University Press, Cambridge, MA (1999).
Rebughini, P. 2008, Costruire nuovi spazi di consumo: i Gruppi di acquisto e il sogno della trasparenza, in L. Leonini, R. Sassatelli (eds.), *Il consumo critico*, Laterza, Roma-Bari.
Ricœur, P. 1981, *Hermeneutics and the Human Sciences. Essays on Language, Action and Interpretation*, Cambridge University Press, Cambridge.

Ricœur, P. 1986, *Lectures on* Ideology and Utopia, Columbia University Press, New York.

Rifkin, J. 2005, *The European Dream. How Europe's Vision of the Future Is Quietly Eclipsing the American Dream*, Tarcher Perigee, New York.

Rosa, H. 2010, *Alienation and Acceleration. Towards a Critical Theory of Late-Modern Temporality*, Aarhus University Press, Aarhus/Malmö (2010).

Rundell, J. 2020, *Imaginaries of Modernity. Politics, Culture, and Tensions*, Routledge & Kegan Paul, London and New York.

Sacchetti, F. 2012, *Alfred Schütz e Paul Ricœur. Percorsi della soggettività tra fenomenologia ed ermeneutica*, Bonanno, Acireale.

Sacchetti, F. 2013, Introduzione, in A. Schütz (ed.), *Tiresia, ovvero la nostra conoscenza degli eventi futuri*, Edizioni Ets, Pisa, pp. 7–48.

Sani, G. 1989, The Political Culture of Italy: Continuity and Change, in G. A. Almond, S. Verba (eds.), *The Civic Culture Revisited*, Sage, Newbury Park, pp. 273–324.

Santambrogio, A. 1994, *I minorenni e la droga*. Una ricerca sulla realtà umbra, Edizioni Scientifiche Italiane, Napoli.

Santambrogio, A. 1997, Sociologia della conoscenza e validità del sapere, *Rassegna Italiana di Sociologia*, v. XXXVIII, no. 4, pp. 507–530.

Santambrogio, A. 1998, *Destra e sinistra. Un'analisi sociologica*, Laterza, Roma-Bari.

Santambrogio, A. (ed.) 2002, *Giovani e generazioni in Italia*, Margiacchi Editore, Perugia.

Santambrogio, A. 2006, *Il senso comune. Appartenenze e rappresentazioni sociali*, Laterza, Roma-Bari.

Santambrogio, A. 2015, *Associazionismo e volontariato in Umbria*, AUR, Perugia.

Santambrogio, A. 2018, Sulla relazione tra genesi e validità del sapere. Per un programma debole di sociologia della conoscenza, *Rassegna Italiana di Sociologia*, v. LIX, no. 3, pp. 427–455.

Santambrogio, A. 2022, *Idee per una sinistra europea*, Mondadori Università, Milano.

Sarantoulias, G. 2019, Mapping the Theme of Creativity in Cornelius Castoriadis's and Paul Ricœur's Social Imaginaries, *Social Imaginaries*, v. 5, no. 2, pp. 11–33.

Sartre, J.-P. 1966, *Being and Nothingness. An Essay in Phenomenological Ontology*, Simon & Schuster, New York (1943).

Sartre, J.-P. 2004, *The Imaginary: a Phenomenological Psychology of the Imagination*, Routledge & Kegan Paul, London and New York (1940).

Scaff, L. A. 2000, Weber on the Cultural Situation of Modern Age, in S. Turner (ed.), *The Cambridge Companion to Weber*, Cambridge University Press, Cambridge, pp. 99–116.

Schluchter, W. 1985, *The Rise of Western Rationalism. Max Weber's Developmental History*, University of California Press, Berkeley.

Schluchter, W. 1989, *Rationalism, Religion, and Domination. A Weberian Perspective*, University of California Press, Berkeley.

Schluchter, W. 1996, *Paradoxes of Modernity. Culture and Conduct in the Theory of Max Weber*, Stanford University Press, Stanford.

Schmitt, C. 2018, The Tyranny of Values, in Id., *The Tyranny of Values & Other Texts*, Telos Press Publishing, Candor, NY, pp. 1–41 (1967).

Schütz, A. 1962, *Collected Papers*, v. I, Martinus Nijhoff, The Hague.
Schütz, A. 1964, *Collected Papers*, v. II, Martinus Nijhoff, The Hague.
Schütz, A. 1966, *Collected Papers*, v. III, Martinus Nijhoff, The Hague.
Schütz, A. 1970, *Reflections on the Problem of Relevance*, Yale University Press, New Haven, CT.
Schütz, A. 1972, *The Phenomenology of the Social World*, Northwestern University Press, Evanston, IL (1932).
Schütz, A. 1996, *Collected Papers IV*, Kluver Academic Publishers, Dordrecht, Boston, London.
Searle, J. R. 1983, *Intentionality. An Essay in the Philosophy of Mind*, Cambridge University Press, Cambridge.
Searle, J. R. 1995, *The Construction of Social Reality*, Free Press, Simon & Schuster, New York.
Sennett, R. 1998, *The Corrosion of Character. The Personal Consequences of Work in the New Capitalism*, W. W. Norton & Company, New York and London.
Spinelli, A. 2006, *Il Manifesto di Ventotene. E altri scritti*, Mondadori, Milano (1941).
Sraffa, P. 1975, *Production of Commodities by Means of Commodities: Prelude to a Critique of Economic Theory*, Cambridge University Press, Cambridge (1960).
Takakusa, K. 2021, Relevance and Cognitive Style: on the Double Characterization of Science in Alfred Schütz, *Sociologia e ricerca sociale*, v. XLII, no. 124, pp. 52–68.
Taylor, C. 2004, *Modern Social Imaginaries*, Duke University Press, Durham and London.
Taylor, G. H. 2015, The Phenomenological Contributions of Ricœur's Philosophy of Imagination, *Social Imaginaries*, v. 1, no. 2, pp. 13–31.
Thompson, J. B. 1981, *Critical Hermeneutics A Study in the Thought of Paul Ricœur and Jürgen Habermas*, Cambridge University Press, Cambridge.
Tucker, R. C. 1973, Culture, Political Culture, and Communist Society, *Political Science Quarterly*, v. 88, no. 2, pp. 173–190.
Van Parijs, Ph. 1998, *Real Freedom for All. What (if Anything) Can Justify Capitalism?* Clarendon Press, Oxford.
von Wright, G. H. 1971, *Explanation and Understanding*, Cornell University Press, Ithaca, NY.
Wallerstein, I. 1998, *Utopistics. Or Historical Choices of the Twenty-First Century*, New Press, New York.
Weber, M. 1949, *On The Methodology of the Social Sciences*, Free Press of Glencoe, Illinois (1904; 1917).
Weber, M. 1969a, Politics as a Vocation, in Id., *From Max Weber: Essays in Sociology*, Oxford University Press, New York, pp. 77–128 (1919).
Weber, M. 1969b, Science as a Vocation, in Id., *From Max Weber: Essays in Sociology*, Oxford University Press, New York, pp. 129–156 (1919).
Weber, M. 1969c, The Social Psychology of the World Religions, in Id., *From Max Weber: Essays in Sociology*, Oxford University Press, New York, pp. 267–301 (1920).
Weber, M. 1978, *Economy and Society*, University of California Press, Berkeley, LA and London (1922).
Wells, H. G. 2006, *A Modern Utopia*, Penguin Books, London (1905).

Wiatr, J. J. 1980, The Civic Culture from a Marxist-Sociological Perspective, in G. A. Almond, S. Verba (eds.), *The Civic Culture Revisited*, Sage, Newbury Park, pp. 103–123.

Wolff, K. H. 1994, Karl Mannheim and Surrender-and-Catch: An Essay in Autobiographical History of Ideas, *Canadian Journal of Sociology*, v. 19, no. 3, pp. 371–377.

Wright, E. O. 2010, *Envisioning Real Utopias*, Verso, London and New York.

Index

Note: Endnotes are indicated by the page number followed by "n" and the note number e.g., 96n19 refers to note 96 on page 19.

Abric, J. C. 57
Adams, J. 113
Adams, S. 84, 98n31
Adorno, Th. W. 32n8, 112, 118–19, 124, 144n33, 148, 171
alienation 77, 104–5, 120–2, 139n1, 141n9, 143n28, 143n29, 158
Almond, G. A. 37–8, 41, 43, 55, 64n1, 66n17, 76, 89
Althusser, L. 141n11
amoral familism 40
anchoring 55–7, 59, 61, 96n19
animalism 139
Anitori, R. 98n29
Apel, K. -O. 110, 142n18
Appadurai, A. 90
Aristotle, 111, 142n19, 169
Aron, R. 101, 108, 132, 142n15
associations 160, 178n9, 183; associazionism 44, 85–6, 90
Athena 29
attitude 38–40, 42, 62, 64n1, 66n17, 70, 78, 95n11, 134, 140n5; group attitude 59–61
authenticity 105
autocracy 135, 176
autonomy 136–8, 158, 160, 169, 173, 181–2
avalutativity 119
awareness 104, 107, 114, 126, 131, 144n31, 173; self-awareness 109, 139n1, 142n20

Bacon, F. 113, 148, 151
bad faith 32n6, 74, 94n9, 101, 106, 123, 140n4
Bakunin, M. 178n6
Banfield, E. C. 39–40
Barry, B. M. 39
Baudrillard, J. 109
Bauman, Z. 80, 135, 177
because-motives 125, 127–8; in-order-to-motives 125, 127–8
Beck, U. 79
belief 2, 55, 58, 63, 67n28, 71, 109, 145n35, 165, 173
Bell, D. 108–9, 123, 132, 142n16, 142n17, 145n36, 157
Bellamy, E. 178n3
belonging 60, 63, 81–2, 85, 87–8, 91–2, 113, 178n10
Belvedere, C. 145n38
Benedictines 150
Bergson, H. 23, 34n15
Bloch, E. 170–5, 177, 179n11, 180n16
Boone, J. 6
Bormann, C. V. 142n18
Bowles, S. 178n7
Brint, M. 66n17
Brubaker, R. 30n1, 31n4
Bruni, L. 5, 90, 98n29
Bubner, R. 110, 142n18
Burke, E. 97n22

Cabanis, P. -J. -G. 73, 114–15, 143n23
Cabet, É. 178n3
Caesar, 122
Campanella, T. 151
Camus, A. 142n15, 142n16
capitalism 65n8, 79–80, 101–4, 134, 140n5, 141n9, 159–60; Fordist capitalism 134; neo-liberal capitalism 80–1
care 161, 175
Castoriadis, C. 3, 98n31, 98n33

cause 127–8, 146n40
change 27–9, 42, 46, 54, 56–8, 63, 67n23, 76, 80, 86–7, 90–2, 122, 145n34, 148, 153–4, 156, 158–61, 164, 170, 179n11; political change 37
charisma 19, 121, 147n46
Chopin, F. 104
Cimmino, L. 5, 178n7
circular economy 138
citizenship 115
City of the Sun 151–2
civic culture (civicness) 38–9, 42, 44, 46, 64n1, 89, 182
civil society 41, 85–6, 88–9, 92–3, 135, 137–8, 146n43, 160, 178n9, 183
Clausewitz, von C. 175
Cleopatra 168
cognitive dissonance 61, 63, 68n31
Cohen, G. A. 141n9, 178n7
Cohen, J. 178n7
coherence 53, 56–8, 61, 63, 76, 79, 87, 91–2, 122, 136, 181; coherence rationality 136
common good 50, 83, 149
common sense 22, 25–9, 54–6, 58–61, 67n23, 69–72, 77, 84–6, 90, 92, 96n19, 97n25, 122–5, 127, 131–2, 134, 136, 145n34, 163, 165–6, 168, 174, 181; deep common sense 27–8, 61, 84
communicative action 142n20
communism 33n10, 88, 102, 107–8, 142n15, 152, 155–6, 159, 166
communitarianism 45, 51, 162
community 42, 44–5, 47, 50, 53–4, 63, 65n8, 69, 71, 93n1, 119, 132, 140n4, 143n29, 148–54, 161, 169, 178n2, 178n10; civic community 43–4; dialogical community 111; political community 85
Compagnoni, G. 114
Condillac, É. -B. 113
Condorcet, M. -J. A. N. de C. 73, 114–15
conflict 74, 82, 85, 88, 92, 108, 115, 135, 148, 175; social conflict 75–8, 97n28, 107–8, 154; class conflict 88; political conflict 134, 138
consciousness 101–3, 105–7, 112, 118, 125, 154, 156, 172; anticipatory consciousness 179n11; false consciousness 101–103, 105–107, 118, 140n4, 141n10; ideological consciousness 102–103, 142n20; social consciousness 100; stream of 125
conservatism 51, 53, 66n20, 75–6, 153; conservative ideal 153
contradiction 158
Cooper, D. 158, 161–3, 165, 173, 178n10
cosmopolitanism 114
Costa, P. 98
Crespi, F. 6, 149
critique 101, 109–11, 119–20, 122, 133, 138, 140n5, 141n9, 143n29, 158, 162; immanent critique 119–21, 132, 158; political critique 139; social critique 114, 138
Croce, M. 163

d'Alembert, J. le R. 113
Damiani, M. 5, 147n45
democracy 37–43, 66n19, 78, 86, 88–9, 92, 100, 115, 119, 133–5, 138–9, 143n22, 146n43, 158, 160, 176, 182–3; direct democracy 160, 162; radical democracy 158–9, 183
democratization 75
de-politicization 134–5; re-politicization 134–5
determinable indeterminacy 166
desire 170–4
Destutt de Tracy, A. -L. -C. 73, 94n8, 114, 116–17, 144n26
determinate negation 119–21
d'Holbach, P. -H. T. 116
Diehl, P. 97n24, 98n31
Dilthey, W. 112
disembedding 78, 80, 84, 87
disenchantment 7–10, 14, 20, 25–6, 32n8, 33n9, 33n10, 55, 84, 99n34, 110
disinterested observer 71–2, 95n11, 124, 136, 166
distrust 134
Dittmer, L. 39
division of powers 104
Dostoyevski, F. 32n6
Dreher, J. 145n38
Dupuis, C. -F. 73
Durkheim, È. 54, 56, 67n22, 67n27, 78, 97n21
dynamic synthesis 50, 112

Eagleton, T. 100, 104, 109, 133, 140n7, 141n12
Edelman, M. 65n10, 68n32
elite 96n19, 134–5, 147n45, 148
Elkins, D. J. 39
Elster, J. 31n4
emancipation 80, 89, 158–9

emotions 24, 38, 57, 63, 81; filled emotions 171; expectant emotions 171
enchantment 91, 173
Engels, F. 102–3, 132, 140n2, 141n10
enlightenment 66n20, 73, 75, 100–1, 107, 113–14, 116, 133, 154
environment 79, 92, 137–8, 152, 160, 177; environmentalism 82, 88
equality 17, 19, 50, 63, 78, 83, 86, 91–2, 118–19, 140n5, 143n22, 151, 161, 165, 178n2; egalitarianism 162; ideology of 118
ethic of ultimate ends 19–21, 32n6, 33n12
ethic of responsibility 19–21, 32n6, 33n12
Euclid 65n11
European society 177
everyday life 22, 25–9, 53, 70–2, 75, 78, 84, 90–1, 94n5, 96n20, 120, 136, 153, 161, 165, 167, 170, 179n14; departure from the everyday 164–6; rootedness in the everyday 165
existential connection of thought 49–50
exploitation 97n26, 101–3, 105, 141n9, 152

fantasying 167
fascism 107, 156
Federici. M. C. 98n29
feminism 140n4; queer feminism 162
Ferrara, A. 5, 30n2, 32n7
Festinger, L. 68n31
Feuerbach, L. 105, 120, 141n13
flexibility 79–81
Foucault, M. 109
Fourier, Ch. 151, 178n2, 178n3
Franciscans 150
Franklin, B. 113–14, 142n21
Fraser, N. 159
freedom 45, 53, 63, 65n8, 66n19, 83, 91, 109, 118–19, 125–6, 128, 130, 134–5, 138, 140n5, 151–152, 155, 159–60, 166, 170, 178n2, 183; economic freedom 134; ideology of 118; political freedom 134
Freud, S. 55, 145n39
Friedman, M. 134
fundamentalism 99n34

Gadamer, H. -G. 110–12, 142n18, 142n20, 181
game theory 168
Gauchet, M. 97n28
gender 145, 159, 175
generation 63, 67n29, 79, 91–2, 96n16, 135, 140n4, 156, 163, 175
Geuss, R. 102
Gibbins, J. R. 64n4
Giddens, A. 78
Giegel, H. J. 142n18
Gili, G. 98n29
Gioia, M. 114
globalization 78, 80–1, 89, 113, 134, 138, 176
Goffman, E. 106
Goldman, H. 20
Grand Inquisitor 10, 32n6
Graziano, P. R. 98n29
Grotius, H. 83, 96n19, 96n20
Guidotti, F. 98n29

Habermas, J. 32n8, 35n19, 35n20, 85, 94n9, 97n22, 110–12, 118, 142n18, 142n20, 176
happiness 149–50, 152, 171–2
Hayek, von F. 134
Head, B. W. 117, 143n26
Hegel, G. W. F. 66n17, 112, 132, 141n9, 141n12, 178n4, 178n7
Heidegger, M. 111
Hélvetius, C. -A. 113
Herder, J. G. 66n17
hermeneutic 109–12; hermeneutic circle 111, 127–8
historical materialism 104, 140n4, 158
Hobbes, Th, 113
Hochschild, A. 31n3
Honneth, A. 144n31, 159
hope 148, 156–7, 161, 167, 171–5, 180n16
Horkheimer, M. 32n8
Husserl, E. 23, 28, 34n15, 35n22, 98n32, 127

identity 60, 66n15, 74–7, 81–2, 87–90, 92, 107, 113, 122, 124, 134, 137–8, 147n46, 158, 174–7, 181–2; political identity 86, 92; sexual identity 88, 92; territorial identity 88, 175
idéologues 73, 113–14, 116–17, 120, 142n22
ideology 3–4, 39, 65n8, 66n20, 73–6, 78, 81–2, 86, 88–92, 94n4, 94n8, 94n10, 96n17, 96n19, 97n25, 100–13, 120, 123, 132–4, 137, 140n2–4, 141n10, 141n11, 142n17, 143n27, 145n36, 156,

173, 181–2; critique of 101, 110, 112, 118–20, 144n33; end of 86–7, 94n11, 100, 106–10, 113, 142n15, 142n16, 153–5, 157–8; general use of the total conception of 75, 86, 107, 155; particular conception of 73–4, 107; theory of 113, 116–17, 120, 124, 133, 182–3; total conception of 74, 107
imaginary 82–3, 94n4, 98n30, 98n31, 99n34, 99n35, 138–9, 173; instituting imaginary 98n33; modern social imaginary 82–6, 97n25, 137, 183; social imaginary 3, 82–6, 90–3, 96n20, 97n24, 97n27, 174, 182–3
imagination 96n19, 98n31, 98n32, 138, 152, 162–6, 169–75, 179n11
immanent analysis 49, 52–3; non-immanent analysis 49, 52–3
individual 54, 58, 61, 66n19, 68n30, 78, 83–4, 113, 134–5, 177n1, 178n5, 182–3; individual opinion 59–61; individualism 50–1, 80, 83; individualization process 60, 78–80, 99n34
Inglehart, R. 39–40, 42, 95n12
integration 78, 82
intellectuals 52, 76–7, 91–92, 108–9, 113–14, 142n22, 152, 175, 183; engagé intellectuals 93, 100; relatively free-floating intellectuals 94n11
intentionality 23–30, 34n14, 36n24, 55, 58, 60, 69, 72, 76–7, 84, 90, 98n30, 112, 122–3, 129–30, 164–6, 169–72, 179n11, 181
instrumental rationality 12–17, 31n4, 32n8, 33n10, 121, 136
interpretation 110–11, 120, 127–8, 136, 146n41
intersubjectivity 22–3, 28–9, 70, 122, 124, 181

Jaeggi, R. 118–21, 133, 140n5, 143n27–9, 144n31–3
Jedlowski, P. 179n13
Jefferson, Th. 113–14
Jesus 32n6, 109
justice 149–51, 160, 176–7

Kant, I. 20, 66n17, 175–6, 180n17
Kennedy, E. 116
Khrushchev, N. 109
Kim, Y. C. 39
Ku Klux Klan, 44, 178n9

La Mettrie, J. O. de 116
language 112, 142n20
law of peoples 180n17
left 3, 5, 62, 133, 135, 142n15, 143n25, 147n45, 178n5
Leonardo da Vinci 65n11
Lerner, M. 145n36, 169
liberalism 51, 62, 75–6, 117, 153; liberal-humanitarian ideal 153, 174; neo-liberalism 134–5
liquid modernity 80
localism 162; social localism 177
Locke, J. 52–3, 66n18, 96n19, 96n20, 113, 116, 143n26
Leopardi, G. 140n6
Lipset, S. M. 108
Lopez, D. G. 145n38
Löwith, K. 18
Lukàcs, G. 105, 141n12
Lyotard, J. -F. 82, 110, 113

Machiavelli, N. 169
MacIntyre, A. 66n15, 98n31, 146n42, 167–9, 179n15
Maffettone, S. 180n17
Majakovsky, V. V. 140n6
Mannheim, K. 1, 4, 33n10, 46–50, 53–4, 65n12, 66n20, 67n29, 71, 73–7, 82, 86–7, 94n10, 94n11, 95n12, 97n25, 107–8, 112, 140n5, 141n9, 153–6, 174, 178n4, 178n6, 183
Manzoni, A. 114
market 132–5, 152, 159–60, 167; market economy 82
Marxism 51, 72, 95n11, 169; analytic Marxism 178n7
Marx, K. 46, 48, 65n8, 66n17, 74, 77, 95n11, 96n16, 97n26, 100–9, 118–19, 121, 132, 139n1, 140n2, 140n5, 141n8, 141n9, 141n11, 141n13, 143n24, 172, 178n7, 180n16
mass media 85, 95n14, 137; social media 90
meaning 21–7, 47, 54–7, 62, 65n13, 67n23, 72, 79, 90, 92, 121–2, 125–9, 131, 133, 136, 144n33, 146n39, 148–9, 164–5, 174–5, 178n4, 179n11, 181–3; intended meaning 21, 24, 26, 29, 35n17, 58, 71, 122–3, 129–30, 165, 181; objective meaning 21–3, 50, 67n25; subjective meaning 21, 24, 28, 59–61, 67n25, 70; ripples of meaning 27–8